At Loggerheads?

Agricultural Expansion, Poverty Reduction, and Environment in the Tropical Forests

Dec 2006

For Chas & Diane Plotnick

with best wishes

A World Bank Policy Research Report

This report is dedicated to the memory of Ricardo Tarifa, who died tragically in an airplane accident in the Amazon forest on September 29, 2006. Ricardo was returning from Manaus, where he had visited and contributed to several major projects focused on conserving the Brazilian Amazon. Ricardo's life and work exemplifies, in a very practical way, the theme of this book—seeking ways to conserve the forest and better the lives of its people.

Ricardo loved forests and the people that live in them. He felt at home with the communities on the banks of the Tapajós river and those in the Amazonas floodplains. A Yale-trained forest engineer, he moved among distant worlds: the world of forest dwellers, of academe, and of World Bank offices—but his preference was clear. Ricardo loved to work in the field. He believed in the power of local action to promote change, to seek local solutions to global problems. Ricardo, and the contributions he was yet to make, will be missed.

At Loggerheads?

Agricultural Expansion, Poverty Reduction, and Environment in the Tropical Forests

Kenneth M. Chomitz

with
Piet Buys, Giacomo De Luca,
Timothy S. Thomas, and
Sheila Wertz-Kanounnikoff

The World Bank

©2007 The International Bank for Reconstruction and Development / The World Bank
1818 H Street NW
Washington DC 20433
Telephone: 202-473-1000
Internet: www.worldbank.org
E-mail: feedback@worldbank.org

1 2 3 4 5 10 9 8 7

This volume is a product of the staff of the International Bank for Reconstruction and Development / The World Bank. The findings, interpretations, and conclusions expressed in this volume do not necessarily reflect the views of the Executive Directors of The World Bank or the governments they represent.

The World Bank does not guarantee the accuracy of the data included in this work. The boundaries, colors, denominations, and other information shown on any map in this work do not imply any judgement on the part of The World Bank concerning the legal status of any territory or the endorsement or acceptance of such boundaries.

ISBN-10: 0-8213-6735-8
ISBN-13: 978-0-8213-6735-3
eISBN-10: 0-8213-6736-6
eISBN-13: 978-0-8213-6736-0
DOI: 10.1596/978-0-8213-6735-3

Library of Congress Cataloging in Publication Data

Chomitz, Kenneth M.
    At loggerheads? : agricultural expansion, poverty reduction, and environment
in the tropical forests / [written by Kenneth M. Chomitz].
       p. cm. -- (World Bank policy research report)
    Includes bibliographical references and index.
    ISBN-13: 978-0-8213-6735-3
    ISBN-10: 0-8213-6735-8
    ISBN-10: 0-8213-6736-6 (electronic)
    1. Deforestation--Tropics. 2. Deforestation--Social aspects--Tropics. 3.
Deforestation--Environmental aspects--Tropics. 4. Forest policy--Tropics. 5.
Agriculture--Tropics. I. Title. II. Title: Agricultural expansion, poverty
reduction, and environment in the tropical forests. III. Series.
    SD418.3.T76C46 2006

                                2006032118

Cover image: ©Michael Fay / National Geographic Image Collection. The cover photo shows the western boundary of Kilimanjaro National Park, Tanzania.
Cover designer: Drew Fasick

 This book was printed using recycled paper.

Contents

Boxes

Figures

Maps

Tables

Foreword

Three billion people—almost half of humanity—live in rural areas of the developing world, and 1.5 billion of them on less than $2 a day. Forests are important resources for the rural poor, with over 800 million people living in forests and woodlands in the tropics alone. However, global deforestation continues at an alarming rate, with annual losses the size of Portugal, as forests are cleared for agriculture or harvested unsustainably. In addition to the implications for poor populations' welfare, forest destruction results in the loss of globally irreplaceable biodiversity and contributes to global climate change, which threatens both the rich and poor.

Forests are integral to the Bank's mission of poverty reduction and commitment to mitigating global environmental problems. The Bank's forest sector strategy is founded on three mutually reinforcing goals of poverty reduction, economic development, and conservation of forest environmental values. While the Bank is committed to engagement in both forest-rich and forest-poor countries in all forest types, this report focuses on the causes, consequences, and connections of deforestation and forest poverty in the tropical world.

Specifically, the report addresses the potential dilemma of trade-offs between poverty reduction and environmental protection. Deforestation causes environmental damage, but it also increases the supply of farmland and generates rural income and employment, sometimes sustainable and sometimes not. Overall, the report suggests that poverty alleviation and environment are not inherently at loggerheads, nor are they automatically aligned. Outcomes depend on the policies adopted and specific conditions on the ground.

The report proposes a typology for three kinds of forests, which face differential kinds of environmental pressure and offer disparate opportunities for growth and poverty alleviation, to appraise policy options. It identifies ample opportunities for "win-win" policies. In particular, anything that boosts labor demand outside agriculture will tend to reduce both poverty and deforestation. Additionally, promotion of some kinds of agroforestry can help to improve the ecological functions of degraded forests while boosting farm output and employment.

Resolving many forest issues requires mediation between stakeholders with conflicting claims on forests. Sorting out and defending land and forest tenure is one key policy challenge. Millions of people live with limited or insecure rights to trees and land, unable to tap forest resources and without any motivation to preserve them. Another challenge is recognizing the environmental externalities associated with forest management. Communities at all levels, from local watersheds to the entire planet, need to find ways of rewarding forest owners and managers whose actions benefit others.

These challenges are difficult even for nations with relatively high capacities for governance, yet many tropical-forested nations rank low on governance measures. Nonetheless, the report is cautiously optimistic that these challenges can be tackled. It points to a number of innovations that could tip the balance toward improved governance and thus to deployment of better policies. The rapidly decreasing cost of information is a critical factor in the emergence of these innovations, as it becomes cheaper and easier to monitor forest conditions, communicate with forest populations, and scrutinize the actions of landholders and of government agencies. Together with new institutional mechanisms such as independent forests observers and third-party certification, these innovations can boost transparency in the sector and restrain environmentally and socially destructive resource grabs.

Global finance for forests could accelerate these institutional changes while directly supporting conservation actions and livelihood improvements. While noting the global demand for biodiversity conservation, the report focuses particular attention on the potential opportunities offered by global carbon finance. This is a topic of current and increasingly intense international discussion. About 20 percent of global carbon dioxide emissions come from tropical deforestation. The costs of abating some of these emissions appear low in comparison to other options. International finance for carbon services could defray the direct opportunity costs of forest conservation while also fostering sustainable agricultural and silvicultural development, which would relieve pressures on protected forests. This is a long-term vision, but it could spur near-term institutional strengthening that would benefit forests and their inhabitants.

The report offers a systematic framework for thinking about how to integrate forest management with rural development in a sustainable way. We hope that this report will help to shape the debate on how best to manage the rural landscape for local and global benefits.

François Bourguignon
Senior Vice President and Chief Economist
World Bank

Katherine Sierra
Vice President, Sustainable Development Network
World Bank

Acknowledgments

This report was written by Kenneth M. Chomitz (Senior Advisor, Independent Evaluation Group) while with the Development Research Group (DECRG), under the general supervision of Zmarak Shalizi (Senior Research Manager) and L. Alan Winters (Director, DECRG). Chomitz was assisted by a research team made up of Piet Buys, Giacomo De Luca, Timothy S. Thomas, and Sheila Wertz-Kanounnikoff. Background papers were written by Arild Angelsen; Dirk Kloss; and William Sunderlin, Sonya Dewi, and Atie Puntodewo. Klas Sander contributed material on Madagascar. The team is grateful for guidance and feedback from an external advisory board consisting of Alain de Janvry, David Kaimowitz, José Sarukhan, and Sara Scherr. Thanks go also to Yasmin d'Souza and Julie Terrell for administrative support; to Paul Holtz for editing; to Susan Graham for managing the production of a particularly complex manuscript; to Nancy Lammers and Stephen McGroarty in the Office of the Publisher; and to Kavita Watsa and Maya Brahmam for assistance in dissemination.

The team thanks management and colleagues from the World Bank's Forest Team, Environment Department, and Agriculture and Rural Development Departments for support and advice. The team benefited greatly from comments, discussions with, and help from many people, including Keith Alger, Eugenio Arima, Philippe Ambrosi, Deborah Balk, Garo Batmanian, Diji Chandrasekharan Behr, Jill Blockhus, Anne Branthomme, Mario Boccucci, Sampurno Bruijnzeel, Malcolm Childress, Chona Cruz, Richard Damania, Robert Davis, Uwe Deichmann, Laurent Debroux, Gerhard Dieterle, Giovanna Dore, Ellen Douglas, Gershon Feder, Erick Fernandes, Douglas J. Graham, Theodore Greenberg, Armando Guzman, Mike Hoffman, Peter Holmgren, Miroslav Honzák, William Hyde, Nalin Kishor, Somik Lall, Nadine Laporte, Franck Lecocq, Daniel Lederman, Karen Luz, Kathy MacKinnon, William Magrath, Edgardo Maravi, Grant Milne, Augusta Molnar, Adriana Moreira, Carlos Muñoz, Polly Means, Andy Nelson, Daniel Nepstad, Peter Ngea, Stefano Pagiola, Kent Redford, Jeffrey Richey, Klas Sander, Jeff Sayer, Robert Schneider, Gerardo Segura, Jim Smyle, Claudia Sobrevila, Fred Stolle, Simon Stuart, Jatna Supriatna, Giuseppe Topa, Juan Manuel Torres, Barbara Verardo, David Wheeler, Tony Whitten, Andy White, Stanley Wood, Greg Yetman, and Liang You. Apologies to anyone inadvertently omitted from this list.

Support from the Knowledge for Change Program, the Trust Fund for Environmentally and Socially Sustainable Development, and the German Consultant Trust Fund is gratefully acknowledged.

Abbreviations and Acronyms

ASB	Alternatives to Slash and Burn Project
CIFOR	Center for International Forestry Research
CO_2	carbon dioxide
CONABIO	Mexico's National Biodiversity Commission
EMBRAPA	Brazilian Agricultural Research Corporation
ETS	Emissions Trading Scheme
EU	European Union
FAO	UN Food and Agriculture Organization
FEMA	[state environmental agency of Mato Grosso]
FRA	Forest Resources Assessment
FRA-RSS	Forest Resources Assessment Remote Sensing Survey
FSC	Forest Stewardship Council
GEF	Global Environment Facility
GHGs	greenhouse gases
GPS	Global Positioning System
ICDPs	integrated conservation-development projects
IMF	International Monetary Fund
INPE	Brazilian National Institute of Space Research
ITTO	International Tropical Timber Organization
IUCN	The World Conservation Union
LSMS	Living Standards Measurement Survey
NGOs	nongovernmental organizations
NPV	net present value
RISEMP	Regional Integrated Silvopastoral Ecosystem Management Project
RL	reference level
SLAPR	Rural Property Environmental Licensing System (Mato Grosso)
TREES	Tropical Ecosystem Environment Observation by Satellite
WWF	Worldwide Fund for Nature/World Wildlife Fund

100 ha = 1 km^2
1 ton carbon is equivalent to 3.67 tons CO_2

Juan Pablo Moreiras / Fauna & Flora International / Comisión Centroamericana de Ambiente y Desarrollo photo archive.

Overview

Over the past three decades tropical forests have captured the world's attention. There have been endless meetings, stacks of reports, demonstrations in the streets, and billions of dollars poured into forest projects.

Why Are Tropical Forests a Concern?

Two broad concerns have driven this attention.

Tropical Forests Are Shriveling before Our Eyes

Satellites allow us to watch forests burn in real time. The tropical forest estate, extraordinarily large at the middle of the 20th century, is shrinking at about 5 percent a decade. By the middle of the 21st century only shreds of this once-vast forest may be left. Unless trends change, the consequences will be severe: 3 billion tons of carbon dioxide (CO_2) added to the atmosphere each year, intensifying climate change; loss not just of many species but also entire ecosystems; and across the tropics, widespread changes in water flows, scenery, microclimates, pests, and pollinators. These environmental damages would touch people near and far.

Pressures on forests will not disappear soon. Croplands, pastures, and plantations are expanding into natural forests and will likely do so for the next 30–50 years. Expansion is driven by both wealth and poverty. A huge rural population relies on low-productivity agriculture for subsistence. A growing, increasingly wealthy urban population demands commodities produced at the forest's edge: beef, palm oil, coffee, soybeans, and chocolate.

The Food and Agriculture Organization predicts that the growth in such demand will slow—but still expects croplands in the developing world to expand by a net 3.8 million hectares a year over the next three decades (Bruinsma 2003). Gross expansion will be even greater, because some farmland is abandoned. And these estimates do not include expansion of pastures and planted forests.

Forests are also under pressure from loggers. Poor people need fuelwood, and a wealthier world demands more wood and pulp—demands only partly met by plantations. Logging thins and degrades forests and helps finance and provide access to farmers and entrepreneurs who burn unsellable trees to establish agriculture.

Forests Are Home to Some of the World's Poorest People

Forests play a crucial role in the lives of many poor people. Almost 70 million people—many indigenous—live in remote areas of closed tropical forests. Another 735 million rural people live in or near tropical forests and savannas, relying on them for much of their fuel, food, and income—or chopping them down for crops and pasture. From a policy viewpoint, what is distinctive about forest poverty relative to other rural poverty? How is it related to deforestation? When are forests a geographic poverty trap—and when are they a route out of poverty?

This Report's Aims, Audience, and Scope

Despite the volume of published material, confusion remains about the causes of forest loss and forest poverty and about effective policy responses. Forest discourse often relies on unreliable generalizations (box 1). Although there is an element of truth in each of these generalizations, uncritical application of them can impede diagnosis of poverty and environmental problems—and without proper diagnoses, prescriptions can go awry. Two examples:

- Kerinci-Seblat National Park, in Sumatra, Indonesia, is one of the world's richest, most distinctive biodiversity sites, containing 4,000 plant species and 3 percent of Earth's mammal species—including threatened ones such as the clouded leopard and small Sumatran rhinoceros. A World Bank–Global Environment Facility project sought to deter deforestation by boosting local incomes. But deforestation in Kerinci was driven not by poverty, but by avarice and opportunity. The region's forests consist of prized hardwoods, and its cool climate and volcanic soils make it one of the best places in the world to grow cinnamon. Modest assistance to local people didn't deter them from deforestation and had no effect on outsiders who sought to cash in on the region's wealth (MacKinnon 2005).

- A Panamanian land-use plan envisioned reforesting 144,000 hectares of pasture to protect the Panama Canal watershed—a project that might cost more than $250 million. But a study found that this investment could have a result contrary to what was expected, reducing rather than increasing water available to the canal during the dry season. Over time, such a change would cost Panama $630 million in revenues and raise global shipping costs by $3 billion (Aylward 2002).

Box 1   Unreliable Generalizations about Deforestation and Poverty

Poverty causes deforestation
Poor people deforest, but so do the rich. Added income may not deter poor people from deforestation.

Deforestation causes poverty
Depending on who does it and why, deforestation can destroy or create assets for poor people.

Highly forested areas tend to be very poor
Many factors muddle this relationship. Remote areas tend to have high forest cover and high poverty rates, but they also usually have low absolute numbers of poor people. Forest dwellers can prosper when they can profitably access forest resources—or suffer when those resources are meager or controlled by others.

Deforestation causes floods and reduces dry season flows
Deforestation's impacts vary considerably depending on the watershed's size and steepness and how the land is subsequently used. It often increases dry season flows, but in some cases could reduce them.

High timber prices promote forest conservation
High timber prices motivate "mining" of unprotected old-growth forests—but can also increase returns to regulated logging and stimulate management of secondary forests and plantations in areas already logged over.

This report seeks to improve the diagnosis of forest problems and facilitate the prescription and application of solutions. It offers tools for tackling two issues related to environmental management and regional development policies:

- Some people benefit, and some people are harmed, when forest is degraded or converted to agriculture. How should society intermediate between these groups?

- How pervasive is poverty among forest dwellers? What approaches are needed to address it? And how do policies for reducing forest poverty relate to those for mitigating deforestation?

The report is directed at people concerned about environmental and poverty policies in the tropical world—particularly those who have to straddle sectors or disciplines. It can help designers of conservation projects assess the plausibility of assumptions about links between conservation and poverty. Local governments and stakeholders might use it to think about their goals and tools for regional development in forested areas. At the national level, it seeks to provide a platform for discussions among environment, agriculture, forest, and finance ministries. It can inform policymakers and voters in formulating equitable, enforceable regulations on land and forest use. Finally, it is intended to contribute to international discussions about the role of forest conservation in mitigating climate change.

The report's cross-sector approach can inform implementation of the World Bank's Forest Strategy (box 2). The strategy recognizes that forests are undervalued because their environmental services fall outside markets and emphasizes the need to reward forest managers for these services. It also recognizes that tapping forests' potential for poverty reduction and sustainable economic development requires politically complex trade-offs between the different groups interested in conservation and production and involves cross-sector coordination.

Though this report has broad ambitions, it is limited in scope. It focuses one spotlight on the causes and consequences of forest conversion to agriculture, and another, somewhat overlapping, spotlight on the nature and location of forest poverty. Those spotlights cover a lot of material, but leave many traditional forestry topics partially shadowed. Such issues—the economics of investing in plantations

---

Box 2   The World Bank's Forest Strategy

The World Bank's 2004 Forest Strategy and Operational Policy has three interdependent parts:

1. Harnessing the potential of forests to reduce poverty by:
   - Strengthening rights of people— especially marginalized groups—to forests and fostering their participation in forest management.
   - Promoting sustainable forestry, community forestry, and agroforestry.

2. Integrating forests in sustainable economic development by:
   - Improving forest governance and introducing legal and institutional reforms.
   - Encouraging investments that catalyze production of forest products, including environmental services.

3. Protecting local and global environmental values by:
   - Establishing protected areas.
   - Improving forest management in other areas.
   - Developing markets and finance for international public goods such as biodiversity and carbon sequestration, and helping governments create national markets for environmental services from forests.
   - Addressing cross-sector links that affect environmental values.

Source: World Bank 2004.

---

and building capacity among small sawmills and furniture enterprises, the policy rationales for stimulating smallholders to grow pulpwood, introducing marketing interventions for community forests, promoting reduced-impact logging, and controlling illegal logging—enter the story, mainly as they affect incentives to maintain or convert natural forests. But readers should not expect detailed or operationally oriented discussions of these topics.

This Report's Arguments and Structure

The report has two parts. The first is diagnostic: it examines the drivers and consequences of deforestation and forest poverty. The second part steps back to see how governance, institutions, and policies shape those drivers—leading to prescriptions. The line of argument is summarized below by chapter and outlined in figure 1.

Figure 1   Structure of This Report's Arguments

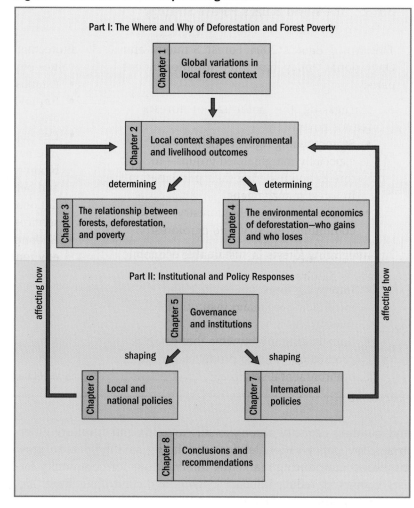

Chapter 1. Forests Differ

Forests differ in the deforestation pressures they face, the extent and depth of poverty they harbor, and the environmental consequences of their conversion. Understanding these differences is essential to prescribing appropriate institutions and policies.

Chapter 1 distinguishes three stylized forest types:

Forest-agriculture mosaiclands—where land ownership is usually better defined, population densities higher, and markets nearer, and natural forest management often cannot compete (from the landholder's perspective) with agriculture or plantation forestry.

Frontier and disputed areas—where pressures for deforestation and degradation are increasing, and control is often insecure and in conflict.

Areas beyond the agricultural frontier—where there is a lot of forest, few but largely indigenous inhabitants, and some pressure on timber resources.

The chapter maps proxies for these types, showing that most forests have few residents—and that most forest dwellers occupy a relatively small portion of the forest estate. The chapter also shows that frontier and mosaic forests have high deforestation rates and threatened or unique biodiversity. These different constellations of economic pressures, forest tenure security, and environmental circumstances require different policy responses.

Chapter 2. Incentives and Constraints Shape Forest Outcomes

People clear and log forests because they gain from doing so. Gains can be unsettlingly small or impressively large (see the "Stage-Setting" section that follows this overview), ephemeral or sustainable. Chapter 2 explores how local conditions, incentives, and constraints determine where and why deforestation occurs, and with what impacts.

A simple economic framework applies to all forest actors: subsistence households and large companies; farmers, ranchers, and loggers. The framework revolves around the relative attractiveness of maintaining forest relative to converting it to agriculture. Landholders and land claimants weigh cultural, economic, and legal considerations when making decisions about land use. A central issue for the report is that some may find agriculture a more profitable, attractive land use than sustainable management of forests for timber and other products.

Low wages, good soils, and higher prices for agricultural goods all motivate deforestation. In addition, high prices for timber can provoke mining of old-growth forests—though it can also stimulate sustainable management of plantations and secondary forests. These relationships are strongly affected by governance and tenure conditions. Where governance is weak and tenure poorly defined, powerful interests can seize forest resources, and smallholders can engage in conflict-ridden races for property rights. But even land-holders with secure tenure may choose deforestation if it offers higher returns.

The report uses empirical examples to illustrate aspects of this general framework as they apply in different contexts. The framework helps explain and predict:

- Where deforestation occurs.

- Private gains and public costs of deforestation.

- How a wide range of policies—involving trade, road expansion, forest tenure, and other areas— are modulated by local conditions to affect poverty and environment.

- Why some places experience forest transitions— deforestation followed by recovery in forest cover— while others follow immiserizing paths of deforestation and increasing poverty.

Chapter 3. Poverty in Forests Stems from Remoteness and Lack of Rights

The relationship between forests and poverty eludes simple general-izations, as shown by the examples in the Stage-Setting section that follows this overview. Asserting that poverty causes deforestation, or vice versa, doesn't provide a fruitful framework for understand-ing the issues.

Empirically, this link is weak. Although poor subsistence farmers cut down trees, so do rich ranchers and plantation owners. Defores-tation can deprive poor people of resources—but it can also provide them with sustainable incomes from cash crops. This chapter pres-ents new data showing weak, inconsistent geographic overlap among forest cover, deforestation, and poverty in several forested countries.

So what is distinctive about forest poverty as opposed to other rural poverty? First, remoteness. Because the best, most accessible farming lands have long been cleared and tilled in many parts of the world, forests and their inhabitants tend to be relegated to remote or unfavorable areas. As a result, areas with high forest cover often have low population densities but high poverty rates.

Second, forest dwellers may be unable to tap forest resources. People living in or near forests derive much of their income from collecting fuelwood, food, and other forest products, or by practicing long-fallow agriculture. If they lack the right to harvest forest resources or to use forest land for cropping, their income can suffer. Sometimes this happens when governments or wealthy interests claim forests and restrict access. In other cases forests effectively belong to no one—with the result that their resources are degraded through overuse.

Third, forest dwellers may lack the resources, capacity, and social organization to profit from managing forests for timber or nontimber products.

Chapter 4. Deforestation Imposes Geographically Varied Environmental Damages

Environmental problems are social problems, and society may be moved to intervene if one person's land-use decisions significantly affect other people's well-being. Chapter 4 traces those impacts, which operate through different channels and depend on the location of deforestation, for instance:

- The most widespread impact—and arguably the one with the most costly damages—is the effect of forest loss on climate change through CO_2 emissions. These greenhouse emissions are associated with all permanent losses of forest, regardless of location. Moreover, their physical impact is reasonably well understood, and society can place an increasingly well-defined economic value on reducing these emissions.

- There is considerable global demand for preventing extinctions and other biodiversity losses, and an increasingly good understanding of where biodiversity is richest and most threatened.

- The impacts of forest loss on flooding, smoke pollution, and water availability and quality are important in some locations but specific to local conditions and changes in land use. Protecting local watersheds can be important for maintaining urban water quality.

- Some theories and evidence suggest that deforestation can cause local and global changes in weather patterns quite apart from its effects through CO_2 emissions.

- Direct economic benefits of forest conservation—such as pollination and pest control—are likely to be greatest in mosaiclands but have not been well quantified in physical and economic terms.

Chapter 5. Improving Forest Governance

Diagnosis of forest poverty and environmental issues reveals two basic problems:

- Many forests are nominally owned by governments, but actual control is unclear or disputed. Elsewhere, private and community rights are not respected. Who should have the right to use and manage forests? How can rights be reliably enforced?

- How should the interests of forest owners in removing trees be balanced against the interests of others—near and far—in maintaining the environmental benefits of those trees?

These are problems of governance that require balancing interests between groups, negotiating solutions, and enforcing commitments. But these problems have been difficult to address.

First, elites tend to capture the institutions that allocate forest resources. Second, there are strong asymmetries of information, power, and organization between the beneficiaries of deforestation and those who bear its burdens. The diffuse interest groups favoring forest conservation find it hard to organize themselves to counterbalance the concentrated interests of forest degradation.

Building on a framework introduced in the *World Development Report 2003: Sustainable Development in a Dynamic World* (World Bank 2002), chapter 5 describes institutional and technological innovations that might help overcome these two barriers to collective action, thereby facilitating implementation of the prescriptive policies described in chapters 6 and 7. These catalytic innovations—which include building constituencies for conservation and better governance, improving public monitoring and disclosure of forest conditions and management, certifying forest and agricultural products, and introducing more flexible, market-like approaches to environmental regulation—can help diffuse groups organize, check abuses of power, and cut the costs of reaching agreements.

Chapter 6. Balancing Interests at the National Level

Nations need to sort out who has the rights to manage forest and how stringently to regulate those rights in the public interest. The challenges play out differently in different types of forests:

In mosaiclands, where agriculture and forests are in close contact, the challenge is to ensure that land managers take into account the benefits of forest maintenance for their neighbors.

At the frontier and in disputed regions, to resolve conflicting claims to forestlands and determine where gains from forest conversion outweigh environmental damages.

Beyond the agricultural frontier, to recognize and defend long-standing indigenous claims, tap and fairly share rents from timber exploitation while avoiding needless forest degradation, and avert disorderly races for property rights when the frontier arrives.

To realize these goals, governments can deploy the following tools, often in combination:

Tenure, zoning, and land-use regulation—revisiting the ownership and management of government lands, implementing systems to enforce property rights, regulating the exploitation of public and private forests, and promoting participatory planning for land management.

Making forest management more attractive relative to agriculture—by funding or facilitating markets for environmental services, researching, developing, and disseminating environmentally friendly land management practices, and removing barriers to sustainable management of forests for timber and other products.

Coordinating regional development interventions (such as road network expansion and agriculture policies)—to exploit synergies between, or minimize trade-offs between, environmental and livelihood goals.

Table 1 shows possible ways to assign property and use rights in forests. Allocating and enforcing property rights and land use regulations is not easy, for reasons described in chapter 5: doing so

Table 1   Alternative Bundles of Forest Rights

Use restrictions	Ownership and/or management		
	State	Community	Private
No restrictions on conversion	State forests zoned for conversion	Some common property	Private lands
Conversion prohibited, sustainable management allowed	Direct state management; forest concessions	Most community forestry	Regulated private forests
Limited or no productive use	Strict protected areas	Some indigenous lands	Private reserves

requires settling disputes between groups and enforcing agreements. Chapter 6 reviews efforts to zone and regulate land use at regional and national levels. These efforts have often foundered due to failure to motivate compliance by landholders and to create reliable institutions for resolving disputes and preventing resource capture by elites. Still, some positive examples are emerging.

Chapter 6 also assesses the pros and cons of different tenure and management regimes:

Protected areas. The establishment of protected areas is perhaps the longest-standing, most widely practiced, and best-funded approach to maintaining forest environmental services. Evidence suggests that such areas can reduce deforestation even in weak institutional settings. Their effects on livelihoods are less documented, but they have been negative when people have been excluded from protected areas that they relied on for forest products. But there is a trend toward permitting multiple uses for protected areas, and the World Bank has instituted strict social safeguards for their creation. Most new protected forest areas are beyond the agricultural frontier, where it is easier to accommodate local residents, and there is less competition from commercial interests.

Indigenous areas. Management and ownership of remote forest areas is increasingly being transferred to indigenous control. Indigenous ownership is sometimes associated

12

with much lower deforestation rates than in comparable areas. But indigenous areas are sometimes prohibited from undertaking commercial logging or large-scale land transformation.

Regulated logging concessions. In frontier areas, where land and forests can be profitably exploited, the biodiversity benefits of protected areas come at an opportunity cost. In principle, regulated logging concessions offer considerable biodiversity protection at a much lower opportunity cost. Where constituencies for protected areas are weak, establishing regulated logging concessions may be a politically feasible alternative that could be far superior—in environmental terms—to agricultural conversion. Innovations in monitoring and control, including certification, can increase public capture of logging profits and reduce environmental damages associated with logging. Efficient regulation—streamlining regulations to ease the burden of compliance and monitoring costs—can also help.

Community forest management. Communities are increasingly sharing management of or taking ownership of public forests. In principle, communities should be better than distant governments at managing and policing their forests, and better suited than individuals to exploit economies of scale in forest management. But successful community management depends on the strength of community organization, the regulations facing communities, and economic and cultural incentives to maintain forests. Communities need strong social capital to enforce compliance with management rules and avoid elite capture of forest resources. Communities may lack the ability to commercially exploit forests or effectively negotiate sales of logging rights to outsiders. Onerous regulations—such as requirements for detailed management plans—can be prohibitively costly. The economics of community management of natural forests can be unfavorable when market access is poor or the density of sellable tree species is low. Still, some communities have overcome these obstacles. Policies to support community forestry include building capacity, fostering markets for less-known wood species, and streamlining regulations.

Privately owned forests. Reconciling agricultural and environmental services has proven difficult in frontier and mosaiclands. Some countries have applied zoning and forest regulations of varying sophistication. Although rigorous impact evaluations are lacking, these regulations do not appear to be heavily enforced on wealthy interests— but may impose costs on poor people, without generating environmental benefits. Systems for environmental service payments and tradable development rights can help secure landholder cooperation in achieving environmental goals. There may also be scope to organize communities in support of land management goals.

Many rural development and agricultural policies have spillover effects on forests and deforestation. Placement of rural roads is especially important for policy attention because it is under direct policy control (though subject to political pressures). Rural roads can have large effects on both rural incomes and deforestation pressures. Thus, careful planning and regulation of road construction, and coordination of road policies with land and forest tenure regularization, can minimize trade-offs between rural incomes and environmental protection. Similarly, policy-induced increases in agricultural commodity prices could benefit rural populations but will tend to increase pressures for forest conversion; these side effects need to be anticipated.

Special attention needs to be paid to the challenges of reducing poverty in remote areas with low population densities. Protecting forest and land rights is a start. Innovative means of delivering services to these areas are also needed.

Chapter 7. Mobilizing Global Constituencies for Forest Conservation

While forests have many environmental benefits, only two command a global constituency with potentially large willingness to pay for those benefits: carbon storage and conservation of globally significant biodiversity. Mobilizing global finance for these environmental services is a crucial long-term challenge.

Global carbon finance offers an ungrasped opportunity for mitigating climate change, supporting sustainable land use, and conserving forests. About a fifth of global CO_2 emissions come from tropical deforestation—and the costs of abating some of these emissions appear low. In Latin America dense tropical forest is often cleared to create pastures worth a few hundred dollars a hectare, while releasing 500 tons of CO_2 per hectare. This implies, at a societal level, a CO_2 abatement cost of less than $1 a ton.

Meanwhile, some observers think that tackling climate change requires paying about $3 a ton for CO_2 abatement—and European Union (EU) members are currently paying up to $20 a ton (though this price is volatile). In other words, deforesters are destroying a carbon storage asset theoretically worth $1,500–10,000 to create a pasture worth $200–500 (per hectare). Yet carbon markets, such as those under the Kyoto Protocol and EU Emissions Trading Scheme, do not reward forestholders for reduced emissions from avoided deforestation.

The failure to grasp this opportunity reflects concerns about the implementation of incentive payments for reducing forest emissions. But a long-term approach could address those concerns by:

Securing global commitment to mitigating climate change, so that reduced deforestation helps reduce the global cost of arresting rising atmospheric CO_2. Reduced deforestation must be part of a long-term global package that includes lower industrial and transport emissions and more rapid research and development on clean energy.

Creating a system of financial incentives, funded by industrial countries, for developing countries to reduce their forest CO_2 emissions. This might be incorporated, for instance, into a change-climate regime whereby industrial countries could meet more stringent requirements for reducing CO_2 emissions partly by funding national programs to reduce deforestation. Developing countries would receive payments tied to measured reductions in deforestation below some agreed level.

Developing national infrastructure for forest carbon—that is, institutions and policies to monitor it and reduce deforestation. In most countries this would be a gradual process. The institutional requirements, though significant, would be consistent with those already required for better forest governance. The policies would not necessarily involve direct payments to forestholders, but would support systems for preventing accidental forest fires, strengthening monitoring and enforcement of regulations, regularizing forest tenure, and increasing returns to forest maintenance relative to agriculture.

Stimulating production of food and timber on degraded lands. This is crucial to counteracting leakages (where pressures on protected forests are diverted to unprotected ones), and is an important avenue through which emission reduction programs stimulate sustainable development.

Providing small payments per ton of CO_2 deferred each year, rather than large upfront payments for unenforceable commitments to perpetual reductions in CO_2.

The spatially concentrated nature of threatened biodiversity lends itself to environmental service payments in which landholders would be paid for maintaining habitat quality. Such markets might be particularly apt for mosaiclands—where biodiversity is highly threatened and land tenure is reasonably well defined—and for community forests—where buyers of conservation services might be able to outbid loggers for concession rights. Auction-based systems for purchasing conservation services have advantages of transparency and efficiency. Such systems could elicit self-assembling biodiversity corridors in biodiversity hotspots where forest remnants persist in areas less attractive to agriculture.

To date there has been no large-scale financing mechanism for payments of this kind. Existing conservation funders—including the Global Environmental Facility (GEF) and nongovernmental organizations (NGOs)—could direct part of their portfolios to such payments. Supplemental funds could be raised if nations, individually or together, create markets for biodiversity offsets to compensate for damages associated with construction, mining, and other projects that harm the environment.

In addition to these long-horizon initiatives, the international community could immediately fund the compilation of information that is critically needed to plan and execute policies for reducing forest poverty and deforestation. Severe but readily remediable information gaps include:

- Rates, locations, and types of deforestation and degradation.

- Poverty levels of forest-dwelling and forest-using populations.

- Monitoring and evaluation of the environmental and economic outcomes of forest conservation projects and policies for devolving forest control.

- Physical and economic impacts of forest conservation on environmental service flows.

Chapter 8. Conclusions and Recommendations

In the long run, rising wages and urbanization will pull rural people away from marginal lands at the forest edge, halting deforestation and in some cases resulting in forest regrowth and recovery. But some forests may never recover, and others may irretrievably lose some of their biodiversity. Better institutions for forest management can help bridge the forest transition—preventing deforestation for small and ephemeral gains while providing more sustainable livelihoods.

Box 3   This Report's Recommendations

International level
- Mobilize carbon finance to reduce deforestation and promote sustainable agriculture.
- Mobilize finance for conservation of globally significant biodiversity.
- Finance national and global efforts to monitor forests and evaluate the impacts of forest projects and policies—including devolution of forest control.
- Foster the development of national-level research and evaluation organizations through twinning with established foreign partners.

National level
- Create systems for monitoring forest conditions and forest dwellers' welfare, make

land and forest allocations and regulations more transparent, and support civil society organizations that monitor regulatory compliance by government, landholders, and forest concessionaires. The prospect of carbon finance can help motivate these efforts.
- Make forest and land use regulations more efficient, reformulating them to minimize monitoring, enforcement, and compliance costs. Economic instruments can help.

Areas beyond the frontier
- Avert disruptive races for property rights by equitably assigning ownership, use rights, and stewardship of these lands.
- Options for forest conservation include combinations of indigenous and community

(continued on next page)

17

Box 3 *(continued)*

rights, protected areas, and forest conces-sions. Still, some forest may be converted to agriculture where doing so offers high, sustainable returns and does not threaten irreplaceable environmental assets.

- Plan for rational, regulated expansion of road networks—including designation of roadless areas.
- Experiment with new ways of providing services and infrastructure to low-density populations.

Frontier areas

- Assign and enforce property rights equitably.
- Plan and control road network expansion.
- Discourage conversion in areas with hydro-logical hazards, or encourage community management of these watersheds.
- Use remote sensing, enhanced communica-tion networks, and independent observers to monitor logging concessionaires and pro-tect forestholders against encroachers.
- Consider using carbon finance to sup-port government and community efforts to assign and enforce property rights.
- Encourage markets for environmental ser-vices in community-owned forests.

Disputed areas

- Where forest control is transferred to local communities, build local institutions with upward and downward accountability.
- Where community rights are secure and markets are feasible, provide technical assis-tance for community forestry.
- Make landholder rights more secure in "for-ests without trees."
- When forest tenure is secure, use carbon markets to promote forest regeneration and maintenance.

Mosaiclands

- Reform regulations so that they don't penal-ize tree growing.
- Promote greener agriculture—such as inte-grated pest management and silvopastoral systems—through research and develop-ment, extension efforts, community organi-zation, and reform of agriculture and forest regulations.
- Develop a wide range of markets for environ-mental services—carbon, biodiversity, water regulation, recreation, and pest control—to support more productive, sustainable land management.

Two Contrasting Cases of Poverty, Wealth, Biodiversity, and Deforestation

This report emphasizes the need for understanding local links among deforestation, environment, and poverty. To set the stage and illustrate the diversity of forest situations, consider two sharply contrasting cases of deforestation. In Madagascar much deforestation is undertaken by poor people for paltry and unsustainable gains. In Mato Grosso, Brazil, large commercial farmers realize substantial monetary gains from deforestation. In both cases the environmental impacts are widely felt.

Poverty, Biodiversity Loss, and Deforestation in Madagascar

If there were a real market for biodiversity, Madagascar would be rich—the sole owner of 11,200 endemic plant species and 144 endemic mammals, including charismatic lemurs. In fact, Madagascar has one of the world's largest assemblages of unique plants and animals.

But there is no organized market for biodiversity, and Madagascar is poor. Despite its $75 million investment in protected areas since 1991—much of it supported by donors—the country's tourism revenue has not risen much. Since 1960

real GDP per capita has fallen from $383 to $246. About 70 percent of the total population and 77 percent of the rural population live below the national poverty line.

Meanwhile, Madagascar's natural capital, priceless but unsellable, is being run down. During the 1990s deforestation proceeded at 0.86 percent a year, and habitat fragmentation threatened the survival of forest species. But forests are not being used to create productive, sustainable assets: they are being converted to low-productivity maize and rice cultivation (photo 1). Averaging 2 tons a hectare, rice yields are barely half the world average (Randrianarisoa 2003; Uphoff 2003). Some fields are rapidly degraded and abandoned, and some forest irreversibly lost. And with stagnant productivity and a rapidly expanding (2.8 percent annual growth) but still largely rural population, pressures on the forest seem likely to continue.

Is poverty responsible for deforestation in Madagascar? At the broadest, most macro level the answer must be yes: people persist in forest-degrading activities with low returns because the economy offers no better alternative. But the poverty-deforestation link blurs if we look closer for

Deforestation in Madagascar's moist forests is undertaken for low-yielding upland rice cultivation.

© Rickey Rogers / Reuters / Corbis.

diagnoses that will help determine policy solutions. Comparing localities and holding other things constant (such as road access and topography), there is not a strong correlation between local poverty and deforestation rates. But deforestation is closely associated with proximity to roads (Gorenflo and others 2006), while poverty is associated with distance from them (INSTAT and others 2003).

These findings suggest that improving the country's dilapidated road network could raise rural incomes by stimulating expansion of farms into forest—leading to a trade-off between poverty reduction and environmental protection. Export-oriented maize farming has been responsible for intense hotspots of deforestation in the country's dry southwestern region. For more subsistence-oriented farmers in the country's humid forests, Ferraro (2002) and Shyamsundar and Kramer (1996) show that restricting their ability to convert forest would translate into lower incomes.

Although policy solutions for deforestation and poverty have been elusive, the search continues. Protected areas seem to be effective in reducing deforestation (Gorenflo and others 2006), but protected area revenues and integrated conservation development projects (often associated with protected areas) have done little to augment local incomes. Experiments with community co-management of state forest areas have also not lived up to expectations (Antona 2002). One hope is that intensifying agriculture in lowland irrigated areas could reduce migration to forest frontiers. In some cases control of upland deforestation may reduce sediment flows that clog lowland irrigation canals—making irrigated rice more productive.

Although the obstacles are formidable, markets for environmental services may offer a partial long-run solution. Deforestation in Madagascar releases carbon dioxide (CO_2) into the atmosphere, contributing to global warming. Although the country's contribution to global warming is tiny, a global market for CO_2 emission reductions could provide financing for sustainable land management in Madagascar. A program for reducing global emissions might be able to offer farmers more for forest conservation than the proceeds of low-yield rice production. And over the very long run, the uniqueness of Madagascar's biodiversity assets and growth in ecotourism demand could yield a lucrative income stream.

Wealth, Biodiversity Loss, and Deforestation in Brazil's *Cerrado*

Cattle and soybeans are displacing *cerrado* (savanna woodland) and forest in Brazil's center-west region (photo 2). Between 1999/2000 and 2004/05 the states of Goias, Mato Grosso, and Mato Grosso del Sul planted an additional 54,000 square kilometers to soy—an area slightly larger than Costa Rica—doubling the area under soy cultivation. At the same time, cattle herds in these states soared from 57 million in 1999 to 71 million in 2004. While some of the soy expanded into former pasture, the combined effect was loss of savanna and forest. The Brazilian National Institute for Space Research (INPE) estimates that 38 percent of total Amazonian deforestation over 1999–2003 occurred in Mato Grosso (INPE 2006). About 5.6 percent of remaining Mato Grosso *cerrado* woodlands were deforested between 1998 and 2002.

Rising profits catalyzed the boom. In 1999 Brazil devalued its currency, which fell against the U.S. dollar by 50 percent or more, making exports more attractive. At the same time, the price of soybeans rose from $184 to $277 in 2004 (USDA 2006), and control of hoof and mouth disease boosted the value of beef exports (Kaimowitz and others 2004).

In effect, there is money lying on the ground for the taking—if trees are removed. In Mato Grosso the price of fields in local currency quadrupled between mid-1999 and the end of 2004. Pastures were worth less, but more favorable lands command higher prices: more than $3,000 a hectare for fields in the most productive parts of Goias state. In 2002 forest conversion in Mato Grosso created farmland with a gross value of about $100 million (Chomitz and Wertz-Kanounnikoff 2005). Most of these values are being appropriated by large farmers and ranchers. Although recent data are not available, the 1995–96 agricultural census found that 72 percent of Mato Grosso farmland (and 58 percent in the entire center-west region) is in establishments larger than 1,000 hectares (IBGE 1998).

Cerrado conversion comes at an environmental price that is large but difficult to quantify. The *cerrado* is home to 4,400 plant species found nowhere else and is one of the planet's most important biodiversity hotspots. Yet this

Recently cleared farmland abuts Amazônian forest in Mato Grosso state, Brazil.

© Louise Cobb / Corbis SABA.

21

irreplaceable biodiversity is hard to monetize. It can't compare with African savannas in terms of large, charismatic mammals (though it does boast a splendid anteater) and so cannot support an extensive ecotourism industry. Its unique plants may contain commercially valuable genetic information, but there is no current market for this information, and a future market probably wouldn't support conservation of the entire area—a modest area might provide all the samples needed. The *cerrado* also has subtle but important environmental links to the rest of Brazil. Deforestation and land degradation in the *cerrado*, for instance, have resulted in higher rainy season flows on the Tocantins River (Costa, Botta, and Cardille 2003). Sediment and agrochemicals run off fields, polluting downstream drinking water.

The result is that landholders face a rather easy choice, Brazilian society a more difficult one. From a landholder's perspective, converting a few hundred hectares of *cerrado* to pasture or soy brings substantial personal gain. From society's perspective, those palpable immediate benefits, and any knock-on local development effects, have to be weighed against large but unmonetizable environmental damages.

Brazil's long-standing forest code enshrines a pragmatic solution to this problem, requiring landholders to set aside 20–80 percent of their properties as forest reserve (depending on location). They also must maintain forests by riverbanks and on hills. But landholders face strong incentives to flout the rules, and authorities have had a hard time monitoring and enforcing these regulations over Brazil's vast territory.

In 2000, in response to high deforestation rates, the state environmental agency of Mato Grosso (FEMA) implemented an innovative environmental control system. Called the Rural Property Environmental Licensing System (SLAPR), it promised a technological and institutional revolution in regulating land use on private rural properties. The system used a multipronged approach to encourage compliance with land use regulations: deterring deforestation on unlicensed properties, encouraging landowners to license their properties, and enforcing regulations on licensed properties. The central innovation was to license large landholders, requiring them to precisely map their allowed land use using a geographic information system. Satellite images were then to be used to monitor compliance by licensed landholders, as well as look for illegal forest burning and clearing on unlicensed properties. Because large properties (larger than 1,000 hectares) were few in number but accounted for most private land, this approach was potentially cost-effective (Fundação Estadual do Meio Ambiente 2001). The system's design called for all licenses to be posted on the Internet to facilitate public oversight of compliance and enforcement—a feature never implemented.

Early studies of SLAPR credited it with reducing deforestation (Fundação Estadual do Meio Ambiente 2002; Fearnside 2003). But it is difficult to separate the system's effects from the annual ups and downs driven by economic factors such as soy and beef booms. Using disaggregated, spatially explicit FEMA deforestation data from 1999–2002, Chomitz and Wertz-Kanounnikoff 2005 found that before 2002, the system did shift landholder behavior in a direction consistent with reduced illegal deforestation.

But subsequent developments showed SLAPR to be ineffective. During 2003–04 deforestation soared in Mato Grosso. Instituto Socioambiental (2005) found that during this period SLAPR failed to achieve what was arguably its main goal: preventing illegal deforestation on licensed properties, where such activity should be easy to detect and prosecute. More spectacularly, in June 2005 a huge network of illegal deforestation and timber trade was uncovered during a federal anticorruption operation. Presumed to have existed for at least a decade, the corruption scheme involved 600 timber companies, dozens of intermediary traders, and numerous public servants from the federal and Mato Grosso environmental agencies (Diário de Cuiabá, December 31, 2005). About 200 people were arrested during the sting—including the director of FEMA, who was charged with contributing to illegal deforestation by issuing environmental licenses in protected areas. (Three main perpetrators have been jailed; other prosecutions are proceeding.)

Moreover, FEMA officials in the state government that entered office in 2003 were accused of issuing environmental licenses and deforestation permits arbitrarily (such as by using alternative land cover maps to define the required proportions of legal forest reserves) and of being negligent in enforcing environmental laws. Major problems with implementation of SLAPR include insufficient spatial coverage and automation, a possibility of falsified satellite images, FEMA's insufficient human and technical capacity, incon-

sistent state and federal environmental legislation, missing institutional cooperation, and inadequate transparency and control of FEMA activities (Lima and others 2005; Barbosa 2006).

FEMA has since been overhauled, and it intends to reinvigorate SLAPR (Araújo 2006). Meanwhile, the neighboring state of Goias is considering an alternative, possibly complementary approach to enforcing the forest reserve requirement. Like Mato Grosso, Goias has experienced an agriculture-led boom. Its private sector is interested in finding ways to continue to grow while complying with environmental laws. Compliance would not only remove legal uncertainties, it could also facilitate financing as well as exports to green global markets.

One possibility is to allow trading of forest reserve obligations. Doing so would allow farmers who lack enough forest reserves to meet their obligations by paying to protect an equivalent amount of forest elsewhere. In principle, this approach could greatly reduce the cost of compliance while boosting the environmental quality of the reserves (see chapter 6). But making it work will require building more reliable institutions for monitoring trades and tracking compliance.

The mosaiclands: A mosaic of citrus plantation and rainforest in Toledo District, Belize.

© Raymond Gehman / National Geographic Image Collection.

PART I

The Where and Why of Deforestation and Forest Poverty

In an Assam (India) forest severely degraded by illegal logging, inhabitants eke out a living selling firewood.

Grant Milne / World Bank.

Frontier areas: A mounted forest patrol returns from a day in the field, northern Sumatra.

Photo by Josef Leitmann, World Bank.

CHAPTER 1

Forests Differ

Forests differ: in the pressures they face, the people they support, and their environmental functions. Three stylized types (forest-agriculture mosaiclands, frontier and disputed areas, and areas beyond the agricultural frontier) in two biomes (forests proper and savanna woodlands) capture much of the social, environmental, and economic variation of tropical forests (box 1.1). This chapter describes these stylized forest types in the tropical world and the challenges they face. It maps the extent of these types, tallies their populations, and assesses their biodiversity. The analysis here sets the stage for subsequent discussions of appropriate policies for different kinds of forests.

Three Stylized Forest Types

How are we to make sense of the staggering diversity of tropical forests? A few factors shape forests' environmental characteristics and human pressures on them—but these generalizations are riddled with exceptions.

A first cut is the distinction between "true" forests and savannas. Forests typically receive more rainfall and (if undisturbed) have unbroken canopies, high densities of wood, and more diverse tree species. These features make them susceptible to selective "mining" for timber, harder to clear for agriculture, and major sources of carbon dioxide emissions and biodiversity loss if cleared. Savannas are grasslands and woodlands dotted with smaller trees and shrubs. Easier to clear, less diverse, and more resilient than rainforests, and less valuable for fine woods, these woodlands are often cut for fuelwood and charcoal.

Box 1.1   This Report's Geographic Scope

To keep this report's scope manageable, it focuses on the developing world's tropical forests and savanna woodlands, with an emphasis on the former. This approach was chosen somewhat reluctantly, since there are important challenges related to the management of boreal and temperate forests, and some forest governance issues cut across all forest types. But tropical forests face distinct issues and challenges. They are home to most of the world's poor forest dwellers and contain the bulk of its forest-based biodiversity, and it is here where almost all deforestation and forest-related carbon emissions occur.

This report looks broadly at ecosystems, rather than narrowly at trees. The focus is on tropical and subtropical forest and savanna biomes—that is, areas originally covered by these types of vegetation, as mapped by WWF (map 1.1). Excluded from these areas but sometimes included in the discussion are xeric shrublands (such as in southwest Madagascar or the Brazilian *caatinga*) and montane grasslands and shrublands (as in the

Map 1.1   This Report's Focus: Tropical Forests and Savanna Woodlands

Biomes
- Tropical forest biome
- Tropical savanna biome

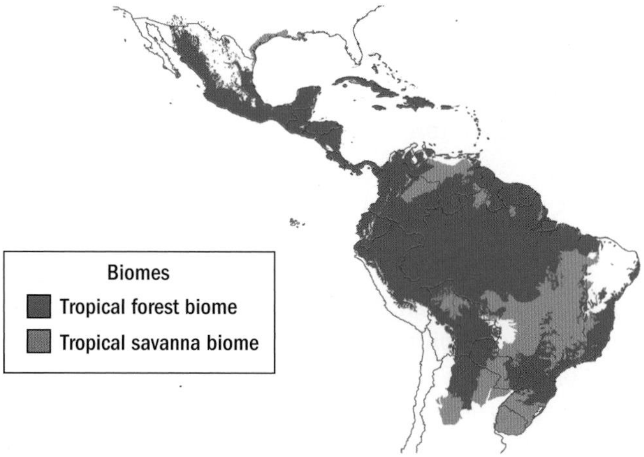

Source: Authors' mapping of data from WWF 2001.

Box 1.1 (*continued*)

highest elevations of the Andes). The report devotes relatively little attention to plantation management.

The report often uses data and examples from Brazil, for several reasons. Brazil contains a large portion of the world's tropical forests, including disparate types: remote, dense rainforests; savannas; and highly fragmented, long-settled forests of extreme biodiversity. It also has a diverse array of forest actors: indigenous people, subsistence-oriented smallholders, extractivists, agrobusinesses. Due to concerns in civil society and government, Brazil has extensive experience grappling with land and forest use regulation—experience from which other countries can learn. Finally, Brazil has superb statistics on its population, economic conditions, and deforestation. Indeed, it is partly because of the Brazilian government's bold decision to regularly monitor and publicize deforestation rates that the world pays more attention to deforestation in Brazilian Amazônia than in other, less transparent regions.

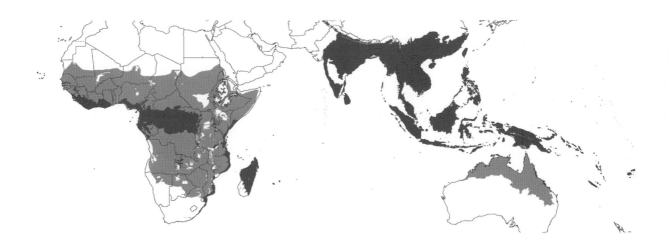

Human pressure on forests is shaped by their market access, suitability for farming, and tenure security. Moreover, these three factors tend to be intertwined, for reasons explored in more depth later. These issues motivate a stylized, three-part typology.

- *Forest-agriculture mosaiclands with better-defined tenure* are settled agricultural areas interspersed with woods, often close to urban centers. They have relatively high population densities and depleted, fragmented forests. These areas account for a minority of the world's forest estate but contain a substantial portion of its forest dwellers, a large share of threatened species, and the bulk of locally valued forest services. Consequently, they are where interactions between people and trees are most intense, and where trees are important sources of incomes and environmental services. Here the potential for both poverty reduction and environmental protection is great—but so is the potential for trade-offs between these goals.

- *Frontier and disputed areas* often suffer from conflicts over land and forest resources. In Latin America and parts of Africa these are places where waves of agricultural expansion are crashing on a broad front of relatively undisturbed forest. In parts of Indonesia large timber and plantation interests, small commercial farmers, and long-time residents are battling for control of forest areas. Elsewhere in Asia and in parts of Africa, ineffectual government control of nationalized forests creates a tragedy of the commons where communities, forest services, and fuelwood extractors dispute woodland control and create degraded landscapes.

- *Areas beyond the agricultural frontier* are outside the reach of most agricultural markets, though not beyond human influence. These include the last great expanses of tropical forest: the Amazon and Congo basins, and some scattered smaller areas. A minority of forest dwellers live here, but they include indigenous populations and some of the world's poorest people.

These types and the challenges facing each are summarized in table 1.1. These categories are meant to help organize thought;

Table 1.1 Forest Types and Their Challenges

Type of area	Features	Poverty and development challenge	Environmental challenges	Governance challenges
Mosaiclands with better-defined tenure	High land value; contain many of the world's forest dwellers but a small fraction of the forest	Managing landscapes for production and environmental services; preventing extinctions of threatened species; mitigating carbon dioxide (CO_2) emissions; fostering carbon sequestration		Agreeing on, committing to, and enforcing property rights over land, trees, and environmental services
Frontier and disputed areas	Agricultural expansion; rapidly increasing land values in frontiers; conflicts over forest use in disputed areas	Fostering more intensive rural development and access to off-farm employment	Avoiding irreversible degradation; mitigating CO_2 emissions; avoiding forest fragmentation	Restraining resource grabs by large actors; averting races for property rights by smallholders; equitably adjudicating land claims
Areas beyond the agricultural frontier	Most of the world's tropical forests; contains a minority of forest dwellers but many indigenous people	Providing services for dispersed populations	Maintaining large-scale environmental processes	Protecting indigenous people's rights; averting disorderly frontier expansion

they are not intended to be rigid pigeonholes into which every forest neatly fits. Rudel (2005) presents a similar but simpler typology, focusing on the distinction between large and small forests—the unbroken blocs of the Amazon and Congo basins and Indonesian forests relative to the fragmented forests of other regions. Rudel also describes deforestation processes by continent—a valuable resource when contemplating forest types.

From Stylized Types to Mapped Domains

It is impossible to map the three stylized forest types because geographic data on forest tenure are weak. But it is possible to map some rough proxies (maps 1.2–1.6). Table 1.2 shows the correspon-

Map 1.2   Domains in Africa's Tropical Forest Biomes

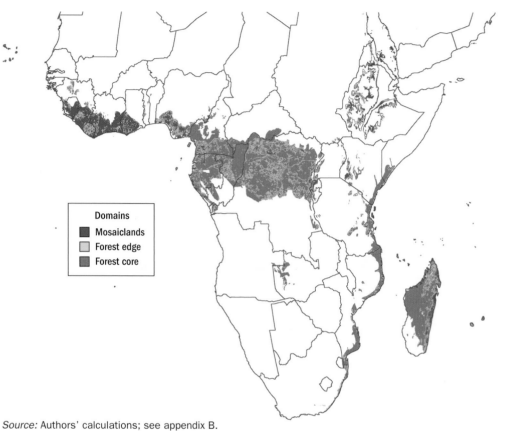

Source: Authors' calculations; see appendix B.

Table 1.2   Stylized Forest Types Have Equivalents in Mapped Domains

Stylized type	Mapped domain
Mosaiclands with better defined tenure	Mosaiclands: agricultural lands, agriculture-forest mosaics, and small forest patches
Frontier and disputed areas	Forest (and savanna) edges: the forested borders of mosaiclands
Areas beyond the agricultural frontier	Forest (and savanna) cores: forested areas well away from mosaiclands

dence between the idealized types and their mapped equivalents—called domains here. Box 1.2 and Appendix B provide more details on the construction of the domains.

The maps, especially those for the "true" forest, capture much of the spirit of the typology. Map 1.5, for instance, clearly shows the mosaiclands that characterize much of Central America and the South American Atlantic Forest. Its depiction of forest edges highlights the expansion of the Amazônian frontier from the south and east, and along roads and rivers. Map 1.4 shows forests remaining beyond the frontier on the islands of Borneo and New Guinea, but

Map 1.3   Domains in Africa's Tropical Savanna Biomes

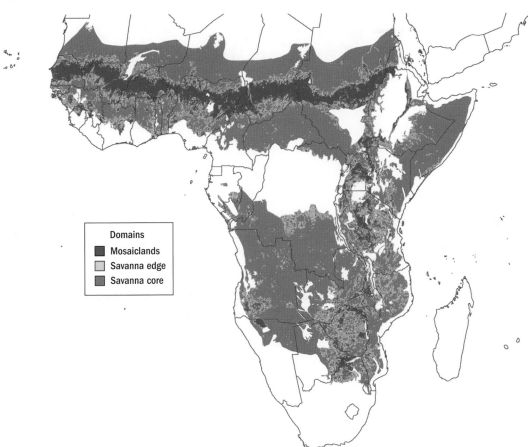

Source: Authors' calculations; see appendix B.

Map 1.4 Domains in Asia's Tropical Forest Biomes

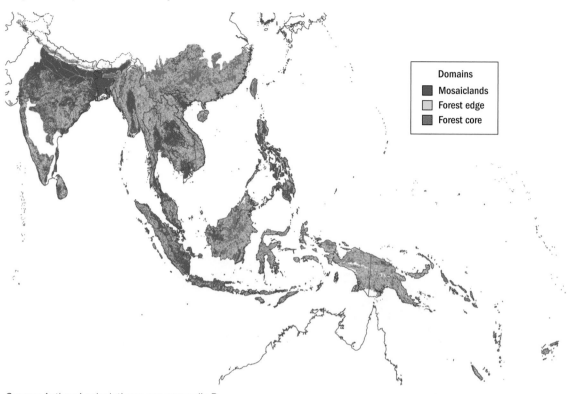

Source: Authors' calculations; see appendix B.

mostly already transformed to frontier in Sumatra and Sulawesi, Indonesia.

The correspondence between stylized types and mapped domains, however, is inexact. Nonremote forest edges could be akin to the mosaiclands they border. In long-settled parts of Asia these edges may be static interstices between scattered settlements. Some of these interstitial forests may be under disputed or insecure tenure. Other forest edges are near cities and have high population densities. These may represent agroforestry rather than frontiers or disputed areas. Thus the maps and tables in this chapter should be considered indicative of broad tendencies, and are not meant to give a definitive classification to any particular spot. They are intended to inspire more detailed work at the national level.

Map 1.5   Domains in Latin American and Caribbean Tropical Forest Biomes

Domains
- Mosaiclands
- Forest edge
- Forest core

Source: Authors' calculations; see appendix B.

Map 1.6   Domains in Latin American and Caribbean Tropical Savanna Biomes

Source: Authors' calculations; see appendix B.

Box 1.2 Mapping the Domains and Tallying Their Populations

To map tropical forest domains, this report uses GLC2000, a global map of land cover based on satellite data (ECJRC 2003). The GLC2000 maps the world in 1-square kilometer cells based on predominant vegetation. Although the GLC2000 is the best available map of global land cover, it has limitations. Remote sensing data at this resolution has difficulty distinguishing agroforestry from forests, and relatively undisturbed savanna woodlands from forest-agriculture mosaiclands.

Mosaiclands are mostly agriculture, mixtures of forest and agriculture, and small clumps of forest surrounded by agriculture. So this domain consists of mosaic forests embedded in a sea of agricultural lands.

Forest edges (a proxy for frontier areas) are forests and woodlands outside mosaiclands, but within 6 kilometers of them. This definition might roughly approximate the radius of household extractive activities or shifting cultivation around a small settlement. Finally, *forest cores* (a proxy for areas beyond the frontier) are more than 6 kilometers from mosaiclands.

The populations of these cells were estimated by overlaying them with data from the Global Rural-Urban Mapping Project (CIESIN and others 2004a, b, c). This data set compiled global census data at a fine administrative level—the equivalent of districts or smaller units, where possible. Residents of towns and cities were distinguished from rural dwellers, who were then assumed to be spread out evenly across the rest of the census district and mapped into 1-square kilometer cells. The assumption of even distribution probably results in an overestimate of the number of people living in forests, because population densities are higher in cleared areas than in forests.

The Uneven Distribution of Forest Populations

In the great forest areas beyond the frontier, people live at densities of less than 1 per 10 square kilometers—while some Asian forests have population densities hundreds of times that. Options for forestry and agriculture are very different in these settings. So is the environmental relationship between people and trees. This section, and much of this report, elaborates on an obvious but crucial distinction: most forest dwellers live in a small part of the forest, and most of the forest has few inhabitants.

It is important to understand the limitations of the data used to map forest populations (see box 1.2). The data assume that rural populations are evenly spread throughout their counties, districts, or municipios. We then tally the number of people in forested areas. This approach results in overestimates, because people tend to occupy unforested areas. Still, the data roughly indicate the number of people living in or around the three domains. The estimates are least reliable for African savannas, where remote sensing sources have difficulty distinguishing small-scale agriculture from savanna vegetation.

The resulting estimates provide guidance on the relative size of the three domains (table 1.3). These tabulations refer only to dispersed rural populations, excluding even small towns with a few thousand people. Some key findings:

- *Forest dwellers outnumber dwellers on purely agricultural lands.* In tropical regions more than 800 million rural people live in or near forests (considered at a fine geographic scale), while about 460 million live on lands that are mostly agricultural. Even keeping in mind that small towns are excluded from this calculation, and that forest dwellers are overstated, this estimate highlights the importance of woodlands in the populated rural landscape.

- *Latin America and the Caribbean have the most forest area, Africa the most savanna.* The area of nonsavanna forest in Latin America—about 10 million square kilometers—exceeds that in Africa and Asia combined. The savanna woodlands of Africa occupy about 11 million square kilometers.

- *Asia has by far the most forest dwellers and the highest population density in forests.* About 350 million people live in the forest edges and cores of Asia, with another 90 million in the Asian mosaic forests. The population densities of less remote Asian edge forests, at about 85 per square kilometer, are high enough to suggest long-settled areas dependent on agroforestry or planted forests. While most of these areas are unlikely to be expansion frontiers, some could be disputed. Africa and Latin America have about 165 million people living in nonsavanna forests, and Africa has 185 million people in savanna woodlands.

- *Forest edges contain most forest dwellers.* In the nonsavanna forests of Asia and Latin America, forest edge

Table 1.3   Forest Populations and Areas Vary by Continent, Biome, Domain, and Remoteness, 2000

Population (millions)

Continent	Biome	Mosaiclands				Forest edges		Forest cores	
		Agricultural lands		Mosaic forest					
		Hours to major city		Hours to major city		Hours to major city		Hours to major city	
		< 8	> 8	< 8	> 8	< 8	> 8	< 8	> 8
Africa	Forests	13.2	2.9	25.5	3.6	22.6	7.9	18.3	12.0
	Savannas	55.4	6.9	28.5	3.6	54.3	11.6	58.9	28.8
Asia	Forests	324.1	12.6	71.5	18.6	256.5	29.5	60.9	6.1
	Savannas	4.7	0.0	0.2	0.0	1.8	0.1	0.0	0.0
Latin America and Caribbean	Forests	31.2	3.2	18.2	1.8	34.8	7.2	7.5	3.9
	Savannas	5.2	0.5	2.8	0.3	4.1	1.0	0.7	0.3
All	Forests	368.5	18.6	115.2	24.0	313.9	44.7	86.7	22.0
	Savannas	65.3	7.4	31.5	4.0	60.2	12.7	59.5	29.0

Area (thousands of square kilometers)

Continent	Biome	Mosaiclands				Forest edges		Forest cores	
		Agricultural lands		Mosaic forest					
		Hours to major city		Hours to major city		Hours to major city		Hours to major city	
		< 8	> 8	< 8	> 8	< 8	> 8	< 8	> 8
Africa	Forests	114	54	440	130	480	466	693	1,206
	Savannas	1,189	480	778	284	1,446	1,012	3,024	4,307
Asia	Forests	1,684	169	636	517	2,045	1,527	594	563
	Savannas	15	1	1	13	8	12	0	3
Latin America and Caribbean	Forests	993	222	922	331	1,622	1,947	647	4,458
	Savannas	566	257	324	170	749	636	259	323
All	Forests	2,792	445	1,998	978	4,148	3,941	1,934	6,226
	Savannas	1,770	737	1,104	467	2,203	1,660	3,283	4,633

Source: Authors' calculations based on CIESIN 2004a, b, c and ECJRC 2003; see appendix B.

populations outnumber core and mosaic forest populations combined. Africa's nonsavanna forest populations are about equally split between the three domains.

- *Remote forest dwellers are relatively few.* Globally, about 22 million people live in nonsavanna forests more than 6 kilometers from the nearest agriculture and more than 8 hours' travel from the nearest city of 100,000 people. An additional 45 million live at similar remoteness, but within 6 kilometers of agriculture.

Figure 1.1 shows how unevenly people are distributed throughout forests. The middle panel shows the cumulative number of forest dwellers in Africa, Asia, and Latin America and the Caribbean as population densities increase, up to 500 per square kilometer. As noted, densities at this level include people who are near forests but not necessarily under forest canopy. An enormous share of these forest dwellers are Asian.

The top of figure 1.1 zooms on the most sparsely populated forests, with population densities below 50 per square kilometer. Dwellers in these forests are presumably highly dependent on forest resources and include shifting cultivators. Most of the 20 million inhabitants of the lowest-density forests (those with fewer than 10 people per square kilometer) are African and Latin American.

The bottom panel of figure 1.1 shows the cumulative area of forest as a function of population density. Most African and Latin American forests (excluding savannas) are occupied at densities of fewer than 20 people per square kilometer. In contrast, most Asian tropical forest is occupied at population densities above 50. These widely varying population densities have divergent implications for livelihoods and forest management.

Trends in Forest Change

With all the attention devoted to loss of tropical forests, one might think that the basic dimensions of the problem—the rate, location, and nature of forest degradation—would be well quantified and understood. They are not. Only a few countries, notably Brazil and India, are measuring and reporting forest status on a regular basis using remote sensing. Some countries, such as Mexico, have undertaken detailed forest inventories that permit assessment of changes in land use over specific periods. For many other important forest

Figure 1.1   Forests Vary Greatly in Population Density, 2000

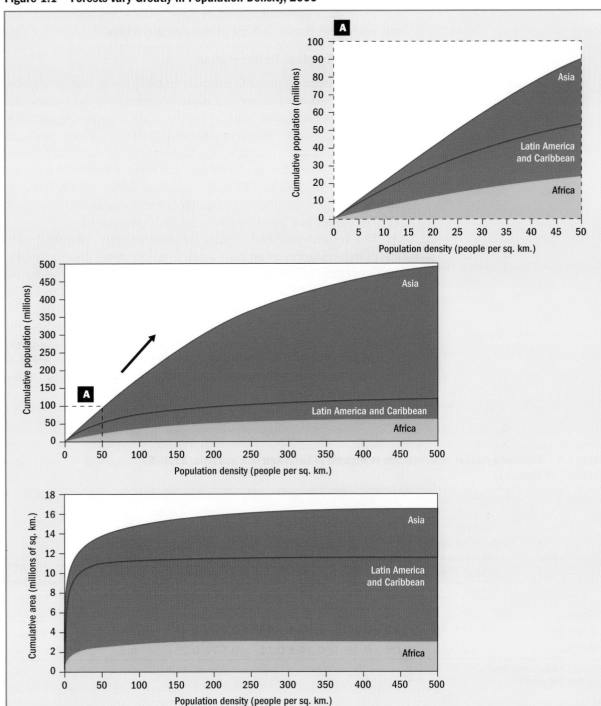

Source: Authors' calculations; see appendix B.
Note: Excludes savannas.

countries, consistent and comprehensive data on forest change do not exist. And overexploitation of forest plants and animals, a serious ecological threat, is hard to monitor anywhere.

Studies on Tropical Deforestation

There have been attempts to estimate tropical forest loss on a global scale. Each has advantages and disadvantages. The most authoritative source is the United Nations Food and Agriculture Organization (FAO 2001b) Forest Resources Assessment (FRA), which produces two sets of estimates. The first, oft-cited set is compiled from national inventories. While the quality of national reports increased substantially between 1990 and 2000, estimates of deforestation rates are affected by low-quality, incompatible, or missing inventories from 1990 or earlier and by inconsistencies between countries.

The less-known FRA remote sensing survey (FRA-RSS) estimates deforestation using high-resolution (30-meter pixels) satellite data covering 10 percent of the world's tropical forests. The results are representative at the continental but not national level. The FRA-RSS also tries to distinguish between kinds of forest degradation. The Tropical Ecosystem Environment Observation by Satellite (TREES) project uses high-resolution sample data to estimate forest loss in humid tropical forests. Achard and others (2004) combined FRA and TREES data to produce the estimates of forest loss shown in table 1.4.

Table 1.4 Estimated Annual Deforestation Is Highest in Latin America and Asia, 1990–97
(millions of hectares)

Type of forest change	Humid forests				Dry forests	
	Latin America and Caribbean except Brazil	Brazilian Amazônia	Africa	Asia	Latin America and Caribbean	Africa
Deforestation	1.08 ± 0.55	1.43 ± 0.88	0.85 ± 0.30	2.84 ± 0.90	1.9 ± 1.1	1.5 ± 0.6
Other degradation	0.61 ± 0.46	0.22 ± 0.21	0.39 ± 0.19	1.07 ± 0.44	n.s.	n.s.
Regrowth	0.20 ± 0.11	0.08 ± 0.11	0.14 ± 0.11	0.53 ± 0.25	n.s.	0.07 ± 0.05

Source: Achard and others 2004.
n.s. Not significant.

In contrast, Hansen and DeFries (2004) used globally comprehensive but low-resolution (8-kilometer pixels) data to map deforestation for the entire tropical realm (map 1.7). In addition to its more comprehensive coverage, their study assesses changes over 17 years instead of the 7 years of Achard and others (2004). But its methodology is less accurate for the dry forests and savannas of Africa and may not be able to detect subtle, small-scale patterns of degradation in forests and mosaiclands.

There is rough agreement between these two sources on the magnitude of gross deforestation on two continents during the 1990s: about 4.4 million hectares a year in Latin America and 2.8 million in Asia. FRA-RSS and TREES also detect substantial forest degradation: about another 1 million hectares a year for each of those continents. DeFries and others (2002) report much more forest regrowth than do the other sources. And the greatest disagreements are for the dry forests and savannas of Africa. The FRA country studies report 5.2 million hectares of annual net forest loss in tropical Africa, while DeFries and others (2002) estimate a net annual loss of just 376,000 hectares.

There is even more uncertainty about the actors responsible for deforestation. What are the roles of loggers, shifting agriculturalists, sedentary farmers, large-scale ranchers, and plantation owners? Because tropical forests are species-rich, loggers are selective in removing trees and rarely engage in clear-cutting. Of the 152 cases of deforestation reviewed by Geist and Lambin (2001), only 5 involved logging without follow-on agriculture. However, logging provides access roads to follow-on settlers, and log sales can help finance the cost of clearing remaining trees and preparing land for planting of crops or pasture. Thus logging can catalyze deforestation.

Moreover, logging can seriously degrade forests. In Indonesia and Malaysia, which have a high density of saleable trees, extraction rates of 150 cubic meters per hectare have been reported (Putz and others 2001). Using new remote sensing techniques, Asner and others (2005) found that the area degraded by logging exceeded the clear-cut area in five Brazilian states. While much of the logged area might eventually be converted to agriculture, only about 19 percent of degraded areas were deforested within three years after logging.

In Africa, forest loss around large cities reflects agricultural expansion and overharvesting for charcoal. The Stockholm Environment Institute (2002) used remote sensing to study forest degradation around Dar es Salaam (Tanzania), Lusaka (Zambia), and

Map 1.7   Hotspots of Tropical Deforestation

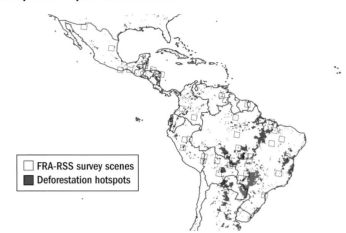

FRA-RSS survey scenes
Deforestation hotspots

Source: Hansen and DeFries 2004 (hotspots); FAO 2001b (survey scenes).

Maputo (Mozambique) during the 1990s. In all three areas there was a reduction in open woodlands and an increase in thicket, bush, and grasslands, due to a combination of charcoal extraction and shrinking fallow periods. Around Lusaka nearly a third of deforestation was attributable solely to charcoal.

The relative importance of small- and large-scale agriculturalists is also debated. A lot of Brazilian and Indonesian deforestation is undertaken by large commercial interests (see chapter 3), and most African and mainland Southeast Asian deforestation is thought to be carried out by smallholders. The only hints to the relative global magnitudes of corporate and "populist" deforestation are provided by the FRA-RSS. Using this data, FAO (2001b) estimated that expansion of shifting cultivation into undisturbed forest represented only about 5 percent of all pan-tropical changes in land use. Intensification of agriculture in shifting cultivation areas represented more than 20 percent of tropical land use change in Asia and less than 10 percent in Africa. Direct conversion of forest area to small-scale permanent agriculture accounted for 60 percent of land use change in Africa, but only a small portion elsewhere. Direct conversion of forest to large-scale permanent agriculture represented about 45 percent of tropical land use change in Latin America and about 30 percent in Asia.

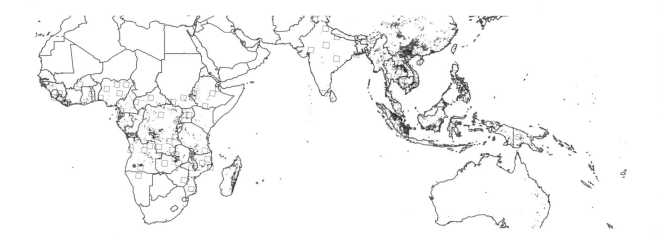

Where Are Forest Degradation Rates the Highest?

Deforestation doesn't occur randomly. Assessing geographic risk factors for deforestation can help in the design of policies that protect threatened forests with high environmental value but little to offer for agriculture.

Table 1.5, based on an original analysis using the FRA-RSS, relates forest degradation rates (including both deforestation and

Table 1.5 During the 1990s Savannas and Asian Forests Experienced Considerable Degradation (percent)

Domain	Tropical forests			Tropical savannas	
	Africa	Asia	Latin America and the Caribbean	Africa	Latin America and the Caribbean
Mosaiclands	11.1	16.8	20.2	11.8	18.4
Forest edges	4.7	9.9	4.3	9.2	8.5
Forest cores	2.7	4.4	0.6	9.6	0.8
Total	5.4	10.9	3.6	9.9	10.8

Source: Authors' calculations based on CIESIN and others 2004a, b, c, ECJRC 2003, and FRA-RSS; see appendix B.
Note: The table shows the percentage of forested 2- by 2-kilometer cells, by condition in 2000, that experienced a reduction in forest cover since 1990.

forest thinning) to the three forest domains.[1] Two features stand out. First, degradation rates are high—about 10 percent—in savannas and Asian forests. Second, degradation rates are quite high in mosaiclands. In Latin American forests, for instance, about 20 percent of mosaicland areas with trees experienced degradation in the 1990s.[2] This includes degradation of forest fragments on largely agricultural lands. Rates are lower on the frontier and lower still on areas beyond the frontier. Because there is relatively little forest left within mosaiclands, the total area degraded is as large or larger outside mosaiclands, even though the degradation rate is lower.

Does deforestation yield valuable agricultural land? Or does it occur on marginal soils with poor prospects for sustainability? Figure 1.2 shows forest degradation rates by suitability for rainfed annual cropping, according to the Global Agro-Ecological Zones assessment (FAO and IIASA 2000). In Africa and Latin America degradation

Figure 1.2 Africa and Latin America Have Higher Degradation on Better Soils, 1990–2000

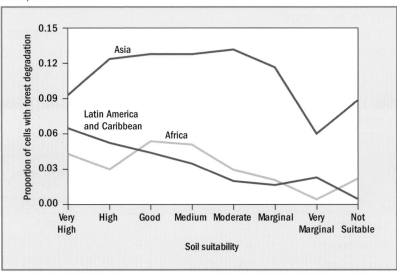

Source: Authors' calculations based on FRA-RSS and GAEZ; see appendix B.
Note: The figure shows the proportion of forested 2-by-2-kilometer cells experiencing loss of forest cover.

rates are higher on better soils, as a simple economic model would predict. This portends significant costs to restraining deforestation in some places. But a lot of forest degradation is occurring on lands considered marginal for annual agriculture. In Asia there is no relationship between agroclimatic conditions and degradation rates. It is possible that in these areas, forest degradation is driven by logging or by conversion to perennials rather than annual cropping. In all three continents this analysis suggests that a substantial amount of deforestation and degradation occurs in areas with little agricultural value—suggesting that it may be possible to reduce some deforestation at relatively low cost.

Threatened Species—Concentrated in Less-remote Areas and Mosaiclands

To support conservation, it is essential to identify and locate species threatened with extinction. The World Conservation Union's Red List is a systematic effort at identifying those species (www.redlist. org). The list classifies species as endangered (extinction probability of 20 percent within 20 years) or critically endangered (extinction probability of 50 percent within 10 years) based on several criteria, including limited or declining ranges or populations. So it is not surprising that threatened species are more likely to be found in nonremote areas with higher human populations and more fragmented habitats.

The World Conservation Union and other conservation groups are also making massive efforts to map the ranges of threatened and nonthreatened species, but are hampered by spotty data. Observations may be outdated. Observers may have favored locations near roads or parks and neglect to look in mosaiclands. And imputed ranges may not take into account actual habitat conditions. Still, the creation of these range maps is a major step forward and provides at least a rough look at the distribution of species.

Information from the Red List and the Global Amphibian Assessment made it possible to map the location of all tropical forest biome cells with at least one threatened amphibian species. The incidence of threatened species is much higher in nonremote areas, at least in Africa and Latin America (figure 1.3). Ricketts and others (2005) apply a stricter criterion to a broader set of species, includ-

Figure 1.3 The Incidence of Threatened Amphibian Species Is Much Higher in Nonremote Areas

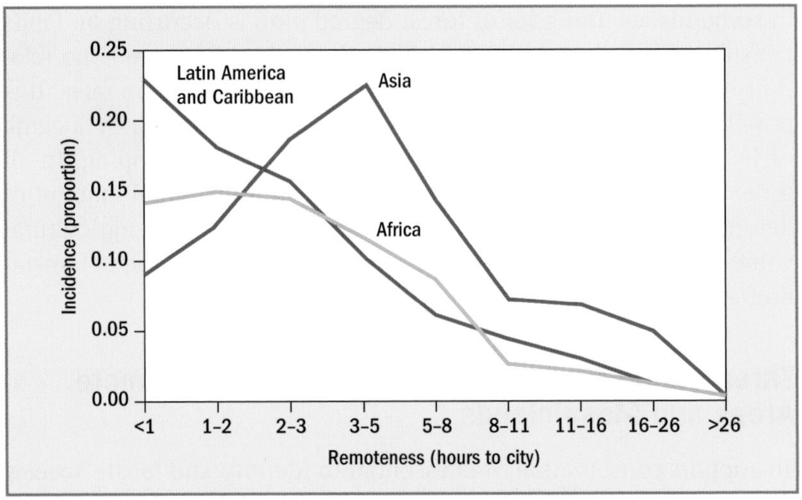

Source: Authors' calculations based on World Conservation Union Red List and Global Amphibian Assessment; see appendix B.

Map 1.8   Imminent Extinction Hotspots

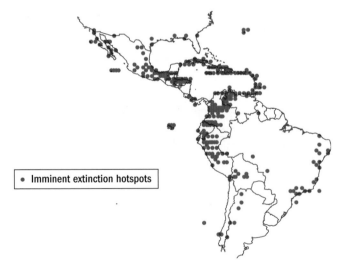

- Imminent extinction hotspots

Source: Updated from Ricketts and others 2005 using data from Alliance for Zero Extinction.

Figure 1.4   Imminent Extinction Sites Are Concentrated Near Cities

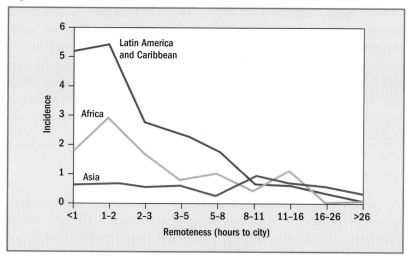

Source: Authors' calculations based on Alliance for Zero Extinction (data set v 2.1).
Note: For each remoteness category, the figure shows the number of imminent extinction sites per 100,000 square kilometers.

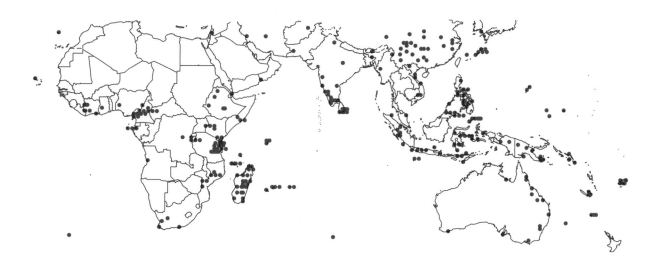

ing birds, mammals, amphibians, some reptiles, and conifers. The authors focus on threatened species found in only one, well-defined location in the world, where the loss of habitat in that location probably implies loss of the species. These locations—dubbed "imminent extinction" locations—tend disproportionately to be on islands and mountaintops, partly because of evolutionary processes (map 1.8). But again, outside Asia the incidence is closely related to urban proximity (figure 1.4). The incidence is much higher in agricultural and forest frontier land than on areas beyond the frontier.

Summary

The world's tropical forests are diverse, with important differences between continents. Asia has most of the world's tropical forest population, living at relatively high population densities and closer to major cities on average than in Latin America and Africa. Asia's deforestation rates are also higher. Latin America has most of the nonsavanna tropical forest area, but only a small proportion of forest inhabitants. Africa has vast areas of savanna.

Populations in nonsavanna forests are quite concentrated, with more than 400 million people occupying the most crowded 2 million square kilometers, and only about 10 million in the least crowded 10 million square kilometers. About a quarter of forest dwellers are in mosaiclands, where agriculture and forests are closely intermingled, though these lands constitute only a small portion of the forest estate. The deforestation rate is particularly high on these fragmented lands. Most forest dwellers live on the edges of these mosaiclands, some in frontier conditions. Biodiversity is most threatened in less-remote mosaic and edge forests. Relatively few people live in core forests or those beyond the frontier. The next chapter examines the geographic and economic forces that shape these patterns.

Endnotes

1. The FRA-RSS estimates are based on a stratified random sample of satellite scenes; sampled areas are represented by the blue rectangles in map 1.7. Note that there are no sample scenes in China, where the map shows deforestation hotspots. Degradation incidence is the proportion of tree-bearing sample points that experience some loss of canopy.

2. This calculation is somewhat biased because the mosaicland classification is based on land cover in 2000, at the end of the period over which change was measured. But the results are qualitatively similar when the outermost cells of the mosaiclands—those in contact with the frontier and thus the most likely to have undergone recent change—are omitted.

Roads often trigger forest conversion to agriculture. This road was opened in Kalimantan, Indonesia as part of a 1980s transmigration program.

CHAPTER 2

Incentives and Constraints Shape Forest Outcomes

Put yourself in the place of a farmer. You have some forest, or are thinking about claiming some forest. Should you log it? If so, should you extract as much as you can now, or plan for sustainable harvesting over the coming decades? Or should you simply clear cut the forest and replace it with crops, pasture, or tree plantations?

Your choices will be shaped by your constraints and abilities, the characteristics of the forest, your rights over it, and the wider social, economic, and political context. Your choices will affect your livelihood—as well as stream flows of your downhill neighbors and climates of people in distant lands. When your interests and other people's diverge, there could be a mediating role for public policy.

Understanding landholders' behavior is essential to understanding how policies and context affect deforestation and forest poverty. Attempts to understand the effects of sweeping policies (such as structural adjustment) on sweeping outcomes (such as aggregate forest loss in a country) are doomed to inconclusiveness. Policy changes typically pull many economic and social levers—changing prices and wages; stimulating one sector, dampening another. Each lever could have a distinctive impact on deforestation and forest poverty, and those impacts might differ between regions. At the national level these impacts might be difficult to disentangle. So this report's strategy is to try to understand how each potential lever works.

This chapter, which draws heavily on Angelsen (2006), offers a simple but powerful model of land use decisions at a particular point in space and time.[1] It then uses that model to examine how forest cover and poverty might evolve over time for entire regions.

The View from the Forest Plot: Comparing the Returns to Forestry and Agriculture

The International Tropical Timber Organization (2006, p. 46) describes the dilemma facing sustainable forest management: "alternative land uses, which usually involve a much more intensive use of the land, are more profitable or provide quicker returns." How and why does this dilemma arise?

Is Sustainable Forest Management Appealing to Landholders?

Culture and experience may impel long-time forest dwellers to maintain forest even if other land uses are potentially more lucrative. Shifting cultivators, for instance, have a long history of sustainable forest management, temporarily clearing small plots for agriculture and cycling over long periods through large tracts of forest. Some forest-owning Mexican communities harvest less than regulations permit or profits might dictate (Bray and others 2003). And cultures around the world protect sacred forest groves.

Still, economics is likely to intrude on the decisions of most forestholders. There are few long-cycle shifting cultivators left in the world—reflecting rising population densities, accelerating fallow cycles, and forests degrading into bush. Elsewhere, as markets approach, forestholders (or would-be forest claimants) balance returns from sustainable timber production against predatory extraction, followed by agricultural conversion.

Though there are exceptions, sustainable timber management is often less lucrative than other options. Exceptional cases involve forests with precious woods, many saleable trees, fast-growing trees, or soils unsuited to agriculture. For instance, sustainable management of Indian teak forests is estimated to confer a land value of more than $5,000 a hectare in net present value (World Bank 2005, vol. II, p. 76).[2] Coniferous forests in Mexico, where nearly all trees are commercially valuable, are another example.

But in old-growth rainforests with diverse, slow-growing species, biological and financial considerations could push landholders away from sustainability. An analysis of logging economics at a Brazilian site by Boltz and others (2001) illustrates a general pattern.[3] Reduced impact logging could net $128 a hectare from an initial selective harvest, leaving the residual forest in reasonably good condition. Left alone (without silvicultural treatment), the forest regenerates, but its value grows by just 2 percent a year—a bad investment. Another harvest is possible in 30 years, but the present value of that harvest, evaluated at a 20 percent discount rate (a reasonable approximation of the discount rate in many developing countries), is only $0.24 a hectare. Even low-return pasture or staple crops offer higher returns to landholders. Of course society, with a lower discount rate and a demand for forest environmental services, may view things differently.

Private Gains from Deforestation: Sometimes Minuscule, Sometimes Huge

How big are the private gains to deforestation? Knowing this is essential to assessing the economic and political costs of encouraging sustainable forest management. The answer—not surprising, but important—is that these gains vary tremendously between places, technologies, and land use systems. Profits from deforestation range from near zero to thousands of dollars a hectare.

Profits are the benefits to landholders from sales of timber and agricultural products, after costs of conversion and production, including labor. For smallholders dependent on unpaid family labor, this concept of profits can be interpreted as income above what family members could earn elsewhere. In other words, a strict measure of profit deducts the opportunity cost of family labor. The resulting measure of net profits per hectare is a convenient measure of the economic pressure for forest conversion—or of the opportunity cost of conservation. However, where labor markets are imperfect, workers and policymakers may consider labor absorption a benefit. So employment per hectare is another way of assessing the benefits of forest conversion.

It is challenging to document the value of forested land in the tropics. In a few places, mostly in Latin America, markets provide a clear indicator of the profitability of land. In theory, prices for pasture or prepared fields in these areas should reflect the net present value of future revenue from farming, including expected gains from road construction and improvements in tenure security.

Elsewhere in the developing world, where land, labor, and product markets are thin, estimates of profitability come from farm studies. The Consultative Group on International Agricultural Research's Alternatives to Slash and Burn (ASB) program has undertaken especially rigorous measurements of economic benefits and environmental impacts of forest conversion in Brazil, Cameroon, and Indonesia (Tomich and others 2005). These measurements, along with other reported land values from forested areas, appear in table 2.1.

Although the land values provide a useful benchmark, they typically overstate the private gains to forest conversion, for two reasons. First, it is necessary to account for the upfront costs of clearing logged-over forest and preparing the land for crops or pasture. In Bolivia, for instance, the cost of clearing and pasture establishment averages $480 a hectare, defrayed only in part by after-tax timber revenues of $227 (Merry and others 2002).[4] These upfront costs are factored into the ASB estimates, but they also need to be deducted from some of the others.

Second, most analyses that compute net present values adopt a 10 percent discount rate, which is lower than typical private discount rates—especially among poor people. At a higher discount rate, the returns to conversion would fall substantially. In Ninan and Sathyapalan (2005) increasing the assumed discount rate from 8 percent to 12 percent cut the net present value in half. Naidoo and Adamowicz (2006) present evidence supporting a discount rate of 15–25 percent for Paraguay; GEF (2006) suggests that discount rates in the developing world are typically even higher. For these reasons the net present values reported in table 2.1 might be two or three times greater than landholder perceptions of returns to forest conversion.

Some highlights from these studies:

- In some places there are huge incentives to degrade or convert forest. In Cameroon oil palm and intensive cocoa cultivation has a net present value of more than $1,400 a hectare. In Brazil's *cerrado* (savanna) region, converting native woodlands to soy results in land worth over $3,000 a hectare. India offers extraordinarily high values for land devoted to coffee cultivation in the Western Ghats, a biodiversity hotspot.

- In contrast, mean land values are just $400 a hectare in another hotspot, the Atlantic forest of Bahia, Brazil—one of the world's most important places for bio-

Table 2.1 Land Values in Forested Areas Vary Enormously

a. Studies Reporting Land Prices or NPV

Study	Location	Year(s)	Land use, type, or location	Price or net present value (per hectare)	Notes
Batagoda and others (2000)	Sinharaja, Sri Lanka	1995	Tea Timber potential	$4,281 $1,129	NPV at 8 percent
Chomitz and others (2005b)	Bahia, Brazil	2000	Median land value	$400	Price
Davies and Abelson (1996)	Bolivia	1992	Mechanized soybeans and maize Traditional farm excl. coca Traditional farm with coca	$1,500 $270 $385	NPV at 10 percent
FNP Consultoría & Agroinformativos	Goias, Brazil (various subregions)	2004	Cerrado (savanna) High-productivity agricultural land	$140–1,290 $1,950–3,150	Price
Fundacão Getulio Vargas	Brazil	2004	Pará Rondonia	$200 $318	Price of pasture
Grimes and others (1994)	Ecuador (Amazon region)	1987–91	Cattle ranching Timber Agriculture Land price	$57–287 $189 <$500 $50–220	NPV at 5 percent NPV at 5 percent NPV at 5 percent Price

Howard and Valerio (1996)	Costa Rica	1994	Cattle ranching
			  Atlantic
			  South
			  North
			Bean crops
			  South
			  North
			Corn (Atlantic)
				
				$1,239
				$1,433
				$880
				
				$2,716
				$2,163
				$2,281
					NPV at 10 percent

Kazianga and Masters (2005)	Cameroon	2001	Land at the frontier	$86	Price
Kishor and Constantino (1993)	Costa Rica	1989	Cattle ranching Clear felling Plantations Managed forestry	$1,319 $1,292 $3,223 $854	NPV at 8 percent (without taxes and subsidies; includes timber revenue)

(continued on next page)

Table 2.1a *(continued)*

Study	Location	Year(s)	Land use, type, or location	Price or net present value (per hectare)	Notes
Merry and others (2002)	Bolivia	Not available	Pasture	$24–500	Price; range reflects accessibility
Ninan and Sathyapalan (2005)	Ghats, India	2000	Coffee on farm <2.5 acres 2.5–5.0 acres 5–10 acres >10 acres	$1,593 $1,819 $4,834 $8,280	NPV at 10 percent; small farms more likely to be in forests
Olschewski and Benitez (2005)	Ecuador	2001	Grazing land North Coast Nearest Quito	$150–500 $400–1,000 $800–2,000	Price
Pinedo-Vasquez, Zarin, and Jipp (1992)	Peruvian Amazon	1988–89	Swidden agriculture (rice, cassava, plantains, fallow)	$1,627	NPV at 10 percent
Ricker and others (1999)	Veracruz, Mexico	1998	Pasture	$210–1,052	Price
Tomich and others (2005)	Brazil Amazônia	1996	Pasture	$2	NPV at 9 percent
Tomich and others (2005)	Cameroon	1990s	Food crop Cocoa Oil palm	$283–623 $424–1,409 $722–1,458	NPV at 10 percent
Tomich and others (2005)	Sumatra, Indonesia	1997	Rubber agroforestry Community forest management Oil palm Unsustainable logging	$1 $5 $114 $1,080	NPV at 20 percent
Wunder (2000)	Ecuador	1994–96	Deforestation cycle (wood, crops, cattle)	$1,721	NPV at 10 percent; includes initial timber revenue
Yaron (2001)	Cameroon	1997–98	Small farming Oil palm and rubber Sustainable timber production	$2,380–4,275 –$2,838 to $96 $45–470	NPV at 10 percent

Table 2.1 (*continued*)

b. Studies Reporting Annual Net Returns

Study	Location	Year(s)	Land use, type, or location	Annual net returns (per hectare)
Naidoo and Adamowicz (2005)	Uganda	1993–2001	Farming	$114
Norton-Griffiths and Southey (1995)	Kenya	1989–93	High potential zone Medium potential Per humid Arable	$151 $91 $38 $54
Olschewski and Benitez (2005)	Ecuador	2001	Cattle ranching North Coast Nearest Quito	 $25[a] $42[a] $110[a]
Zelek and Shively (2003)	Philippines	1994–96	Low-input maize	$260

NPV stands for net present value.

a. Returns are net of costs except labor.

diversity conservation. Only small fragments of forest remain in this long-settled region. The study also finds that remaining forest sells at a steep discount relative to other land with similar characteristics. This disparity may reflect the effect of laws, even though imperfectly enforced, against deforestation. It may also reflect relegation of the poorest-quality land to forest; after decades of occupation, most agriculturally suitable land has already been cleared. Both effects may be present in other biodiversity hotspots where forests have been heavily fragmented.

- At the Latin American frontier, forest is being converted to low-value uses that generate little employment. Conversion of forest to traditionally managed pasture in Amazônia yields pasture worth only a few hundred dollars a hectare. Pasture at the Ecuadorian frontier is worth $150–500 a hectare; at the Bolivian frontier, $24–500. After accounting for costs, ASB estimates that converting a hectare confers a net present value of only $2 and provides just 11 days of employment a year. But values are much higher near cities and on well-managed farms using improved production systems.

- Low-value land uses are also reported in Indonesia, Uganda, and the Cameroonian forest frontier.

- Sustainable forest management typically provides lower returns and employment than does commercial agriculture. In Sumatra, for instance, management for non-timber forest products employs 0.3 people a hectare per year and returns a net present value of just $5 a hectare—while oil palm cultivation employs 108 people a hectare per year and returns $114 a hectare. Agricultural returns outstrip those from sustainable forest management in Cameroon, Costa Rica, India, and Sri Lanka.

In summary, there is great variation across pantropical forest margins in the strength of incentives for deforestation. Where conditions are amenable to crops such as soybeans, oil palm, or cocoa, and where old-growth timber is still standing, deforesters are rewarded with thousands of dollars a hectare. On marginal lands, lands far from markets, or where agricultural technologies are unavailable, there may be little incentive beyond the ability to eke out a living at the going wage.

How Do Agroclimate, Prices, Technology, Tenure, and Other Factors Affect Deforestation and Income?

This section considers how the environmental, social, and economic context of a forest plot affects the relative returns to forest maintenance and agriculture. The discussion here helps in understanding how policy levers affect outcomes in the forest domains described in chapter 1. Table 2.2 summarizes the discussion.

Richer Farmers Are Better Able to Finance Deforestation

A poor household can't afford to clear much forest. In Bolivia clearance and land preparation costs range from $350–605 a hectare (Merry and others 2002); in Costa Rica clearance costs $78 a hectare (Howard and Valerio 1996). Sometimes these costs can be partly or fully defrayed by sales of timber; sometimes wealthy interests are willing to finance clearing by smallholders on their behalf. Where these markets are lacking, successful deforesters must be able to mobilize a lot of family or community labor—50 to 70 person-days

Table 2.2   Predictions of How Changes in Local Variables Will Affect the Environment and Welfare

Element	Effect on environment − Promotes deforestation + Inhibits deforestation	Effect on welfare − Reduces welfare + Enhances welfare
Access to credit markets; own assets	−	+
Lower discount rates	+ with exceptions	+
Good soils, moderate rainfall	−	+
Higher prices for extensive farm output	−	+
Higher prices for intensive farm output	+ Where labor markets are imperfect, could decrease deforestation by attracting labor away from extensive production − Where capital markets are imperfect, could increase deforestation by funding forest conversion	+
Higher prices for timber	− Spur deforestation of old-growth timber − Increase deforestation in open access areas + Encourage sustainable management of secondary forests where there is secure tenure + Spur reforestation in forest-poor areas	± Effect on local poverty depends on who extracts the timber and wider economic effects; poverty may increase if outsiders degrade forests on which locals depend
Higher off-farm wages	+ Where labor markets are imperfect or in-migration is limited, draw labor away from deforestation of marginal areas − Could fund deforestation	+
Higher-yielding agricultural technologies	− If labor and capital can migrate to forest margins + If marketwide effects lower prices + If technologies absorb labor and in-migration is limited	+ (though indirect negative effects are possible)
More secure land tenure	+ Reduces deforestation as a means of claiming land + Makes sustainable forest management more attractive − Makes investments in land improvements (including perennial crops) more attractive	+
Road extension or improvement	− Increases farmgate prices of outputs, lowers prices of inputs, makes in-migration more attractive	+ (unless outsiders displace locals)

a hectare—or to hire workers, chainsaws, and bulldozers. This point suggests that cash and credit constraints hamper smallholder deforestation. Relaxing those constraints—through transfers, stronger credit markets, and better opportunities for off-season employment—could increase both incomes and deforestation.

Good Land Is Cleared First

Soils, topography, and climate (agroclimate, for short) strongly affect land rents. Differences in soils and climates explain most county-level variations in land values in Brazil, India, and the United States (Mendelsohn, Dinar, and Sanghi 2001). In Bahia rural land prices increase with soil quality but decrease with slope, holding constant other characteristics such as road access (Chomitz and others 2005b).

Deforestation occurs more quickly on lands that offer higher rents. Studies of deforestation at the farm or local level generally find that deforestation rates are lower on hillsides, other things constant (appendix table A.1). These studies also find a strong correlation between soil quality and deforestation. In periurban areas of Latin America and Asia tree cover is about twice as high on the poorest soils as on the best soils for rainfed agriculture (see chapter 1).

High densities of saleable trees can also promote deforestation. Roads built by loggers and revenue from timber sales can help finance agricultural clearing. If the density is high enough, extraction can lead to deforestation even in the absence of agriculture. This is thought to be true in Southeast Asia, where lowland forests have high densities of valuable dipterocarp trees. For instance, logging is blamed for deforestation in sparsely populated, protected areas of Kalimantan, Indonesia (Curran and others 2004).

Deforestation skirts areas with high rainfall, which is inimical to cultivation of annual crops and discourages cattle ranching—especially when there is no dry season. A study of Brazilian Amazônia by Chomitz and Thomas (2003) found that, controlling for road access, higher rainfall is associated with lower deforestation, more land abandonment, and lower grazing densities.

Higher Prices for Farm Output Induce Forest Conversion and Benefit Farmers

Other things being equal, higher prices for crops and lower prices for farm inputs will spur faster deforestation. This prediction is important because many policies can affect farmgate prices, including taxes, tariffs, subsidies, road improvements, and exchange rate policies.

The prediction can be tested by looking for variations in prices across the landscape within a country, between countries, or over time, and correlating prices with deforestation rates. Doing so is difficult. Within a country, at a single point in time, there may be little price variation. Comparisons between countries and over time are problematic because there are many other confounding influences, and because measurements of deforestation may be inconsistent. So there are only a few relevant studies.

Most of these studies find a strong link between higher agricultural prices and more rapid or extensive deforestation. The degree of price sensitivity varies but tends to increase with more localized measurements. For instance, an analysis of remote sensing data shows that, after controlling for other factors, deforestation rates in Brazilian Amazônia are closely linked to farmgate prices of beef (figure 2.1). This analysis focuses on unprotected lands (excluding land reform settlements) and shows the strong effect of rainfall levels and farmgate prices on deforestation rates. In areas with moderate rainfall (less than 2,000 millimeters a year) near roads, deforestation over 2001–03 was 8 percent where the beef price was above R$600 a ton, 4 percent where the price was R$400–600, and 0.5 percent where the price was below R$400.

In a study of Mexico, Deininger and Minten (1999) examined the relationship between deforestation and proximity to buyers of

Figure 2.1 Deforestation in Brazilian Amazônia Is Shaped by Rainfall and Farmgate Prices of Beef, 2001–03

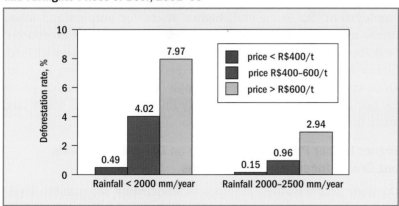

Source: Authors' calculations; see Appendix B.
Note: Rate is deforested area/initial forest area.
Excludes protected areas and land reform settlements.

maize—the main forest-competing crop. Because maize is bulky, closer proximity translates into lower transport costs and higher farmgate prices. The authors found that an increase of one standard deviation in buyer density corresponded to a 40 percent increase in the deforestation rate. Barbier and Cox (2004) examined mangrove deforestation (due to shrimp farming) in Thai provinces and found that a 10 percent hike in shrimp prices would boost deforestation a modest 1.6 percent—while a similar hike in the price of ammonium phosphate (an input) would reduce deforestation by 4.5 percent. But not all studies find strong effects. Gbetnkom (2005), for instance, finds that changes in prices of coffee, cocoa, and food have negligible effects on forest clearance in Cameroon.

The impacts of price changes become more complicated when two other land uses compete with forest. Suppose that one use is extensive: long-fallow cultivation of a staple food (such as cacao, irrigated rice, or coca). Suppose that the other is much more intensive, using far more labor per hectare (say, shifting cultivation of maize, rice, or plantains). Suppose too that the labor supply is limited, and outsiders cannot easily move in to exploit new opportunities. Then, theory says, an increase in the returns to the intensive land use could absorb labor from the extensive one, at least in the short to medium run.

There is evidence that this happens. Coxhead and Demeke (2004), in a study of upland farmers in the Philippines, find strong cross-effects between vegetable and maize production. An increase in the price of vegetables, the more intensive crop, is predicted to slightly reduce the total area under cultivation.

Higher prices for farm products benefit land owners and increase employment. So in general, higher prices for outputs and lower prices for inputs will reduce rural poverty—with two exceptions. First, because farmers with tiny plots might be net buyers of food, higher food prices will hurt them. Second, substitution between crops could indirectly hurt poor people. For instance, higher prices for beef or soy—which use relatively little labor—could divert land away from more intensive cultivation.

Higher Timber Prices Put Pressure on Old-growth Forests but Create Incentives for New Ones

Do high timber values promote or undermine sustainable forest management? The answer depends on the state of the forest (von Amsberg 1998) and how it is regulated. New roads or new markets can confer enormous value on old-growth forests. Individual trees can be worth thousands of dollars.

In the absence of regulation, rising prices induce loggers to sweep deeper into old-growth forests, mining sellable trees (Stone 1998). But where societies are willing and able to require forest owners to practice sustainable forest management, higher timber prices make such regulation less onerous. And where forests have already been depleted, higher timber prices make it more attractive to raise trees—especially plantations of fast-growing ones—as a crop.

Higher Off-farm Wages Discourage Deforestation in Marginal Areas

Many, though not all, forest dwellers have opportunities to earn wages. The opportunities may be on neighboring farms or plantations, in nearby market towns, or in distant cities. As these opportunities become more lucrative, there is less incentive to use forest for subsistence or low-value crops. Kaimowitz and Angelsen (1998) found broad support for this proposition.

A dramatic long-run example of this is the abandonment of the hillsides of Puerto Rico. By 1950 almost all the island's hillside forests had been converted to coffee plantations or other agriculture, leaving only 9 percent of the island under forest. Subsequently, there was massive out-migration from the hillsides as people sought better-paying employment in San Juan and the United States. The result was regeneration of the deforested area: by 1990, 37 percent of the island was under forest (Rudel, Perez-Lugo, and Zichal 2000; Lamb, Erskine, and Parrotta 2005b).

Between 1994 and 2002 Coxhead and Demeke (2004) observed a wage rise of about 50 percent among hillside farmers in the Philippines, as transportation and communications improved. According to their analysis, this increase would by itself reduce land cultivation by about 20 percent. But wage increases can also affect deforestation in other ways. Barbier and Cox (2004) found that higher wages were associated with higher clearance of mangroves for shrimp farming in Thailand. They suggest that this was because shrimp growers, faced with higher wages, had ways of substituting land for labor. Wage increases can also increase the demand for fuelwood and food, spurring additional deforestation.

Whatever their effects on deforestation, increases in off-farm wages are essential to poverty alleviation. A growing literature documents the potential role of off-farm employment in alleviating rural poverty (Reardon, Berdegue, and Escobar 2001).

Agricultural Technology Promotes Growth
—With Ambiguous Implications for Deforestation

Technological improvements in agriculture are crucial to raising rural welfare (through higher farm incomes) and consumer welfare (through lower food prices). But the gains from these improvements may be unequally shared. And except in special circumstances, technological improvements are likely to increase pressures on forest. To explain why, this section draws on Angelsen (2006) and Angelsen and Kaimowitz (2001).

To be adopted, a technical innovation generally has to save a farmer's time or increase farm output. But any innovation that makes farming more profitable is likely to prompt the expansion of farms into forests or attract new farmers to the forest frontier. And anything that reduces labor requirements could release unemployed farmers to search for new frontiers. For instance, Ruf (2001) claims that in Sulawesi, Indonesia, the introduction of herbicides and mechanical cultivators in lowland rice production released workers to engage in upland deforestation.

Consider too the impact of improved soybean varieties in Brazil's *cerrado* (savanna) region. The region's poor soils and short days had been unsuitable for cultivating traditional soy varieties. So EMBRAPA, the Brazilian agricultural research agency, bred varieties adapted to the region. As a result soy cultivation exploded—at the expense of pasture, biodiversity-rich *cerrado,* and, recently, dense forests. The area cultivated jumped from nearly zero in 1970 (Warnken 1999) to 117,000 square kilometers in 2004 (IBGE 2006). Soybean and soy product exports were $9.8 billion in 2004 (Economist Intelligence Unit 2005).

For a technological innovation to simultaneously increase farmer welfare and reduce forest pressure, one of the following conditions must apply:

- The innovation increases food production so much that food prices fall, easing pressure to convert forested uplands. This might happen in isolated locales cut off from markets. Or it might happen if the productivity increase is so large that it depresses national or even global markets. Some analysts think that the green revolution is an example, positing that improvements in irrigated rice yields reduced pressures for upland deforestation.

- The innovation boosts the productivity of subsistence farmers not closely linked to food markets. This could reduce their need for clearing and might occur in areas beyond the frontier.

- The innovation boosts both productivity and labor use per hectare. Moreover, labor supply is limited, either because of remoteness or because local residents have secure tenure over large amounts of land and prefer not to rent or sell to newcomers. In these conditions—more characteristic of frontier areas than mosaiclands—some intensive farming systems could absorb labor away from extensive, more forest-damaging ones. Holden (2001), Shively and Pagiola (2004), Shively and Martinez (2001), and Coxhead and Demeke (2004) present examples of how expansion of intensified land use systems can draw labor away from extensive, deforesting land uses. It is uncertain, though, whether over the long run inflows of labor might counteract this effect.

- The innovation stimulates nonfarm employment. Returning to the example of soy in Brazil's *cerrado,* the direct beneficiaries were soybean farmers, including large and industrial growers. But related growth in services, transportation, and processing has contributed to the rapid development of urban centers in the soybelt, and during the 1990s these cities accounted for substantial employment growth. However, the size of the link between soy expansion and urban employment has not been quantified.

Tenure Is Good for Landholders, but Has Uncertain Effects for Deforestation

Landholders with secure tenure are more likely to make physical improvements, invest in perennial crops, and plant and maintain forests. They worry less about defending their property and lives from thieves. They are better able to tap credit markets. And large landholders with secure tenure are more inclined to rent out land to tenants or sharecroppers, rather than keeping it idle or under pasture. For all these reasons, tenure security boosts incomes of rural landowners and workers (Deininger 2003).

Poorly defined tenure is generally bad for people and forests. In many parts of the world, governments have nominal control of forests but are too weak to effectively regulate their use. This can lead to a tragedy of the commons where forest resources are degraded.

The relationship between tenure and deforestation is more ambiguous. In frontier areas deforestation is a common way of laying claim to land and securing tenure, in both practice and law. This setup encourages a destructive race for property rights at the frontier (Schneider 1995), where land is prematurely deforested—that is, before it generates any economic rent—in speculation that roads or government will eventually confer value on it. And in countries with pressure for land reform, large landholders will feel pressured to deforest just to demonstrate "productive use" of the land and so avoid invasion or expropriation. That has been especially common in Brazil, where uncertainty over land rights has led to violent fights over forested properties.

But secure tenure does not guarantee that landowners will spare forests. As noted, landholders will likely first extract and sell large, mature, slow-growing trees. Landholders will then weigh the relative advantages of forest maintenance and cropping. With secure tenure, investments in perennial crops such as black pepper or oil palm may be more attractive.

Roads Provide the Path to Rural Development —and Forest Clearance

Providing road access is the most effective determinant of deforestation that is under policy control. The theoretical argument is strong: it says that road provision increases farmgate prices for outputs and decreases farmgate prices for inputs, with all the effects just reviewed. Property-level studies of land values in Nepal (Jacoby 2000) and the Atlantic forest area of Brazil (Chomitz and others 2005b) support this linkage. This means that improving access to a forest plot generally creates strong pressures to deforest it.

The theory allows for exceptions. In rural areas where tenure is strong and immigration is limited, better road access might allow residents to work in towns, or shift them from extensive production of subsistence crops to more intensive production of commercial crops. Deforestation might then fall as long as residents can and will exclude in-migrants. Road links to nearby towns might boost local wages more than farmgate prices, attracting farmers away from marginal lands. And where forests are already exhausted, better road access could trigger tree planting for poles, firewood, and timber.

But an extensive empirical literature strongly supports the proposition that roads tend to promote, rather than inhibit, deforestation. A major challenge for this literature is determining causality when road development and deforestation occur together. Did the roads facilitate deforestation? Or were they built in response to settlement that would have occurred in their absence?

One approach to answering these questions is through case studies of deforestation (for example, Arima and others 2005). One analysis of 152 case studies finds that road access was a driver of deforestation in 93 cases (Geist and Lambin 2001), and another metareview concurs on the importance of road access (Kaimowitz and Angelsen 1998).

Another approach uses spatial econometric analysis to relate the incidence of deforestation to road proximity. Investigators compare small geographical regions, or even individual points on the landscape, in order to account for confounding factors such as soil fertility, climate, slope, or elevation. This helps to control for the possibility that roads are a symptom rather than cause of deforestation. This report reviewed 33 such studies, most of them at the finest level of geographic analysis (appendix table A.1). Twenty-one found a statistically significant, positive relationship between road proximity and deforestation. Eight found complex or ambiguous patterns, for instance when several measures of remoteness were used, or when there were differential effects on different groups. The remainder were inconclusive.

Road access also facilitates hunting of large mammals. In central African forests this is a more severe environmental threat than deforestation, and a study in Gabon found fewer mammals near roads (Laurance and others 2006).

Rural roads are generally believed to raise rural incomes and alleviate poverty, for the same reasons our model suggests they promote deforestation: by raising farmgate prices, lowering prices of urban manufactured goods, and promoting more intensive demand for labor. Rural roads also facilitate access to nonfarm employment in towns, which is often crucial to alleviating poverty in rural areas. For these reasons rural road provision is a mainstay of rural development strategies.

Considering the importance of rural roads to development strategies, the literature on their impact is thin. This report reviewed 26 studies and two metareviews covering 56 others. Though they were almost unanimous in finding positive impacts, the magnitude of the impacts varies greatly. Few of the studies used rigorous, quasi-experimental evaluations of how roads affect income and welfare. One of the most rigorous evaluations compared Peruvian villages that had received rehabilitated road links with similar control villages (Instituto Cuanto 2005). After five years, male (but not female) wages in the villages with rehabilitated roads rose by 20 percent relative to the control villages. In subsequent hard economic times, poverty in the control villages increased by 4–6 percentage points more than in the villages with rehabilitated roads.

Two recent simulations are of particular interest because they examine countries with extensive forest cover. In Papua New Guinea a study assessed the impact of reducing to three hours the access time to a road of all households that required more time (Gibson and Rozelle 2003). This potentially expensive undertaking would cut the number of poor people by 12 percent. The other study found that providing all-season roads to the 50 percent of Laotians lacking them would release 5 percent of the population from poverty (Warr 2005).

Other studies involve econometric analysis of district or provincial data, attempting to control for other potentially confounding factors. Fan and Chan-Kang (2004) summarize some of these studies, reporting astounding returns to road investment—hundreds of percentage points—in China, Uganda, and rain-fed regions of India. Other reported returns are far more modest, but still positive (appendix table A.2).

The inconsistent relationship between rural roads and poverty alleviation reflects a variety of factors. First, it may be modulated by other policies and conditions. Finan, Sadoulet, and de Janvry (2005) find that rural Mexicans with both road access and primary education earn about 10 times more from an extra hectare of land than do those without either asset. Second, where immigration is possible, roads may cause an increase in workers rather than wages.

Forest Trajectories: Roads, Markets, and Rights Shape Outcomes for Environment and Income

Astronomers teach us that the farther into space we peer, the farther back in time we see. So too, when we stand in an urban center and look toward the remote forest frontier, we see not only a changing spatial pattern of forests on today's landscape, but also a history of how that landscape evolved. Seen from the other direction, conditions near contemporary towns—old frontiers—provide hints about the future prospects of today's frontier regions. This section builds on our understanding of landholders' behavior, expanding from a single plot to an entire landscape, and from a snapshot to an evolving pattern.

From Urban Center to Forest Frontier: A Stylized View of the Landscape

Let's first take a stylized journey from an urban center to a forest frontier, at a moment in time. Our guide is Johann Heinrich von Thünen, the 19th-century economist. Von Thünen's enduring insight was that farms and forests closer to towns are more valuable, other things (such as soils and topography) being equal. The reason is simple: if the price of rice or wood is determined in a town's market, then nearby farmers bear lower costs in getting their products to market. Because they make higher profits, their land is worth more—that is, its rent for agriculture is higher.

Rents fall with distance to town, rapidly for bulky or perishable commodities (vegetables, milk) and more slowly for others (beef, coffee, hardwood timber; see figure 2.2). As land values decrease, land uses become more extensive, with pastures displacing crops and rotating fallows replacing permanent fields. After a certain distance farmers can no longer profitably supply crops to market, and their land has no agricultural *rent*. This is the agricultural frontier; beyond it there are only subsistence farmers and standing forests. Thus this stylized model predicts concentric rings of land uses centered on urban areas. There is evidence that this model, inspired by German landscapes of the early 19th century, describes landscapes across the developing world (Chomitz and Thomas 2003; Barnes, Krutilla, and Hyde 2005).

How does forestry fit into this picture? There is an important distinction between one-time extraction of old-growth trees and sustainable management of planted or natural forests. Big, valuable, old trees tend to get extracted as soon as they are accessible. Smaller,

Figure 2.2   A Stylized Model of How Land Use Changes with Remoteness

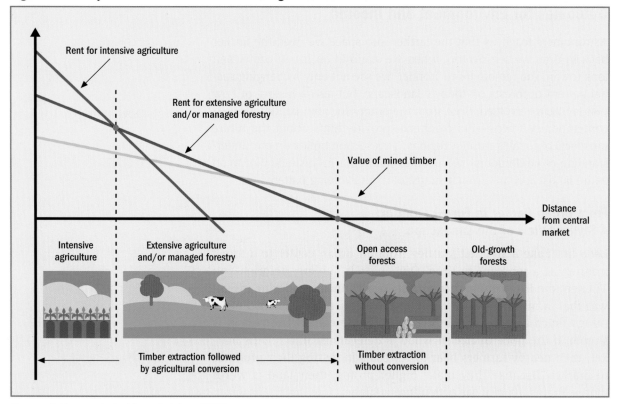

Source: Authors, adapted from Angelsen 2006.

less valuable trees are often sold as a byproduct of clearing for agriculture in von Thünen's inner rings—especially if the central town has an appetite for fuelwood or charcoal. Only when natural forests are depleted does it become attractive to manage them, or plant new ones, for sustained harvest over time. When that happens, a forest ring can emerge at the edge of the agricultural ring.

Of course, real landscapes don't look like archery targets. Two elaborations are needed to make the model more realistic. First, as noted, the effects of distance are strongly modulated by soil, climate, and topographical features. Forests may remain on steep slopes near cities. Remote areas with excellent soils may attract early colonization. And different combinations of accessibility, soil characteristics, and topography may appeal to different land uses and users. Chomitz and Gray (1996), for instance, used extremely detailed land cover, topography, and soil data for Belize to elucidate the determinants of land use. They found that semisubsistence shifting cultivators—those who can't afford fertilizers and don't sell much in the market—favor hilly areas with nitrogen-rich soil and are only moderately sensitive to distance from town. In contrast, commercial cultivators—those who can afford fertilizers but rely on tractors—favor flat lands, regardless of soil fertility, and tend to be closer to markets.

Second, security of land tenure is a crucial part of the picture. Although the determinants of land tenure are complex and rooted in history and institutions, they follow an important geographic pattern. Typically, the more remote a plot of forest from settled areas, the more difficult it is to establish and defend property rights. So, elaborating von Thünen's model, the cost of defending property likely rises with distance from town. (Moreover, defending a managed forest is typically more costly than defending a pasture.) At some point—the frontier—the cost of defending property rights exceeds the profitability of land. Beyond that point it doesn't make economic sense to invest in establishing a farm or actively managing a forest plot.

In sum, von Thünen's theory tells us that agricultural lands give way to forests with increasing remoteness. Figure 2.3, based on pantropical data, shows that the theory does a good job of describing today's tropical world.

Figure 2.3   As Remoteness Increases, Mosaiclands Are Displaced by Forests, 2000

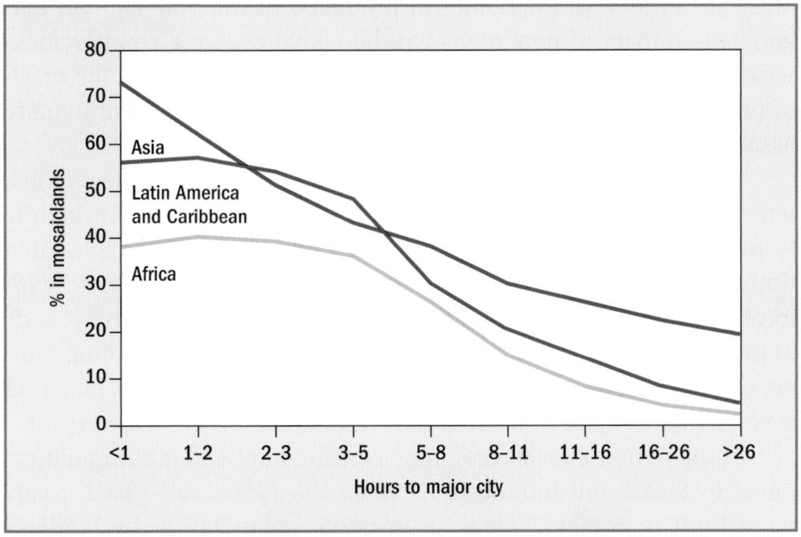

Source: Authors' calculations based on ECJRC 2003; see appendix B.
Note: Covers only nonsavanna areas.

From Forest Frontier to Urban Center:
A Stylized View of Forest Dynamics

Let's now take a return journey, starting at the frontier. But this time we'll take the trip in a time machine, looking in a stylized way at the dynamics of change and the role of institutions, markets, and geography in shaping the trajectories of poverty, development, and environment. Some of these trajectories will end up at an urban center; others will not.

Arrival of the Frontier

The journey begins beyond the agricultural frontier. Population is sparse, and inhabitants are mostly long-residing indigenous peoples. An increase in forest rents triggers the arrival of the frontier. Gradually or suddenly it becomes worth mining forests for timber, or worth defending plots of land to establish farming or pasture. Areas that had been beyond the frontier are now under contention. A race for property rights—or a dispute—begins.

There are a number of triggers, some linked. Sometimes, as in Madagascar, the trigger is the growth of populations engaged in subsistence farming. This increases demand for land and lowers effective wages and can be visualized as a shift upward in the rent curve for agriculture.

But the most important trigger is the construction or substantial improvement of major roads, which make it possible to exploit new areas for timber and agricultural products. In the von Thünen diagram the impact of new roads can be visualized as a counterclockwise rotation of rent curves. The cost of transport falls and the reach of property rights is eventually extended, shrinking the rent penalty associated with remoteness.

There are several spurs for the construction of major new roads, which may coincide with other triggers. First, it may be worthwhile to finance roads precisely because they offer returns in exploitable timber and raise land value. Farmers do this on a small scale with local road construction. Mahogany loggers, seeking lucrative stands of timber, can finance forest roads hundreds of kilometers long. Miners can open new roads. And state or national governments may find it beneficial to open new areas to forest extraction and conversion.

At the national level, economic considerations blur with political ones. In Brazil and Indonesia between the 1960s and 1980s, roads were built in forested areas to promote colonization by landless farmers. Road expansion, though without organized colonization schemes, was important in the opening of the Bolivian and Peruvian

Amazon during the same period. Forest road construction is sometimes geopolitically motivated—aimed at increasing government or military presence in remote and border areas. Elite interests and corruption also play a role, if the rents created by road construction are funneled to politically connected interests (Ross 2001).

Finally, frontier expansion can be triggered by market and technological changes. These can include booming markets for forest-competing commodities such as cacao, oil palm, coffee, and beef. Agronomic technology can also change incentives for deforestation. As noted, the breeding of soybean varieties adapted to low latitudes facilitated conversion of Brazilian savanna areas to cultivation.

Trajectories Out of the Frontier: Disappearing or Rebounding Forests, Immiserization or Growth

When the frontier arrives, people jockey for rights to trees and land. Depending on who obtains possession of those resources, under what circumstances, and how they dispose of them, different trajectories of forest cover, income, and population evolve (table 2.3). Some of these trajectories correspond to the forest transition (box 2.1).

- *Intensification with deforestation.* In this trajectory, changes in markets or roads increase the value of both standing timber and agricultural land in areas with favorable soils and climate. The resulting rush to claim timber and land often leads to conflicts between large and small actors. Profits from timber sales are used to finance the costs of clear cutting and of establishing crops. Agricultural development and timber harvesting may stimulate the growth of market towns with sawmills, slaughterhouses, and other agriculturally oriented service and processing businesses. This in turn increases the local population and demand for land. Land values rise, benefiting landholders; the results may be good or bad for equity depending on whether large or small landholders appropriate the land. Labor demand rises, either on farms or in processing and servicing centers, with possible benefits for poverty alleviation. Forest cover stabilizes at a low level, with remaining forest occupying slopes or poor-quality land. Agriculturally favorable areas, especially near cities, would be expected to follow this trajectory. The soybean areas of the Brazilian savanna provide an example.

Table 2.3 Five Trajectories of Forest Cover, Income, and Population

Trajectory	Agricultural rent curve	Managed forest rent curve	Forest cover trend	Poverty and population trend	Location or identifying characteristics
Intensification with deforestation	Shifts up due to increasing urban or international demand and improved tenure	Is everywhere dominated by agricultural rent	Deforestation continues and stabilizes at low forest cover	Landowners prosper, labor demand probably increases, wages, and/or workforces increase, with labor growth possibly in towns	Periurban, good soils, high-input agriculture, and higher population density
Intensification with reforestation	Shifts up due to increasing urban demand, increasing returns, and improved tenure	Shifts up due to increased demand, exhaustion of mined sources, and demand for environmental services	Decreases, then rebounds	Landowners prosper, labor demand increases, and wages and/or workforces increase	Periurban, medium to good soils, medium- to high-input agriculture, and medium to high population density
Abandonment with regrowth	Shifts up due to increasing urban demand, then down due to rising wages	Shifts up due to improved tenure and increased demand for wood and environmental services	Decreases, then rebounds	Poverty decreases due to out-migration	Likely on marginal lands: hillsides and/or semiremote, forested, or low population density
Abandonment and irreversible degradation	Shifts up, then down due to land degradation	Never surfaces, either because of high costs of tenure or irreversibility of degradation	Decreases toward zero	Out-migration without poverty alleviation	Marginal lands, not near cities; nutrient-poor soils, slopes, or high incidence of fire; grasslands in forest biomes
Immiserizing deforestation	Shifts up due to falling wages and increasing food demand	Shifts down due to soil degradation, increases disputes over forest tenure	Decreases toward zero	Larger but poorer population	Probably not near cities; anomalously high population density given remoteness and agroclimate

---

Box 2.1   The Forest Transition

The concept of the forest transition, introduced by Mather (1992), describes a tendency for forest cover to decrease in response to colonization, development, and population growth, then rebound—a process that has occurred over the past two centuries in Western Europe, Japan, and the United States. Rudel and others (2005) describe the two forces behind such a turnaround. The forest transition can arise because higher wages, associated with the opening of more productive farmlands, induce the abandonment of marginal farmlands, leading to forest regrowth. The second route occurs when deforestation makes wood so scarce that it is worth replanting trees.

A number of developing economies appear to be experiencing this transition. According to Rudel and others (2005), rebounds in forest cover have been documented in Bangladesh, China, Costa Rica, Cuba, the Dominican Republic, The Gambia, the Republic of Korea, peninsular Malaysia, Morocco, Puerto Rico, and Rwanda. India and Vietnam may also be experiencing a forest transition. Note that it is possible for forest cover to show a net increase due to planting or secondary forest regrowth even while old-growth natural forest is being lost in another part of the country.

- *Intensification with reforestation.* The dynamics of intensification with reforestation are similar to those of the previous trajectory. But here, forest depletion leads to wood scarcity, and better tenure makes it possible for households and communities to manage forests. Under some conditions it becomes profitable to convert fields and pastures to woodlots or to tend and manage secondary forests. The result is a mosaic of croplands and managed forests. Examples include India (Foster and Rosenzweig 2003), Kenya (Tiffen and Mortimore 1994), and Tanzania (Monela and others 2004). This is one route to the forest transition described in box 2.1.

- *Abandonment with regrowth.* Here one possible trigger may have been population expansion onto marginal lands. After this trigger, rents are low and barely provide subsistence livelihoods for landholders. So if development elsewhere in the economy leads to higher wages, local populations migrate to better opportunities and these marginal areas are abandoned to natural forest regeneration. This is the most familiar manifestation of the forest transition, and it summarizes the forest experiences of Western Europe, Japan, and the United States. For instance, the U.S. state of Vermont was largely cleared for agriculture in the early 19th century, despite its unfavorable terrain and climate. Vermont's fields were then abandoned as western frontier expansion and better transportation brought new more productive farmlands into the market. Among tropical areas, Puerto Rico is a striking and well-documented example, noted earlier. Other potential reasons for abandonment include a decline in the size of the youth cohort or in the price of agricultural commodities. Costa Rica's strong forest regrowth during the 1990s may be an example of the latter, if pastures were abandoned in response to declining beef markets.

- *Abandonment with irreversible degradation.* This trajectory is similar to the previous one, except that the land uses of in-migrants prove unsustainable. Soil fertility collapses due to nutrient exhaustion, compaction, or invasion by persistent weeds. The rent curve collapses, but natural regrowth doesn't occur. Examples include millions of hectares of *imperata* grasslands in Southeast Asia and large areas of apparently abandoned pastures near Belem, Brazil.

- *Deforestation and immiserization.* Here the trigger could be population expansion. A combination of stagnant technologies and immobile labor continues to push the rent curve out, but is combined with declining returns to labor and increased poverty. Poor agronomic conditions and inappropriate land use may further reduce incomes and increase pressure for nutrients from fresh deforestation. In environmental terms the outcome is similar to the abandonment with degradation trajectory. It differs in having a larger population and higher poverty rates. The humid forest of Madagascar exemplifies this scenario.

Summary

Soils, climates, markets, and governance shape pressures for deforestation across space and over time. Changes can be driven slowly, as when population and income growth boost demand for food; or abruptly, as when new roads, crop varieties, or markets create pressure to convert forests. Formerly valueless land becomes more valuable without forest cover than with. The resulting forest rents can range from barely more than zero to thousands of dollars a hectare. Landholders, especially newcomers, respond rationally to these incentives, deforesting their lands to capture the rents. Positive feedbacks kick in: for instance, burgeoning populations demanding food, fuel, and secure land rights. So do negative feedbacks, such as deteriorating soil quality. The balance of these forces determines the regional trajectory of environment, income, and population.

Different trajectories are possible and imply different associations between poverty and deforestation (Sunderlin and others 2005). A prominent win-lose trajectory has historically been associated with rural development: the conversion of forest to intensive agriculture. Here forests shrink but employment and incomes increase. Sometimes forest cover will rebound as wood becomes scarce, approximating a win-win outcome, but the recovered forest may not be equivalent in biodiversity or carbon storage to the previous forest. Alternatively, forest conversion can result in stagnant agriculture, providing subsistence income to a poor population that might be even worse off if denied access to this land. And in the worst, lose-lose case, forest conversion provides only an ephemeral income.

This chapter stresses that policies and conditions that make forestland valuable for agriculture will result in a negative association between deforestation and poverty. More valuable land tends to result in more rapid deforestation but also higher incomes.

Endnotes

1. It draws also on Chomitz and Gray (1996), Hyde and others (1997), and Hyde (forthcoming).

2. Land values in this report are net present values unless explicitly qualified as annual flows or as market prices or rentals.

3. See Boscolo and Vincent (2000) for a similar bioeconomic analysis from Malaysia, and Pearce, Putz, and Vanclay (2003) for a literature review.

4. The total value of timber was $324. But since the landholder may have the option to sell selectively extracted timber without clear cutting, the gross conversion cost is probably more relevant than the net cost in assessing the profitability of forest conversion.

Rural residents depend on forests and woodlands for fuelwood and other resources. Here, women carry firewood in the spiny forest region of Madagascar.

CHAPTER 3

Poverty in Forests Stems from Remoteness and Lack of Rights

Poverty is pervasive in the tropical world—especially in rural areas. What is special about forest poverty? Why does it deserve policy attention? Do forest dwellers constitute a substantial proportion of all poor people? Are poor people the majority among forest dwellers? What poverty reduction policies might be tailored to forest dwellers?

This chapter argues that it is fruitless to seek simplistic connections between forests and poverty. Empirically, the links are weak. Some people derive wealth from forests, others from converting forests to agriculture. Many poor people live in marginal lands without trees.

There are three distinctive forest poverty syndromes, with different causes, locales, and possible remedies. First, remote areas tend to have high forest cover, high poverty rates, and low population densities. This remote forest and poverty syndrome poses a challenge for development because most standard approaches are inapplicable or extremely costly. A corollary is that forest-poverty relationships are quite different in remote and nonremote areas. Second, forest dwellers depend on forest resources for food, fuel, medicine, and income. But many interests compete to control or exploit forest resources. So changes in rights or access to forest resources can profoundly affect the livelihoods of people who live in and near forests. Third, there can be impediments—in policy, technology, or marketing—to commercializing forest products.

Building on chapter 2 and Sunderlin, Dewi, and Puntodewo (2006), the discussion here uses a geographic lens to examine spatial overlaps between forests and poverty. This raises another question that may seem simple but is not: what do we mean when we say that an area is poor?

Poverty Rates and Poverty Density: Two Ways of Viewing Poor Areas

Let's set aside, for the moment, the question of how poverty should be measured at the level of individuals and households. Whatever the measure, a common approach to identifying high-poverty areas is to map, by province or district, the poverty *rate*: that is, the pro-

Map 3.1a   Poverty Rates for Brazil, 2000

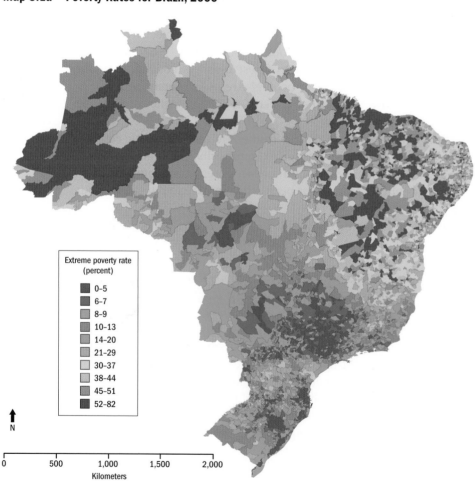

Extreme poverty rate
(percent)

- 0–5
- 6–7
- 8–9
- 10–13
- 14–20
- 21–29
- 30–37
- 38–44
- 45–51
- 52–82

N

| 0 | 500 | 1,000 | 1,500 | 2,000 |

Kilometers

Source: Authors' mapping based on UNDP.

portion of inhabitants who are poor. Map 3.1a shows this strikingly for Brazil: poverty rates are very high in Amazônia.

But high-poverty areas can also be defined as places where the poverty *density* is high. Places with high poverty densities have a lot of poor people per square kilometer. Map 3.1b presents this measure for Brazil—where, as in many places, the two maps are like photographic negatives of one another. Areas with high poverty rates tend to have low poverty densities, and vice versa.

Which is the better definition of high-poverty areas? Later this chapter argues that each type of high-poverty area has distinct needs and policy implications. But first it examines the forces that shape

Map 3.1b   Poverty Densities for Brazil, 2000

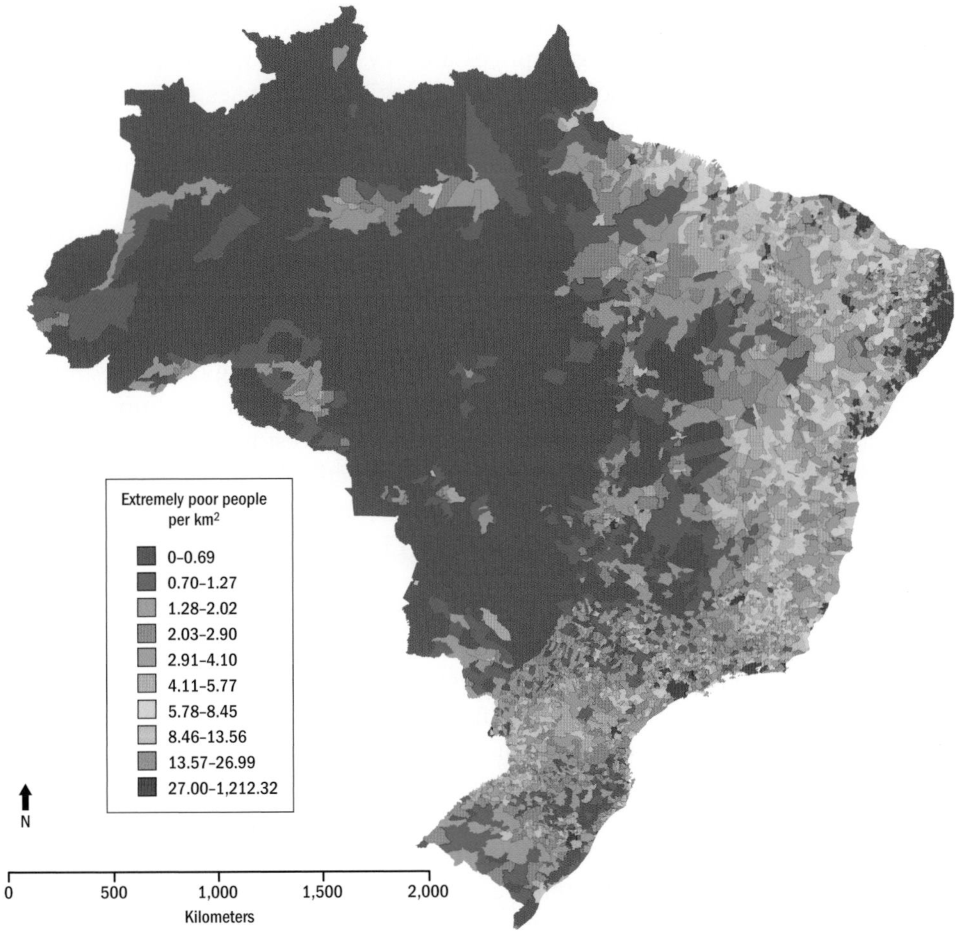

Extremely poor people
per km²

■	0–0.69
■	0.70–1.27
■	1.28–2.02
■	2.03–2.90
■	2.91–4.10
■	4.11–5.77
□	5.78–8.45
■	8.46–13.56
■	13.57–26.99
■	27.00–1,212.32

N

0   500   1,000   1,500   2,000
Kilometers

Source: Authors' mapping based on UNDP.

the geographic distribution of forest cover, deforestation, and poor people.

Remote Forests—High Poverty Rates, Low Poverty Densities

Remoteness mediates strong connections between forests, poverty, and population (see chapter 2). Because it is expensive to send produce to markets from remote areas, it is rarely worth growing crops or harvesting timber for commercial use—meaning that deforestation is low and forest cover high. The situation is even worse if areas have remained remote because they offer poor prospects for agriculture. In remote areas low land rents lead to low incomes because farm profits are negligible and off-farm employment opportunities missing. Hence poverty rates are high.

Because farmgate prices are low, it is not worth applying much labor to a plot of land. Only extensive land uses such as pasture, shifting cultivation, and forest extraction are feasible. This means that population density is low—probably so low that poverty density is also low. Low population densities, together with distance from administrative centers and poor communications, mean that forest dwellers have little voice in regional and national affairs. The problem is compounded if, as is likely, they are indigenous people not yet displaced by farmers or ranchers. Disempowered, they are subject to neglect or exploitation by elites seeking timber or mineral wealth. Finally, remoteness from law and communications and low population density mean that land and forest tenure are likely to be insecure. Table 3.1 summarizes predictions about remoteness and its effects on poverty and the environment.

Evidence

These relationships are evident in Nicaragua, a small country with a dominant city (Managua) and a forest frontier (Chomitz 2004). Extreme rural poverty rises sharply and smoothly with increasing travel time to Managua (figure 3.1). Population density falls just as smoothly and even more sharply, causing poverty density to decrease with increasing distance (figure 3.2). In addition, the ratio of rural workers to farmed land falls with remoteness, as expected. Forest cover rises with remoteness—though not as smoothly, partly because some nonremote areas are on slopes (figure 3.3). Tenure is less secure in frontier areas on the Atlantic side of the country:

Table 3.1   How Does Increasing Remoteness from Markets Affect Poverty and the Environment?

Indicator	Effect
Population density	Decreases with remoteness
Poverty rate	Increases with remoteness
Poverty density	Decreases with remoteness
Land productivity	Decreases with remoteness
Labor intensity	Decreases with remoteness
Tenure security	Decreases with remoteness
Forest cover	Increases with remoteness

a substantially lower proportion of farms have titles. This part of the country also has a prominent indigenous population. And unlike western Nicaragua, the Atlantic side has uniformly poor soil quality, as measured at the *municipio* level.

Areas near Managua (within about four hours' imputed travel time) make up only a quarter of the nation's area but contain half of its extremely poor rural population. The most remote areas (those

Figure 3.1   Extreme Rural Poverty Increases with Travel Time to Managua

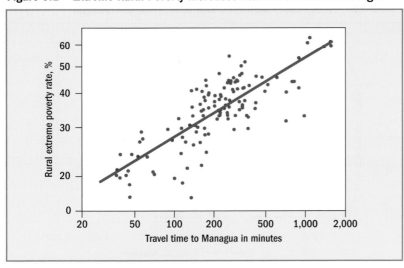

Source: Chomitz 2004.
Note: Excludes Managua department.

Figure 3.2   Rural Population Density Decreases with Travel Time to Managua

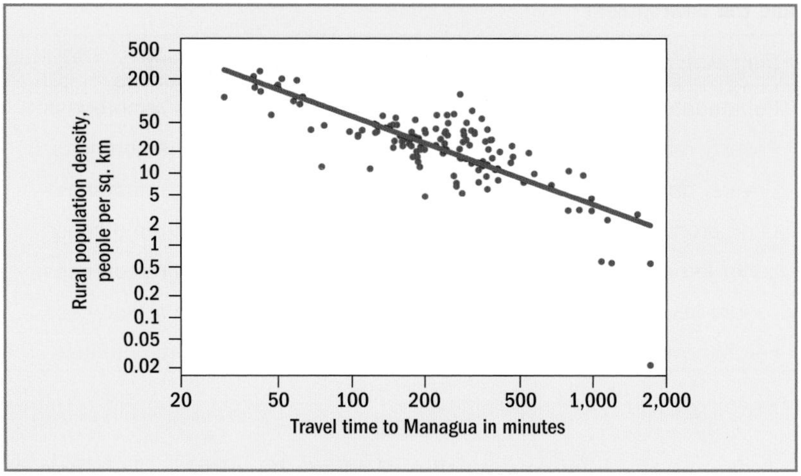

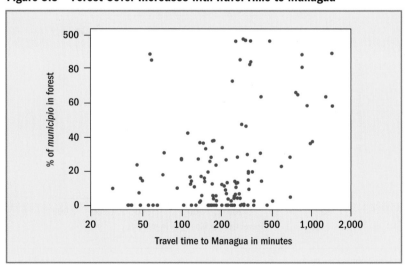

Source: Chomitz 2004.
Note: Excludes Managua department.

more than 16 hours' journey) occupy about a third of the nation's area but contain only about 10 percent of its extremely poor rural population. The most remote areas have abundant forests; areas near Managua, sparser forests except on mountainsides.

Figure 3.3   Forest Cover Increases with Travel Time to Managua

Source: Chomitz 2004.

Implications

The remoteness connection points to a distinct poverty-forest syndrome. At the extreme end are places with relatively undisturbed forest cover and low population densities—perhaps 1 or 2 people per square kilometer, or less. Limited empirical and anecdotal evidence suggests that these people are extremely poor in terms of consumption, assets, and health indicators (such as child mortality). For instance, detailed measures of poverty for Vietnam in 1998 found that 73 percent of northern upland minority groups and 91 percent of central highlands minority groups lived below the poverty line, compared with 30 percent of the majority population (Baulch and others 2004, p. 278).

Although data are lacking, indigenous people account for a large share of remote forest dwellers, and a disproportionate number of indigenous people live in remote forest areas. For instance, Baulch and others (2004, p. 291) found that Vietnamese upland and highland minority members were four times farther from a market and six times farther from a telephone than were majority group members. Being indigenous compounds the difficulties associated with remoteness. Indigenous people have historically been subject to severe discrimination and exploitation. Despite legal and social progress in some countries, indigenous people remain disadvantaged. A recent study of indigenous people in Latin America found that:

- Indigenous children in Ecuador, Guatemala, and Mexico are twice as likely to be stunted (an indicator of severe malnutrition) as nonindigenous children. About half of indigenous children are stunted.

- Indigenous adults have 2.3–3.7 fewer years of schooling than do nonindigenous.

- Indigenous people earn significantly less than do nonindigenous, and about half the gap cannot be explained by differences in education or other personal characteristics (Hall and Patrinos 2005).

These differences would presumably be even larger if attention were limited to remote forest dwellers.

Remote communities, indigenous or not, face enormous challenges. For example, providing education and health care is difficult and expensive in remote areas (Chomitz and others 1998). Infrastructure is also difficult to provide in remote communities. Water and electricity systems cannot exploit economies of scale or density. Building and maintaining feeder roads is expensive in rainy, swampy, or mountainous environments, and their unit costs skyrocket if they serve few people and little traffic.

Lack of roads is also an obstacle to realizing the potential of forestry. Community forestry is often considered a development option that combines environmental and livelihood benefits for remote forest communities. Timber is, apparently, the main commercial resource that these communities have in abundance. But to benefit communities, that timber has to get to market. Poor roads mean high transport costs, and high transport costs reduce the stumpage value of timber—the value received by communities. Roper (2003) identifies poor roads as one of the main barriers for commercializing the forests owned by indigenous people of Nicaragua's Atlantic region. Transport costs of $0.34 a cubic meter per kilometer eat into wood values, for these communities, of about $20 a cubic meter.

In sum, there is not necessarily a strong relationship between forest cover and poverty rates, though poverty densities tend to be lower in forested areas. But some forest areas suffer from poverty because of their remoteness from agricultural markets and because low population densities make it difficult to deliver services and infrastructure.

Incomes of Forest Dwellers Depend on Rights and Access to Forestlands

Forests provide food, fuel, fodder, wood, and medicine to their inhabitants and neighbors, for personal consumption and for sale. Though these resources represent a substantial portion of forest dwellers' income, it is difficult to measure forest income and dependence. It seems reasonable to suppose that households' degree of reliance is inversely related to population density. People living at extremely low densities—say, fewer than five per square kilometer—probably rely heavily on the forest for their livelihoods. These people are numerous in aggregate, but spread thinly across the world. For logistical and cultural reasons, they are hard to survey.

Because Living Standards Measurement Surveys (LSMS) usually omit remote, low-density districts and provinces, there is little quantitative information about this most forest-dependent population. On the other hand, there are hundreds of millions of people in high-population-density forests and forest-agriculture mosaics. Here the problem is accurately enumerating, measuring, and attributing cash values to the extraction of dozens of forest products. Standard survey instruments probably underestimate this income stream. A further issue is that forest products serve as a safety net, relied on more heavily in times of crop failure and other hardship. One-time surveys could easily miss this feature.

With these concerns in mind, Vedeld and others (2004) conducted a metareview of 54 case studies that measured income from forest products. The studies are not a representative sample, so their data are merely indicative. Forest income (averaging $678 a year, adjusted for purchasing power parity) accounted for about a fifth of household income in the sample—a significant contribution, particularly for families near the survival line. Wild food and fuelwood were the most important products, accounting for 70 percent of forest income (although some products, such as fodder, are probably underreported in the sample).

Forest income was higher the farther that households were from markets—suggesting that for remote communities, a lack of alternative income opportunities and an abundance of forests lead to greater dependence on such resources. Reinforcing this, the most forest-dependent half of the sample cases (earning an average of 42 percent of their income from forest products) lived in more remote areas, had less education and livestock, and averaged only about half as much income per household. The few studies that examined the distribution of income within communities found that because poor people depended more on forest products, forest income reduced inequality. The average Gini coefficient (a common measure of inequality) was 0.51 when forest income was excluded but fell to 0.41 when it was included.

Forest Control and Tenure Can Affect Income

Because rural poor people are dependent on forest resources, anything that affects their rights or access to those resources merits attention. Three policy concerns arise here. The first is a potential tragedy of the commons. Although some forests are effectively managed by communities as common property resources, others are open access—managed by no one, exploited by all. If these forests are degraded, local income streams are destroyed.

Second, forest regulations from colonial times, or recently imposed on environmental grounds, may restrict forest dwellers' ability to gather fuelwood, food, and other forest products. Forest officials can also use these regulations as a source of rents, extracting bribes from poor forest dwellers.

Third, changes in legal or de facto ownership of forests affect local dwellers' ability to undertake commercial forestry and agriculture, both of which can provide a route out of poverty.

Open Access Forests Suffer Degradation

There is a long history of concern that rural households, dependent on woodlands for fuel, suffer when those woodlands are depleted. A thorough recent literature review by Arnold, Kohlin, and Persson (2006, p. 604) concludes that "the body of information now available suggests that the greater part of rural populations in both Africa and South Asia do not face serious welfare implications due to decreasing access to biomass, but resource poor areas and households can face a problem, in particular landless people without access to common pool biomass stocks."

It is difficult to measure the extent and depth of deprivation due to degradation of open access forests. Given the substantial proportion of income derived from forests, forest degradation may translate into lower consumption or increased workloads as it becomes harder to glean resources from thinned-out woodlands. But it is hard to measure consumption of forest resources and local access to them, and to control for other correlates of resource availability.

This point is illustrated by Bandyopadhyay, Shyamsundar, and Baccini (2006), who marshal unusually detailed and comprehensive data to assess the impacts of biomass scarcity in Malawi. They report that deforestation and forest degradation reduced biomass, nationwide, by 16 percent over 1990–2004, and that fuelwood accounts for about 12 percent of the value of household consumption. Gathering fuelwood takes an average of 1.5 hours a day—and 84 percent of this burden falls to women.

In this setting one might hypothesize a vicious circle of poverty and degradation. As forests thinned, people would be expected to reduce their consumption of fuelwood or to devote more time to gathering it. But Bandyopadhyay, Shyamsundar, and Baccini (2006) find that, other things being equal, households in lower-density forests did not spend more time gathering fuelwood, and that fuelwood gathering did not come at the expense of agriculture. In the rural south of Malawi, where forests are more degraded, the authors found that a 10 percent lower biomass density was associated with

0.2 percent lower consumption. This modest association suggests that households adapt their fuel sources or strategies as forest resources dwindle. But because this effect applies to every household in a neighborhood, forest degradation might be significant in areas with higher population densities.

On the other hand, the study found that consumption actually fell with higher levels of biomass in less degraded areas. This may be a spurious association: high-biomass areas are likely more remote and less suitable for agriculture. But the study's bottom line is that low biomass densities are not associated with drastic poverty burdens—meaning that people are resourceful in adapting to exhausted biomass or that proper measurement is extremely difficult. More studies like this are needed in a wide variety of settings before general conclusions can be drawn.

Another potential tragedy of the commons could result from overexploitation of bushmeat. Some 2.2 million tons of wild mammals and other animals are exploited for food each year in the Congo Basin, representing a major source of animal protein for the region (Fa, Currie, and Meeuwig 2003). Bushmeat accounted for about 10 percent of household production in a very poor village surveyed by de Merode, Homewood, and Cowlishaw (2004), and was especially important in the lean agricultural season. But bushmeat extraction already exceeds the sustainable supply by more than 25 percent in Cameroon and the Democratic Republic of Congo (Fa Currie and Meeuwig 2003). Population and income growth, increased road access, and shrinking animal populations threaten to make exploitation increasingly unsustainable.

Regulations Can Limit Forest Use

Forest regulations may restrict forest dwellers' ability to gather firewood or other forest products, to market timber, or to convert forests to agriculture. For instance, Cameroonians cannot legally sell trees they grow as part of a cocoa agroforest (Gockowski and others 2006). Facing depressed prices, their timber stock is undervalued by $1,460 a hectare. In Indonesia regulations discourage farmers from selling rubber trees they cultivate in an agroforestry system. The potentially valuable wood is burnt instead (Joshi and others 2002).

Dwellers Are Often Dispossessed of Land and Forests

When wealthy interests seize or degrade forests, poor local populations can suffer. These situations do not lend themselves to controlled study, so evidence is anecdotal. For instance, Davis (2005) estimates that 100,000 Cambodians depend for their livelihoods on tapping forest dipterocarp trees for oleoresin, a commercially valuable product. Davis, McKenney, and others (2004) and McAndrew and others (2004) report that illegal logging and conversion of forests to acacia plantations have deprived resin tappers of access to trees.

Establishment of protected areas has sometimes involved displacement of and loss of assets by local populations (Ghimire and Pimbert 1997; Geisler and De Sousa 2001). (See chapter 6 for a discussion of efforts to emphasize comanagement of parks as an alternative to displacement.) Cernea and Schmidt-Soltau (2003) and Schmidt-Soltau (2003) review the establishment of nine national parks in central Africa and conclude that about 51,000 people were displaced. In only two of the nine cases were there formal resettlement policies. In two cases no compensation was made to the displaced populations, and in most of the other cases compensation was inadequate. The loss of assets could be thousands of dollars per capita depending on the potential surrendered stumpage value of timber, but this valuation is complicated by the need to estimate transport costs from these remote areas.

Ferraro (2002) analyzes how the establishment of Ranomafana Park in Madagascar affected its inhabitants, who were subsequently denied park access and forced to rely on buffer zones for agriculture and forest extraction. The analysis accounts for different time paths of resource degradation under the unsustainable agricultural technologies used by the residents. Access to the park allows them to defer the long-term effects of soil fertility decline and timber exhaustion. Ferraro finds that park exclusion imposed a mean annual cost of $39 a household—equivalent to 14 percent of household income. This is consistent with a survey by Shyamsundar and Kramer (1996) that asked households how much they would require in compensation for resettlement.

Forests without Trees Are a Widespread Dilemma

Large swathes of tropical Asia are legally forestland but devoid of trees:

- In Indonesia between 333,000 square kilometers (Contreras-Hermosilla and Fay 2005) and 370,000 square kilometers (Boccucci, Muliastra, and Dore 2005) of land are under Forest Department control but devoid of forests. Of this, about 100,000 square kilometers was designated for conversion to oil palm, timber, or pulp plantations that never materialized. The rest represents deforestation of forests gazetted for conservation, watershed protection, or sustainable timber production.

- In India 20 percent of reserved forest—at least 100,000 square kilometers—is without trees (Ministry of Environment and Forests 2005).

- In the Philippines a 1981 presidential decree declared all land with a slope greater than 17 percent to be within the public domain. Today only a small fraction of these 150,000 square kilometers retains any forest (Fay and Michon 2005).

- In Thailand 70,000 square kilometers of state forestland was treeless when a 1992 reform sought to rezone the forest domain (Fay and Michon 2005).

Treeless forests are problematic because they are inhabited by people without secure land rights. The populations are large—at least 40 million in Indonesia alone (Boccucci, Muliastra, and Dore 2005). But lack of security makes it hard for them to invest in land improvements, such as reclaiming degraded grasslands or planting trees. Weak tenure depresses land values and reduces access to credit (Deininger 2003).

Forests, Poverty, and Deforestation: Ambiguous Relationships

The search for win-win solutions to poverty and environment dilemmas motivates the hypothesis that there is substantial spatial overlap between areas with high poverty rates and areas with high forest cover, high deforestation, or both. This chapter and the previous one offer several reasons to expect those relationships to be muddled:

- Remoteness is associated with high poverty rates and forest cover, but low deforestation.

- Insecure tenure may be associated with high deforestation and either low or high poverty rates, depending on the deforestation process.

- Deforestation is sometimes undertaken by wealthy commercial interests.

- Deforestation can create valuable agricultural assets for smallholders.

- On the other hand, deforestation may reflect the expansion of subsistence-oriented populations onto increasingly unsuitable lands.

Empirical studies reflect this ambiguity. Sunderlin, Dewi, and Puntodewo (2006) analyze associations between poverty rates, poverty densities, and forest cover in seven countries. In three of the seven they find a significant positive correlation, at the district level, between poverty rates and forest cover. Vietnam is a clear example, with high poverty rates, low population densities, and high forest cover in the remote mountain regions of the north and central parts of the country. In three countries there is no significant relationship.

Only one country has a significant negative relationship: Brazil. At the national level, across all forest types, the relationship is negative because the semiarid region of northeast Brazil has high poverty rates and low forest cover—while the wealthy southernmost part of the country, well into the forest transition, has low poverty rates and high forest cover. This national-level correlation result obscures the relationship evident in map 3.1: remote western Amazônian forests have high poverty rates and high forest cover.

Deininger and Minten's (1999) study of Mexico related municipal poverty to deforestation, controlling for a host of biophysical and socioeconomic factors including slope, elevation, rainfall, indigenous proportion of population, and land tenure. They found a strong partial relationship, statistically and quantitatively, between deforestation over 1980–90 and poverty rates in 1990. Other things constant, a one standard deviation increase in poverty was associated with an increase of almost 3 percentage points in the annual deforestation rate. But rainfall and hilliness were strongly negatively associated with deforestation and positively associated with poverty. So it is likely that the simple correlation between poverty and deforestation is negative.

The rest of this section uses newly available, fine-scale data to examine spatial relationships between poverty rates, population densities, forest cover, and deforestation in four important forested countries: Brazil, India, Indonesia, and Madagascar. Keep in mind that measures of poverty, forest cover, and deforestation are not comparable between countries.

Deforestation and Poverty in Brazilian Amazônia Are Largely Unrelated

Deforestation of Brazilian Amazônia is sometimes blamed on poor people. But evidence suggests that poverty and deforestation problems in Amazônia are largely separate problems requiring separate approaches:

- Poverty and deforestation are spatially localized, with limited overlap.

- Most deforestation is undertaken by large-scale, well-capitalized actors.

- Much of this large-scale deforestation occurs on public land and so represents a regressive transfer of public resources.

- Deforestation is profit-driven, but typically yields modest profits per hectare.

Scale of Deforestation

Remote sensing data suggest that poor people are responsible for less than a fifth of deforestation in Brazilian Amazônia (figure 3.4).[1] Because clearing is expensive and large clearings require mechanical

Figure 3.4   Most Deforestation in Brazilian Amazônia Reflects Large- and Medium-scale Clearing, August 2000 to July 2003

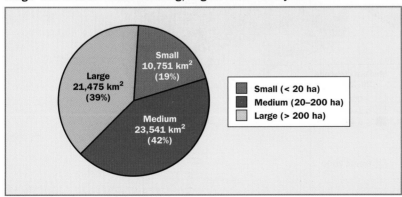

Source: Wertz-Kanounnikoff 2005.
Note: Categories reflect size of clearings, not properties.

equipment, there is a strong correlation between clearing size and the deforester's wealth or access to capital. Subsistence farmers are unlikely to be able to afford to clear more than 20 hectares a year, and most probably clear far less.

About 39 percent of deforestation occurs in incremental clearings larger than 200 hectares, which likely represent wealthy interests. This finding is consistent with Chomitz and Thomas (2003), who find that agricultural establishments of 2,000 hectares or more contain 53 percent of privately owned, cleared land in Amazônia. It is also consistent with the description by Margulis (2004) of large-scale ranching activities in the Amazon.

Map 3.2 Amazônian Deforestation 2000–03 Showing Rates and Predominant Clearing Size

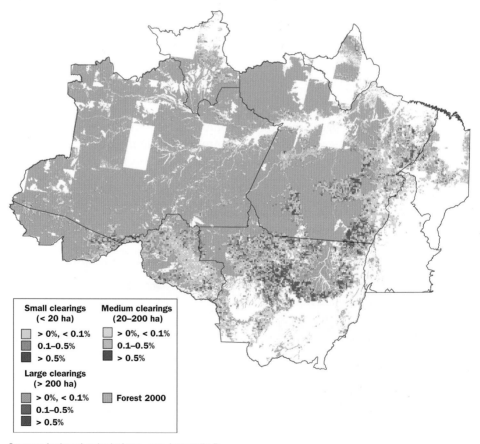

Source: Authors' calculations, see Appendix B.
Note: Rate = deforested area/total area.

Location of Poverty and Deforestation

Map 3.2 shows the concentration of deforestation in Brazil between 2000 and 2003, following a broad arc extending from Maranhão to Rondônia. The map, based on data from the Brazilian National Institute for Space Research (INPE), includes only deforestation of mature Amazônian forest, excluding deforestation of *cerrado* (savanna) woodland and secondary regrowth. Darker colors correspond to more rapid deforestation. The colors represent predominant shares of deforestation by size of incremental clearing, a proxy for the scale of the actors involved. The map shows that large-scale clearings predominate in Mato Grosso and southern Pará along the

Map 3.3 Amazônian Deforestation Rates and Rural Illiteracy Densities

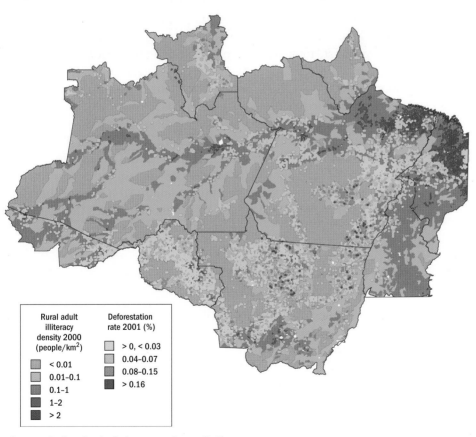

Source: Authors' calculations, see Appendix B.
Note: Rate = deforested area/total area.

forest-cerrado boundary. Small-scale clearings—and thus, presumably, small-scale landholders—are scattered throughout but are most prominent in Rondônia and parts of Pará.

Map 3.3 shows the density of rural adult illiteracy in Brazil in 2000, overlaid by deforestation rates in 2001. Most of the deforestation hotspots of Mato Grosso and Pará are in areas where rural adult illiteracy density (a proxy for poverty density) is extremely low—from 0.01–0.1 per square kilometer. These densities are too low for poverty to be a plausible cause of deforestation, reinforcing the conclusions drawn from the predominance of large-scale clearings in these spots. But there are places where deforestation hotspots and higher illiteracy densities coincide, as in central Rondônia.

About 12 percent of deforestation in Brazil between 2000 and 2003 occurred on lands known as *terras arrecadadas*—unambiguously public lands. This represents private appropriation of public lands. It is not known how much of this transfer was legal. Some, perhaps most, took place through an opaque process called *grilagem*,[2] which results in an award of title to land of uncertain status (Margulis 2004). What is clear is that about half of this deforestation occurred on incremental clearings of 20–200 hectares, and another quarter on clearings more than 200 hectares. (The properties themselves are presumably much larger than the clearings.) The breakdown of deforestation by size is similar in the regions for which tenure status is unknown. These regions contain *terras devolutas*—unallocated and undemarcated public lands. So it is plausible that much deforestation in Brazilian Amazônia constitutes the appropriation of public lands by large private actors, in nontransparent and possibly illegal ways.

India Contains Net Reforestation with Patches of Deforestation

Despite its huge poor rural population and limited arable land, India has experienced a forest transition (see box 2.1). Between 1971 and 2003 forests grew from 10 to 24 percent of national area (Foster and Rosenzweig 2003).

This expansion conceals a welter of local processes. One explanation may be a supply response to a long-term increase in the price of fuelwood. While some of this response may have occurred on private lands or in regenerating forests under joint forest management, it is also due to the Indian government's massive investments in tree plantations—on a nominal scale of about 1 million hectares a year since 1980. At the same time, forests dwindled in villages where the green revolution increased the value of putting land into agriculture (Foster and Rosenzweig 2003). A 1980 decree forbade deforestation for agriculture and probably restrained large government-sponsored projects (Rudel 2005).

Still, deforestation continues in places. Many forests are thinning under human pressure, so the proportion of very dense forest is only 7.5 percent, or 1.5 percent of the national area (Ministry of Environment and Forests 2005). In sum, there is continuing conversion and degradation pressure on India's remaining native forests, while planted forests—already about half of the forest estate—expand.

Figure 3.5 shows the relationship in India, at the district level, between forest cover and illiteracy—a rough indicator for poverty.[3] There is no clear relationship. Districts with more than 50 percent forest cover contain just 3.6 percent of the country's illiterates. Additional analysis finds examples of both coincidence and divergence of forest cover, illiteracy, and tribal populations. The role of joint forest management in stimulating reforestation and reducing poverty remains to be comprehensively investigated.

Figure 3.5 Illiteracy and Forest Cover Have No Clear Link in India

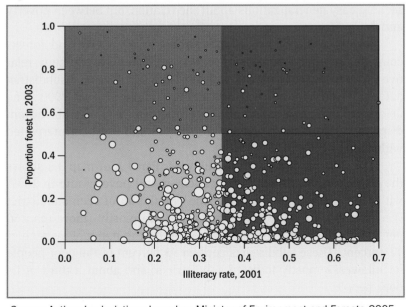

Source: Authors' calculations based on Ministry of Environment and Forests 2005 and Census India 2001.
Note: Bubble sizes are proportional to population.

Indonesia Is a Complex Pastiche of Deforestation Processes

In Indonesia the relationship between corporate interests and small-holders, poverty, and deforestation is complex and varies across the archipelago. FWI and GFW (2002), like other sources, surmise that most deforestation is due to clearance by timber, pulp, and oil plantation interests. In some, perhaps most, cases these parties used conversion permits to obtain timber or pulp, but failed to install promised plantations.

There are no nationwide, reliable, quantitative estimates of the importance of corporate relative to smallholder deforestation. In a detailed study combining ethnography and remote sensing data, Dennis and others (2005) examine nine disparate sites in Sumatra and Kalimantan, sometimes finding multiple agents of deforestation at a single site. They find smallholders converting forest to com-mercially oriented permanent agriculture in two sites, smallhold-ers engaged in short-rotation shifting agriculture in six sites, and land clearance by large plantation companies in six sites. Deforesta-tion was also caused by arson connected with land tenure disputes between communities and companies, and by escaped fires lit by hunters in search of easier paths to deer, fish, and turtles. This kalei-doscope of actions by rich and poor actors illustrates the futility of seeking easy generalizations about the relationship between poverty and deforestation.

Here is a tale of two islands: one where poverty and forests coincide, another where deforestation appears to accompany rela-tive prosperity (see maps 3.4 and 3.5). The tale uses new subdistrict data on poverty, forest cover, and deforestation over 1990–2000. (The deforestation data, although the best available, were assembled from disparate and possibly inconsistent sources and must be interpreted with caution.)

Consider first the island of Sulawesi. Panel A of map 3.5 shows the relationship between its forest cover and poverty rate in 2000, with the bubble sizes indicating the population of each subdistrict (*kecamatan*). In many subdistricts that are mostly (more than 50 percent) forested, the poverty rate exceeds the national average of 17 percent. These subdistricts contain 95 percent of the poor people in Sulawesi's mostly forested subdistricts, and about a third of its poor people.

Panel B of map 3.5 shows that most of these high-forest, high-poverty districts are in the remote central portion of the island, far from the urban centers at the tips of its "arms." Panel C shows the slightly negative relationship between the deforestation rate and poverty rate, with the bubble sizes showing initial forest cover. In sum, Sulawesi conforms with the remoteness–high poverty rate–high forest cover syndrome and does not show a strong positive association between poverty rates and deforestation.

Kalimantan, to the west, presents a different picture (map 3.4). Some areas have high forest cover and high poverty rates (panel A). Again, these are mostly in the remote center of the island (panel B) and are large in area but have few people. A much larger population lives in subdistricts that are mostly forested and have lower than national average poverty rates (green areas of panels A and B). Overall, the poverty rate in the high-forest areas is 19 percent—scarcely more than the national average. Panel C of map 3.4 shows that the subdistricts undergoing the most rapid deforestation tend to have much lower poverty rates than more stable subdistricts.

Why the difference between the two islands? Kalimantan has a much more active logging industry than Sulawesi. An hypothesis, to be confirmed, is that there is a pulse of income and deforestation at the logging frontier. This would be consistent with case studies of two forest communities, one on each island, by Deschamps and Hartman (2005). The remote Kalimantan site is inhabited by forest- and agriculture-dependent groups; the forest is threatened mostly by logging. The Sulawesi site abuts a national park, and here the threat is conversion to rice, cocoa, cloves, and other cash crops.

The authors find that all three groups (the two in Kalimantan and the one in Sulawesi) receive similar agricultural incomes per household. The agriculturally oriented groups earn about as much again from forest extraction. The forest-oriented Kalimantan group, however, earns three times as much from forest extraction than from agriculture. It can draw on commercially valuable wood and gaharu (a prized nontimber forest product)—neither of which is plentiful at the Sulawesi site. Further investigation is needed to determine whether these income gains are sustainable. High poverty rates in low-forest areas hint at unsustainability and may reflect populations living in degraded forests without trees, with insecure land rights.

Map 3.4   Poverty, Forests, and Deforestation in Kalimantan

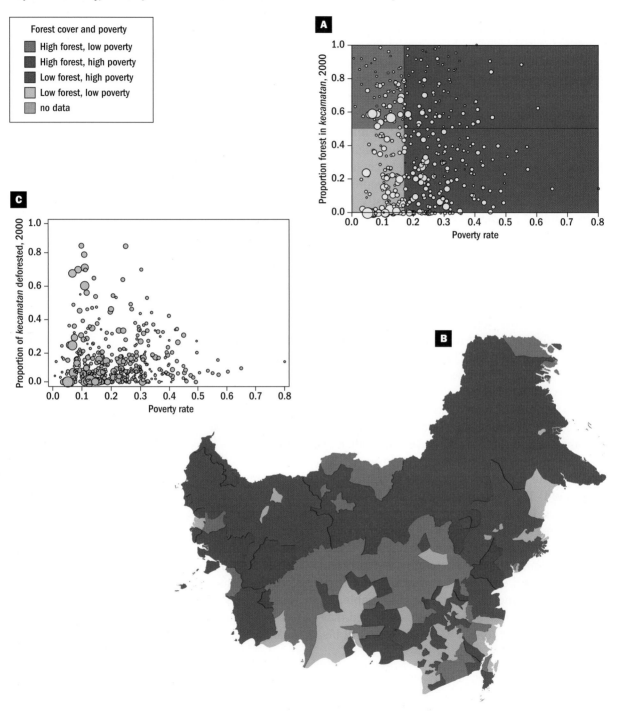

Map 3.5   Poverty, Forests, and Deforestation in Sulawesi

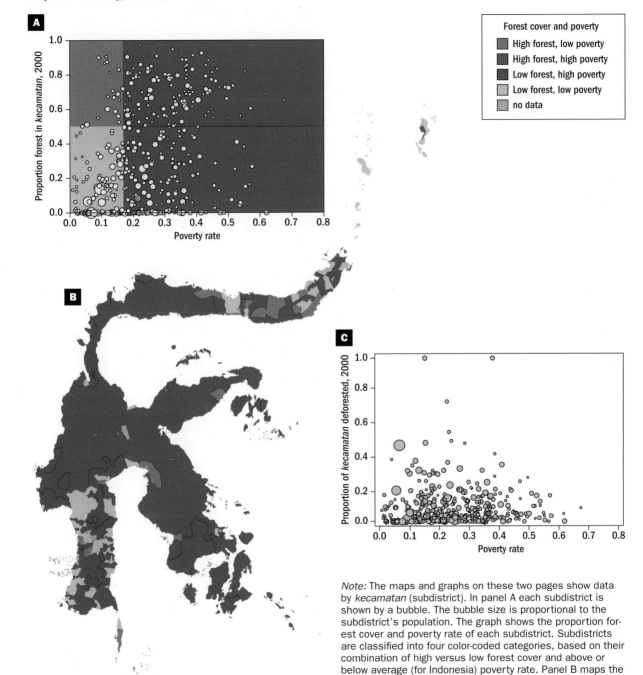

Note: The maps and graphs on these two pages show data by *kecamatan* (subdistrict). In panel A each subdistrict is shown by a bubble. The bubble size is proportional to the subdistrict's population. The graph shows the proportion forest cover and poverty rate of each subdistrict. Subdistricts are classified into four color-coded categories, based on their combination of high versus low forest cover and above or below average (for Indonesia) poverty rate. Panel B maps the subdistricts according to these categories. Panel C shows the poverty rates and deforestation rates for each subdistrict. The rate is defined as forest loss/total subdistrict area.

103

Madagascar Shows a Spatial Association between Forests and Poverty, with Other Factors at Work

In Madagascar much deforestation is undertaken by people who are extremely poor by absolute standards. About three-quarters of the population lives below the national poverty line. How, then, are we to understand the relationship between poverty and forests within the country? Map 3.6 presents some perspectives, using district data on poverty in 1993 and deforestation over 1990–2000.

About 10 percent of the country's poor people lived in districts with high forest cover (more than 50 percent forested). Almost all lived in districts that were mostly forested and had higher than average poverty rates (red areas in map 3.6). Areas with the highest poverty rates also tended to have higher deforestation rates. But the overwhelming majority of Madagascar's poor people live in areas with low forest cover—including formerly forested areas that have become degraded.

The link between poverty and deforestation in Madagascar unravels, however, when other factors that might affect forest clearance are taken into account. Gorenflo and others (2006) assessed the impact of poverty on deforestation, controlling for road access, topography, and the presence of protected areas. These factors were powerful correlates of deforestation. Holding them constant, there was a mild partial correlation between poverty and deforestation in most of the country's subregions. But in the southwest, where commercially oriented maize cultivation prevails, poverty was negatively associated with deforestation—suggesting that deforestation is at least temporarily associated with higher incomes.

Summary

Beware of facile generalizations about poverty, forests, and deforestation. In general, forest cover is an unreliable indicator of poverty rates, and poverty is a poor proxy for deforestation. In Brazil, India, Indonesia, and Madagascar only a small proportion of poor people live in mostly forested districts. In India and Indonesia there are forested places with low poverty rates (by national standards) as well as high. A more reliable generalization is that highly forested areas tend to have low densities of poor people.

But there are several important forest-poverty linkages that can guide policy. First, remote, forested areas in transfrontier zones often

Map 3.6 Forest Cover, Deforestation, and Poverty in Madagascar

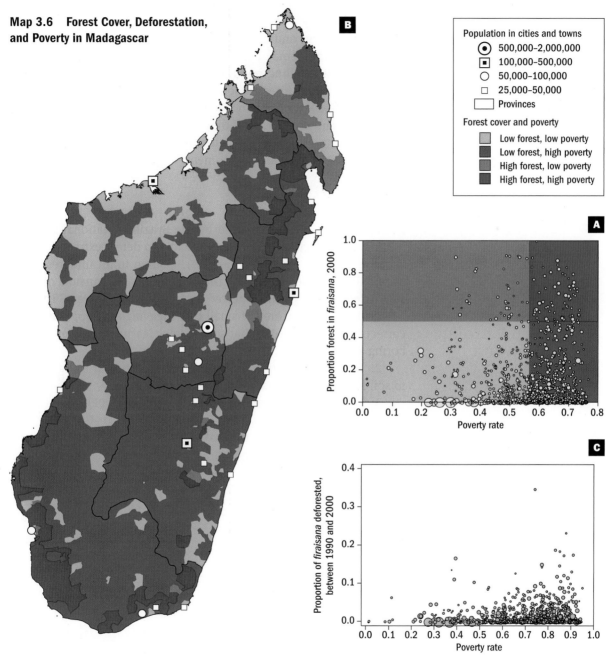

Note: The maps and graphs on this page show data by firaisana (subdistrict). In panel A each subdistrict is shown by a bubble. The bubble size is proportional to the subdistrict's population. The graph shows the proportion forest cover and poverty rate of each subdistrict. Subdistricts are classified into four color-coded categories, based on their combination of high versus low forest cover and above or below average (for Madagascar) poverty rate. Panel B maps the subdistricts according to these categories. Panel C shows the poverty rates and deforestation rates for each subdistrict. The rate is defined as forest loss/total subdistrict area.

have high poverty rates, especially when timber markets are distant. Providing services and development options in these areas is a great challenge, but they may benefit some of the world's poorest people. Second, forest-dwelling populations may face legal or bureaucratic obstacles to using forest assets. The scope of this problem is not well quantified, but it could be quite large. Third, tens of millions of people occupy hundreds of thousands of square kilometers of forests without trees. More secure tenure in these areas could improve both livelihoods and the environment.

Endnotes

1. The satellite sensor used by the Brazilian National Institute for Space Research (INPE) may be unable to detect extremely small clearings (on the order of a hectare), leading to an underestimate of smallholder clearings. But the incremental expansion of such small clearings might be detected over two or three years. Thus on a statistical basis the area of small clearings might be approximately correct. It is also possible that some large clearings represent neighboring small clearings.

2. The word is said to derive from the practice of using crickets to soil forged documents to make them look antique.

3. Population data are from Census of India (2001). Forest cover data are from Ministry of Environment and Forests (2005) and include forests outside the tropical forest biome and both native and planted forests. Data are missing for some states and districts.

Harpy eagles, found in Latin America, exemplify the need to manage land-scapes to ensure biodiversity survival. A nesting pair of harpy eagles re-quires 100 km^2 of forest to provide enough prey for sustenance. A viable population of harpy eagles requires dozens of times as much.

Juan Pablo Moreiras / Fauna & Flora International / Comisión Centroamericana de Ambiente y Desarrollo photo archive.

Forest loss typically increases total annual water flows, potentially exacerbating chronic (but not necessarily catastrophic) flooding.

Juan Pablo Moreiras / Fauna & Flora International / Comisión Centroamericana de Ambiente y Desarrollo photo archive.

CHAPTER 4

Deforestation Imposes Geographically Varied Environmental Damages

What environmental problems are associated with deforestation—where and when do they occur, and who suffers from them? Forests have diverse environmental values and functions. This chapter unbundles those functions, which include provision of biological goods, maintenance of genetic diversity, regulation of water flows, and storage of carbon. The approach used here helps explain who suffers when those functions are impaired by forest degradation and the costs of maintaining or substituting for those functions.

This review is necessarily highly selective. The Millennium Ecosystem Assessment (2005), on which this report draws, provides a comprehensive synthesis of ecological relationships between forests and people. A motivation for that assessment, and for this report, is that social and economic policies often do not incorporate scientific insights. That shortcoming can result in poor prioritization of problems and poor choices of instruments for addressing problems. Two questions underscore this chapter's discussion: What are the most compelling reasons for reducing deforestation, and where do they apply?

Before starting the discussion, it is useful to offer a framework for thinking about environmental damages. The essence of environmental problems is the concept of an externality—where one person's actions unintentionally benefit or harm another person. For instance, I may remove the trees along my river banks, heedless that the consequent erosion will pollute your drinking water with sediment. In principle, society as a whole would be better off if externalities were factored into environmental decision making. If I gain $100 from felling my trees but you have to pay $1,000 to filter your drinking water, the potential damages from pollution far outweigh the potential profits from deforestation. There should be a way to arrange to keep the trees standing.

The nature of that arrangement depends on whether society assigns me the right to cut the trees or guarantees you the right to clean water. If the latter, your right trumps mine. My potential $100 gain is too little to compensate you for your $1,000 loss, so I won't bother to cut the trees. But if I have an absolute right to cut my trees, you would find it worthwhile to pay me up to $1,000 for the environmental service of preserving the trees and reducing erosion. Either way, the trees would remain standing. And the assignment of rights determines who benefits and who loses.

But there are transactions costs involved in enforcing rights and negotiating payments. Those costs can be high if there are diffuse sources of the externality and many on whom it impinges. Costs escalate further if sources and impacts are distant, with no shared institutions to help mediate the problem. Unfortunately, many of the environmental externalities associated with deforestation are characterized by a difficult combination of diffuse sources, diffuse impacts, and lack of intermediating institutions.

Biodiversity Loss—A Local and Global Concern

Biodiversity is an ambiguous term, and ambiguity can create confusion. The term is used in several senses. Sometimes it refers to biological resources: timber, fuelwood, fish, medicinal plants, pollinating bees. Sometimes it describes the diversity of microorganisms or cultivars within a plot of cropland. And sometimes it denotes the diversity of species, genes, or ecosystems considered from a local or global viewpoint.

These different senses of biodiversity all refer to valuable natural assets, and they overlap to some degree. But failure to distinguish between them can lead to conceptual and policy errors. For instance, there is evidence that diversity of rice cultivars within a farm plot increases yield and reduces costs. But that doesn't mean that conservation of plant and animal biodiversity in a nearby forest will necessarily boost productivity in a farmer's field.

Biological Resources Provide Locally Valuable Services

Local biological resources and local biodiversity are probably the aspects of forest biodiversity most immediately relevant to livelihoods and welfare. The most obvious benefits are related to extraction of biological resources such as fuelwood, timber, food, and fodder. These constitute a significant though inaccurately known share of income for people living in or near forests (see chapter 3).

Other local biodiversity services may be extremely important but inadequately recognized. According to Cassman and Wood (2005, p. 759) at least 80 percent of the world's 100 most important food crops are pollinated by wild pollinators. Ricketts and others (2004), in a study of Costa Rica, show that bees from forest fragments contribute substantially to coffee productivity and profits on adjacent farm plots—a pure, uncompensated externality. Forests may also support natural antagonists of crop pests. Or they may provide food for those beneficial creatures during the fallow season when there are no pests to feed on (Cassman and Wood 2005, p. 759).

These subtle relationships can be easy to miss—and easy to disrupt unintentionally. In principle, because most occur at a very local scale and contribute directly to livelihoods, it should be possible to set up local management institutions to handle them. In practice, these ecological benefits may not be immediately apparent to land managers, and solid scientific quantification is often lacking.

Extinction Threats Draw Attention to Globally Significant Biodiversity

This chapter focuses on conserving globally significant biodiversity: genes, species, and ecosystems at risk of extinction. Given the global nature of the externalities involved, this is a serious challenge. Conservation of globally significant biodiversity is motivated by the growing threat of irreversible loss. According to the Millennium Ecosystem Assessment (2005), current extinction rates are about 100 times the rate they were before humans existed and could increase by another 10–100 times.

There are two reasons for the world to be concerned about this looming, irreversible loss. The first is instrumental: conserve biodiversity because it provides specific economic services or averts specific risks. The second is intrinsic: conserve biodiversity because people attach aesthetic and spiritual values to it, or because their values demand it. Proponents of this rationale justify conservation of diversity as an inherent goal, of the same kind as reducing child mortality or preserving the great artworks of earlier civilizations.

Can conservation of globally significant biodiversity be justified on instrumental grounds? Many valuable pharmaceutical products are derived from tropical plants. But this has so far failed to spark a significant market for bioprospecting rights: drug companies have not been willing to pay much for the right to prospect in particular areas. Simpson, Sedjo, and Reid (1996) provide a convincing explanation for why. A standard approach to bioprospecting is unfocused—simply hoping that randomly selected organisms will yield promising chemicals for treatment of target diseases. But given a low rate of success and substantial overlap in genetic contents between forest plots, no individual plot is unique enough to command much of a premium. Drug companies could continue to find ample specimens for evaluation, for decades to come, even with rapid deforestation. Accordingly, such bioprospecting has failed to provide sufficiently "bankable" benefits to pay for conservation.

Better-focused bioprospecting might confer higher economic values for conservation. For instance, forests that harbor the wild relatives of commercially exploited species such as coffee, vegetables, and fruits might be an enduring source of useful genetic information for global agriculture, including information about pests and their natural enemies. More systematic searches for particular kinds of biological activity, combined with better information about biodiversity distribution, might generate high bioprospecting rents for particular locales.

Finally, the Millennium Ecosystem Assessment (2005) argues that biodiversity loss and associated large changes in forest cover could trigger abrupt, irreversible, harmful changes. These include regional climate change, including feedback effects that could theoretically shift rainforests to savannas; and the emergence of new pathogens as the growing trade in bushmeat increases contact between humans and animals.

These instrumental arguments for conserving global biodiversity are still rather speculative and unfocused. In contrast, the intrinsic rationale for conservation—conservation as a fundamental value—has deep resonance in ethics, aesthetics, and religion. These different approaches lead to a formulation of biodiversity policy that places an "existence value" on maintenance of diversity. Surveys suggest substantial willingness to pay for this diversity, at least in industrial countries, though the validity of these stated preferences has been questioned. Funding for the Global Environment Facility and for large, conservation-oriented nongovernmental organizations (NGOs) is a palpable demonstration of willingness to pay.

The science of biogeography provides important insight into the design and geographic targeting of forest policies aimed at reducing extinctions. First, biogeography tells us that species and other aspects of biodiversity are unevenly distributed across the Earth (Mace, Masundire, and Baillie 2005, pp. 90–91). Species of vertebrates are much richer near the equator. Endemic species (those with limited ranges) tend to cluster on islands and mountaintops. And an analysis of biodiversity hotspots has found that half the world's vascular plant species are located on just 1.4 percent of Earth's land surface (Myers and others 2000). Other conservation scientists emphasize the desirability of preserving places with distinctive ecological processes, such as mass migrations of wildlife, or locations that appear to be generating new species (Burgess and others 2006).

Second, one of the most well-established regularities in ecology links habitat area to number of species in the habitat. As habitats shrink, there are fewer niches for specialized species, and there is less room for predators that need large ranges to maintain viable populations. As usually formulated, a 90 percent reduction in area is associated with about a 30 percent reduction in the number of supported species. For an optimist, this is not too bad a result: the mostly empty glass is still, in effect, more than half full. Conserving just 10 percent of the original forest biome could theoretically maintain more than half of its original biodiversity.

Third, however, forest fragmentation further reduces the survival prospects of species and their ecosystems. Relative to a large chunk of forest, small chunks with the same total area are more exposed to natural and human pressures such as wind, fire, and hunting. Forest-specialist species requiring large contiguous blocks of habitat fare poorly in fragments that are widely scattered through an inhospitable matrix of fields or settlements (Laurance and others 2002). As fragmentation increases and connectivity weakens, prospects for these species get dramatically worse (box 4.1).

Fourth, extinctions respond with a lag to loss of habitat. The relation between species and area holds over the long run. Places that have suffered rapid habitat loss may still contain their original complement of species, but may not be able to for much longer. Brooks, Pimm, and Oyugi (1999) estimate that a newly isolated 1,000 hectare fragment experiences about half its eventual species

---

Box 4.1   Forest Fragmentation Can Trigger Local Ecological Collapse

Imagine a checkerboard arrangement of forested properties or plots of land in an area that is a biodiversity corridor. Initially the land is entirely forested, and a key animal species is free to roam from one side to another. Then settlers arrive and randomly convert some properties to fields that are inhospitable to the animal. How does the amount of converted land affect the animal's ability to traverse the corridor?

A remarkable mathematical result is that the animal can *always* find a path when the proportion is below 41 percent, but *never* when the proportion is above that threshold. Although this is a highly stylized result, it points to the possibility of rapid and unexpected ecological collapses as deforestation proceeds. It also underscores the potential importance of landscape-level management for biodiversity in places where forests and farms are intermixed. Farm-level decisions about cropping, maintenance of gallery forests, and establishment of living fences can make a big difference for biodiversity conservation.

Source: Based on Forman 1995.

---

losses in 50 years. Rosenzweig (2001, 2003) takes a longer, starker view. He says that in the very long run, species loss is proportional to habitat loss because climate and disease shocks continue to cause extinctions, while the rate of creation of new species is proportional to habitat area. So he argues that a 90 percent habitat loss implies an eventual 90 percent species loss. He doesn't specify whether that adjustment takes centuries, millennia, or longer.

Finally, the rapid pace of climate change provides another reason why connectivity is important, and why Rosenzweig's drastic adjustment may come sooner rather than later. Plant and animal species are adapted to particular temperature ranges. As global temperatures rise, the survival of some species will depend on their ability to migrate to cooler areas, on higher slopes, or at higher latitudes. If there is insufficient connectivity in existing habitats, these species may be unable to migrate and will get caught between rising temperatures and inhospitable surroundings. Climatically triggered diseases could make things worse.

This foray into biogeography provides important policy lessons.

- Conservation of globally significant biodiversity requires focusing attention and resources on certain places. This approach may clash with other norms for allocating resources between countries and places. A country's share of global biodiversity, for instance, may differ from its share of global population or poverty.

- The most urgent extinction threats will largely be in and around fragmented mosaiclands where habitat has drastically shrunk and become fragmented. Here, species and ecosystems are living on borrowed time. There is a brief opportunity—the next few decades—to refurbish these landscapes and make them more habitable to most threatened species, while maintaining their usefulness for agriculture and human habitation (McNeely and Scherr 2003; Rosenzweig 2003). Reducing fragmentation and encouraging connectivity are important parts of this program.

- Threats are low in large, unfragmented forest tracts. But these species-rich areas are the last irreplaceable examples of large-scale ecological processes in quasi-natural habitat. They also offer insurance against climate change, allowing species uninterrupted pathways for migration in response to rising temperatures. Policy interventions today to head off a dynamic of uncontrolled conversion could determine whether, over the coming century, these tracts retain ecological vitality or whether they grow fragmented, placing their species at threat of extinction.

How Does Deforestation Affect Water, Air, and Weather?

Clean water flows from forested hillsides, muddy torrents from steep denuded slopes. These observations have often been used reflexively to justify forest conservation. But in recent decades scientific research has refined people's understanding of how forests and land use affect flooding, sedimentation, landslides, and dry season flows. Although some aspects of these relationships remain debated, the overall message is clear: the forest-hydrology relationship is highly nuanced. The effects on hydrology of changes in forest and land use depend, systematically and explicably, on how and where changes occur.

It is important to get the science straight. For instance, Aylward (2005) reports on a study of the potential effect of reforesting pasturelands around Costa Rica's main hydropower reservoir to reduce sediment inflow. The study found that reforesting 1 hectare would reduce sedimentation and estimated the benefit, in increased reservoir life span, to be $74 per hectare reforested. But the study also found that higher water consumption by the trees would draw down the reservoir—imposing potentially larger, countervailing costs due to decreased electric output during dry years.

Consider too the diagnosis of the catastrophic 1998 floods on China's Yangtze River. The floods were blamed on deforestation, and a swift policy response was the shutdown of the Chinese logging industry. This move disrupted domestic employment and placed increased extractive pressures on forests of high biodiversity significance in Southeast Asia and elsewhere. But to what extent was deforestation to blame?

Subsequent analysis suggests a complex picture (Yin and Li 2001). Beginning with the construction of the Great Jinjiang Levee in 1548, and accelerating in the past 50 years, many land use changes have reduced the ability of the Yangtze watershed to handle peak water flows. The flows, which formerly covered vast floodplains, have increasingly been constricted by levees and dikes. Since 1949, 50 cubic kilometers of lakes have been reclaimed for agriculture, reducing lake storage capacity by a third and thus crippling a major buffer against flooding. Heavy siltation has raised the river bed, increasing the risk of flooding. Deforestation and other land use changes have increased the proportion of the basin subject to erosion, and so over the long run have presumably contributed to siltation. But observations over a 30-year period did not show any link between siltation and deforestation, suggesting that it may take decades for erosion to end up as sediment in the river. Thus in the context of the complex hydrodynamics of a large basin, it is not at all clear to what degree the logging ban has reduced the risk of future floods or how it compares to alternative watershed management strategies.

To help get the science straight, this section relies heavily on comprehensive and incisive reviews by Bruijnzeel (2004) and Bruijnzeel and others (2005). It also draws on Bonell and Bruijnzeel (2005), Calder (2005), CIFOR and FAO (2005), and van Noordwijk and others (2006). Interested readers can refer to these works for more detailed treatment.

From Farmer's Field to River Basin: Policy at Different Scales

Interactions among people, precipitation, soils, and vegetation play out differently at different scales. First, many phenomena important at smaller scales become attenuated at larger ones (Kiersch and

Tognetti 2002; Calder 2005). Consider erosion and sedimentation. Erosion can be severe on steep fields, clogging local streams with sediment. At this scale, actions to prevent erosion and sedimentation can have more or less immediate effect. But at the level of a large watershed, new upland erosion doesn't translate immediately to sedimentation far downstream. This is because any individual bit of sediment has to follow a long journey of short trips from mountainside to river mouth. That journey could take decades—or it may never be completed—because the sediment gets lodged somewhere along the way (Chomitz and Kumari 1998).

Second, the economics and politics of watershed management vary with scale. In small watersheds (10–100 square kilometers) it may be relatively easy to organize local communities to deal with clearly perceived issues such as erosion or landslide risk. Larger basins require more complex, wide-ranging institutions to negotiate interests between upstream and downstream populations. But the payoffs to cooperation at this scale might be considerable. Urban populations might be willing to pay substantial sums to reduce flood risk, sediment damage to reservoirs, or pollution of urban water supplies. If they could do so by paying poor upland populations to conserve forests, it would be a happy outcome on many grounds: reducing flooding and poverty, with biodiversity conservation as a by-product.

Against this background, consider how changes in forest cover and land use affect hydrological functions that people care about, at two scales: local and far-field.

Local Hazards Depend on Many Variables

Forests modulate water flows in various ways. In the popular conception, trees are sponges, soaking up water and releasing it later. But this is an inadequate and incomplete metaphor (Bruijnzeel 2004). Forest floors, with their leaf litter and porous soils, easily accommodate intense rainfall. Water infiltrates the ground until soils are saturated. In this sense forest soils act like sponges. But trees behave like fine-misted fountains, pumping water out of the ground and transpiring it as water vapor into the air.[1] Rain also clings to tree leaves, from which it evaporates without ever touching the ground. The effects of deforestation on water availability, flash floods, and dry season flows depend on what happens to these countervailing influences of infiltration and evapotranspiration—the sponge versus the fountain.

Replacing a mature forest with a mature agroforest doesn't much change evapotranspiration and so has little effect on water yield. But permanent conversion of forest to pasture, annual crops, or short perennial crops reduces evapotranspiration and thus increases the water yield from a plot. On this point there is strong scientific consensus. Converting a tropical moist forest is roughly equivalent, in water yield, to increasing rainfall by 300 millimeters a year. That's why South Africa's Working for Water program pays for the removal of invasive tree species—to increase water availability in parched regions. The program employs 21,000 poor people and provides water to Capetown at a cost 90 percent below the alternative: construction of a dam (van Wilgen and others 2002).

Floods and Flow Regularity

Deforestation's effect on the timing of flows—on floods and dry season flows—is more difficult to predict and is sensitive to the balance between infiltration and evapotranspiration effects. Deforestation tends to increase flooding for two reasons. First, with a smaller "tree fountain" effect, soils are more likely to be fully saturated with water. The "sponge" fills up earlier in the wet season, causing additional precipitation to run off and increasing flood risk. Second, deforestation often results in compacted soils with little ability to absorb rain. Locally, this causes a faster response of streamflows to rainfall and thus potential flash flooding. That is why some Costa Rican run-of-river hydropower plants invest $1.50–5.00 in watershed protection per kilowatt generated each year (Rojas and Aylward 2002). These small plants (6–17 megawatts) have no storage reservoirs, so their output is greatest when water flows evenly at their turbines' capacity.

Dry Season Flows

More controversial is the impact of deforestation on dry season flows. Here there is strong divergence between the popular view that deforestation dries up springs, and scientific evidence that strongly indicates higher—not lower—flows after deforestation. A thorough review by Bruijnzeel (2004) finds only a couple documented cases of lower flows. But he stresses the need for more observations. In theory, deforestation could decrease dry season flows under certain conditions:

- New land use patterns result in severely compacted soils, so losses of rain to runoff exceeds gains from shutting off the "fountain" (Bruijnzeel 2004). This might happen where cattle or machinery have caused severe compaction, where there has been extensive road building, or where fires have degraded the landscape. In other words, postdeforestation land use matters more than just deforestation.

- Annual rainfall is high and concentrated in the wet season.

- Soil has considerable water holding capacity or is in an important recharge zone.

Sedimentation and Erosion

Think about sediment, and you will understand why watershed management involves more than simple decisions about how many trees to retain or plant (Van Noordwijk and others 2006). First, people place different values on sediment. Reducing sediment is a service to downstream irrigators, reservoir owners, and water filtering plants—but not to farmers who depend on it for renewed soil fertility.

Second, deforestation doesn't necessarily increase erosion, the main source of sediment. As with flooding, what matters is how land is used after forest is removed, and especially whether leaf litter is maintained. Typical erosion rates are 0.2 tons a hectare under forest and 0.6 under plantations with ground cover, but more than 50 tons a hectare may be observed under plantations without leaf litter (Wiersum 1984, quoted in Bruijnzeel 2004). Forest roads generate far more erosion per hectare than do agricultural uses. Ziegler and others (2004), in a study of a northern Thai watershed, found that unpaved roads delivered as much sediment to streams as did agricultural fields—though the fields occupied 24 times more area.

Third, the spatial arrangement of land use matters. Van Noordwijk and others (2006) simulated the effect on sedimentation of different combinations of clean-weeded coffee plantation and forest on a Sumatran hillslope. Retaining 25 percent forest at the bottom of the slope reduced sedimentation by 93 percent relative to no forest. Forest retention elsewhere on the hillslope was much less effective. In sum, watershed management for sediment reduction involves many choices, with different consequences for incomes, biodiversity, and other environmental outcomes.

Landslides

Forests can provide protection against shallow landslides. Perotto-Baldiviezo and others (2004) studied the incidence of landslides after Hurricane Mitch in a Nicaraguan watershed. They found that less than 1 percent of forested lands were affected by landslides, regardless of slope. For plots under bare soil (recently harvested) this incidence jumped from near zero on flat land to 7.5 percent on land with

10 percent slope, and 10 percent when slope was 20 percent. But some deep-seated landslides occur regardless of forest cover.

Water Quality

Urban water protection is potentially one of the most important services that forests provide. Filtering and treating drinking water is expensive. Forests can reduce the costs of doing so—either actively, by filtering runoff, or passively, by substituting for housing or farms that generate runoff. An example is New York City's watershed (National Research Council, Water Science and Technology Board 2004, pp. 156–58). For many decades the city had drawn its water, untreated, from its 5,000 square kilometer watershed. In the mid-1990s water quality began to deteriorate, and authorities were faced with the prospect of committing $6–8 billion (in operating and future maintenance costs) for a treatment plant to meet safety standards.

Instead the city developed an innovative program for watershed protection, at a cost of $1.0–1.5 billion. About $250 million was used to purchase and protect land (though not necessarily forestland). But the plan also involved activities to reduce water pollution. Importantly, it worked with dairy farmers to manage manure and nutrient runoff.

This example may be widely applicable. Dudley and Stolton (2003) found that 18 of the world's 42 largest tropical cities draw their water directly from protected areas. An extension of this study might usefully identify cities that draw their drinking water from small, steep, forested watersheds. Under these conditions the public value of watershed protection is likely to counterbalance private rewards to forest conversion or degradation.

Geography of Local Hazards

Nelson and Chomitz (2006) examine the potential spatial coincidence of local hazard risk and poverty in two hilly Central American countries, Honduras and Guatemala. The authors define a watershed's critical zone as where forests meet agriculture on slopes. This is where deforestation might be most rapid and might lead most rapidly to erosion. They then define a watershed's "sensitivity" as its proportion in a critical zone.

In Guatemala highly sensitive watersheds (more than 20 percent critical) occupy 22 percent of the country but contain 43 percent of its poor people and 54 percent of its montane forest. The poverty rate in these watersheds is 70 percent, compared with 53 percent for

Figure 4.1 Guatemala Critical Watersheds Have High Poverty Rates

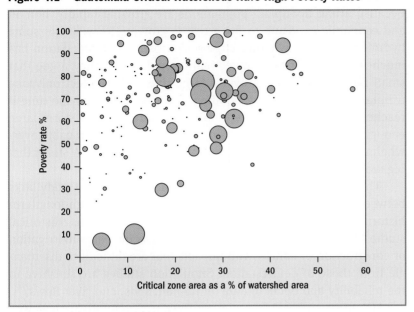

Source: Nelson and Chomitz (forthcoming).
Note: Bubble size indicates absolute number of poor people in watershed.

the country as a whole. Figure 4.1 shows that all of the most sensitive watersheds have high poverty rates. Nelson and Chomitz (2006) also find that the relationship between hydrological vulnerability and poverty is stronger when smaller watersheds are considered. This focuses attention on highly local externalities, with poor people both causing them and bearing their burden.

At the global scale, Dilley and others (2005) used topographic and geological criteria to identify areas around the world at risk of landslides. Areas with the highest imputed mortality risk from landslides—including along the mountainous spine of Latin America, the islands of Sumatra, New Guinea, and the Philippines, and the border between India and Myanmar—are shown in map 4.1.[2] Because mountain peaks tend to host distinctive, restricted range species, the landslide risk map is strikingly similar to the imminent extinctions map (see map 1.8).

Far-field Impacts Can Be Major

We turn now from local impacts of deforestation to far-field impacts—those felt tens or hundreds of kilometers away.

Distant Floods

Because urban floodplain populations are growing rapidly, human and economic exposure to flood risk is growing as well. But some hydrologists doubt whether large-scale upstream deforestation has much impact on distant downstream populations. They argue that small rainstorms, passing over a large river basin, affect only one tributary at a time, so any flooding effect is diluted by the time it reaches a city down the river's main branch. The rare storm large enough to drench the entire basin, they argue, would probably overwhelm the basin's ability to absorb water into the soil. A storm that big would cause a flood regardless of tree cover.

This argument is hard to test. There are two ways to study links between deforestation and floods in large basins: through long-term historical studies and by simulation. Each has limitations. Historical studies may face confounding trends—such as increases in irrigation or construction of dams—with impacts that are difficult to disentangle from those of deforestation. Simulation studies are sensitive to the reliability and detail of data on rainfall, soils, and river flows.

Historical studies yield contrasting results. Several studies reviewed by Bruijnzeel (2004), mostly in Southeast Asia, found no marked increase in river flows following basinwide deforestation. In contrast, Costa, Botta, and Cardille (2003) found a substantial impact on far-field flows of deforestation in the 175,000 square kilometer Tocantins River basin. They compared flows over 1949–68 and 1979–98. Only 6 percent of the basin had been converted to planted pasture or cropland in 1960, but by 1995 it was 49 percent. The study found that, despite similar rainfall, wet season river flows increased 28 percent between the two periods. The authors speculate that the difference between their results and those in Southeast Asia reflect the faster natural regeneration in the Asian study areas. A change from primary forest to plantations or secondary regrowth may have little effect on hydrological flows (though possibly a profound effect on biodiversity).

Because it is hard to isolate the effect of long-term, large-scale changes in land use through observations, researchers have turned to hydrological simulations. Advances in hydrological modeling have resulted in tools that can reproduce watershed behavior with some accuracy, such as the Distributed Hydrology Soil Vegetation Model (Wigmosta, Vail, and Wittenmaier 1994). These models trace water and sediment flows over the landscape, incorporating effects of vegetation and geology. Their accuracy is validated by comparing model predictions, based on historical precipitation records, with streamflow records.

Map 4.1 Mortality Risks from Landslides

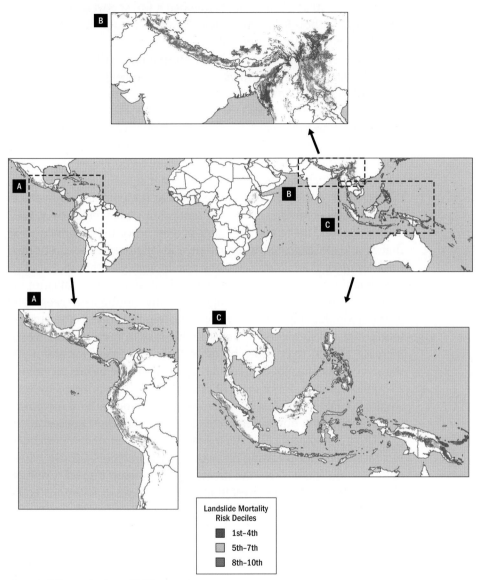

Landslide Mortality
Risk Deciles

■ 1st–4th
□ 5th–7th
■ 8th–10th

Source: Dilley and others 2005.

Scientists are beginning to use these models to assess the impacts of land cover change in the tropical world. An example is Thanapakpawin and others (2006), who constructed and validated a model of the 3,853 square kilometer Mae Chaem watershed (in northern Thailand) using limited data on soils and precipitation. The

123

authors used the model to assess, retrospectively, the impact of the loss of about 10 percent of the watershed's forest cover. Other things being equal, they found that deforestation would have increased wet season flows by 2 percent and dry season by 4 percent. But expanded irrigation more than counterbalanced the deforestation effects, reducing net outflows by up to 6 percent in the wet season and 16 percent in the dry. Ongoing work extends this to larger basins and shorter periods.

Douglas and others (2005, forthcoming) have conducted similar simulation studies in large river basins throughout the tropics. Their work seeks to determine whether and where forest losses would have significant effects on biodiversity and water flows. For this purpose, they simulated the hydrological impacts of the complete conversion to agriculture of all forests deemed "critical or endangered" by WWF.[3] They calculated the resulting change in river flows and identified areas that would be expected to experience an increase in mean annual flows of more than 25 percent. The assumption was that increases of this magnitude could be associated with chronic if not catastrophic flooding. (The exact impact is highly sensitive to the local geography of the floodplains and to daily and hourly peak flows.) The authors found that the hypothetical catastrophic loss of these forests would increase annual river flows by more than 25 percent for about 100 million people, most of them on floodplains. In nine basins containing 55 million people, more than 100 people would be affected by each square kilometer of forest conversion—a crude indicator of the potential for mobilizing downstream interest in upland forest conservation.

The hydrological cost-effectiveness of forest protection might be increased by concentrating on hydrological hotspots—those where deforestation might have the greatest downstream impact. Combining spatial models of deforestation and hydrological functions could help pinpoint these locations.

Water Quality

Does it make sense to manage land over a very large basin to reduce sedimentation for downstream users? Although sediment travels slowly over slopes, it can be mobilized fairly rapidly from riverbanks over a wide area. A simulation study found that sediment load in a 2,500 square kilometer watershed could be cost-effectively reduced by revegetating steep croplands close to the river (Khanna and others 2003). Although this finding sounds obvious and mirrors the local area results noted earlier, it contrasts with a strategy of protecting forested uplands far from major rivers. In generalizing this analysis, it is important to keep in mind that vegetation other than trees can intercept sediment without using as much water as trees do.

Effects on Air and Climate

Forest fires release noxious smoke and smog, disrupting transport and industry and triggering respiratory illness. These are chronic problems. In Brazil smoke from forest and land fires is cited as a major environmental problem by *municipio* governments that represent 39 million people. These problems are worst in dry (El Niño) years. Tacconi (2003) estimates that the Indonesian fires of 1997–98 affected 110,000 square kilometers in Indonesia and Malaysia, imposing costs in damaged health and industrial disruption of $676–799 million.

Deforestation affects wind flows, water vapor flows, and absorption of solar energy, so it's plausible that it affects local climate. But it's difficult to assess these impacts, which may operate differently at different scales, from field to continent. One study found that deforestation on lowland plains moved cloud formation and rainfall to higher elevations (Lawton and others 2001). Another study found strong changes in land-sea breeze patterns affecting cloud formation and upland rainfall in tropical island and coastal settings (van der Molen and others 2006). Yet another study simulated the impact on regional climates of a plausible scenario for global deforestation during this century. It predicted that Amazônian temperatures will rise by 2 degrees Celsius, in addition to effects from global warming. It also predicted possible disruptions of Asian monsoon patterns (Feddema and others 2005). Finally, van der Molen and others (2006) and other researchers intimate the possibility of global impacts of widespread deforestation—especially for coastal and island deforestation, which disrupts atmosphere-wide wind patterns.

Deforestation Spurs Climate Change

There's no need to repeat here the vast literature on climate change; for authoritative summaries, see the work of the International Panel on Climate Change (Watson and Core Writing Team 2001) and the Millennium Ecosystem Assessment (2005). Still, three points are crucial.

First, climate change is a real and growing threat to people, economies, and the environment. Arctic communities already face permafrost that is no longer permanent. Andean populations need to begin planning for the impending loss of glacial icepacks on which their water supply depends. Poor Sahelian farmers and pastoralists, already coping with a difficult and volatile climate, may soon experience deteriorating conditions. Looming behind the predictable threats, however, is the real but unquantifiable possibility of rapid, catastrophic changes—such as a shutdown of Atlantic Ocean currents or massive changes in regional climates.

Second, tropical deforestation is an important source of greenhouse gases, releasing 3.8 billion tons of carbon dioxide (CO_2) a year (Achard and others 2004). Such deforestation also accounts for about 20 percent of human-generated CO_2 emissions (House and others 2006).

Third, preventing deforestation and encouraging forest regeneration have the same effect on atmospheric CO_2, no matter where they occur. This is in marked contrast to other environmental benefits of forest conservation, which depend on local conditions.

Forest management has global effects on greenhouse gases. But does it make economic sense to actively manage forests to reduce atmospheric CO_2 emissions (box 4.2)? What might be the costs and benefits to landholders? How do the costs of reducing CO_2 through forest management compare with those of abating CO_2 emissions from transportation, electricity generation, and manufacturing?

Consider first the cost of reducing CO_2 emissions from deforestation. The cost to landholders depends on:

- The per hectare profits forgone by maintaining forest rather than converting it.

- The difference in carbon storage between a conserved forest and a field or pasture.

These two considerations vary tremendously depending on the factors discussed in chapter 2: agroclimate, market opportunities, and technology. Rigorous data on these trade-offs have been assembled by the Alternatives to Slash and Burn program for a number of land use systems in the moist forests of Brazil, Cameroon, and Indonesia (Tomich and others 2005). For each land use, researchers calculated the net present value of profits (a measure of the value of land devoted to that use), the amount of carbon stored, and the level of biodiversity conserved.

Drawing on these data, figure 4.2 shows the implicit costs of reducing carbon emissions through forest conservation. These costs were calculated by comparing the profits and carbon storage of each

---

Box 4.2   Trees and Carbon: Lessons from Biology for Forest Policy

Many of us vaguely remember learning, in a biology class long ago, that trees absorb carbon dioxide (CO_2) and produce oxygen. But that's only part of the story, because trees also use oxygen for respiration and release CO_2, just as animals do. A growing tree absorbs more CO_2 from the atmosphere than it emits, embodying the carbon as wood, leaves, and other biomass.

A tree that dies, or is cut down, rots or burns. The carbon in its biomass is then released into the atmosphere as CO_2. Soil carbon may also be exposed and lost into the atmosphere. In a regenerating forest, growing trees outnumber dying ones, so carbon accumulation is vigorous. But as forests mature, their net accumulation of CO_2 slows. (There are debates about the rate at which old-growth forests continue to sequester carbon.)

What does this mean for the impact of alternative land uses on carbon storage?

- Converting forests to agriculture or pasture releases CO_2 into the atmosphere, so protecting a threatened forest could reduce greenhouse gas emissions.

- Mature standing forests maintain carbon stocks, but have at most a low per hectare rate of accumulation.

- Reforestation and afforestation absorb CO_2 out of the atmosphere, storing it as wood and biomass as long as the forest endures.

- Pulp and timber plantations absorb CO_2 as they grow. The carbon they embody is transformed into wood or paper after harvest. It may be released rapidly into the atmosphere if these products are discarded or incinerated. But timber used for enduring structures may stay out of the atmosphere for a long time.

- Plantations can create fuel from thin air by absorbing CO_2 and transforming it to biomass. When burned as charcoal or biofuel, the same amount of CO_2 is returned to the atmosphere, in a closed cycle. So sustainable biofuel plantations are carbon neutral—they don't add net CO_2 to the atmosphere—and can substitute for fossil fuels, which do augment global warming.

- Logging releases CO_2 from damaged trees, though forest recovery may partly offset this effect over time. The harvested timber may release its carbon quickly to the atmosphere, if burned or discarded to rot, or slowly if used for construction.

---

land use system and an assumed forest baseline. (The Cameroon and Indonesian examples assume a baseline of already logged, depleted forest.) The figure shows the tremendous variation in the potential costs of conserving carbon.

At one extreme, traditional pasture management in Acre, Brazil, entails a loss of 145 tons of carbon per hectare but creates only $2 a hectare in land value (in net present value of all future earnings). So the cost of conserving carbon is, in principle, just $0.03 a ton C (or less than $0.01 per ton of CO_2). Similarly, traditional rubber agroforestry in Indonesia provides lower per hectare profits and a significant loss of carbon relative to community agroforestry—although it creates much more employment. In contrast, the most profitable land use, for intensive cocoa in Cameroon, entails a carbon loss of 103 tons per hectare, confers a land value of $1,149, and provides 93 days of employment. Here the theoretical cost of conserving carbon is $11 a ton ($3/ton CO_2).

These calculations assume that the costs are borne by landholders, in forgone profits, and that workers can find alternative employment at the same wage. This may be a reasonable assumption when deforestation is related to frontier migration. Otherwise, workers bear a burden—because of lower-paying work—that should be included when calculating the cost of emission reductions.

For extensive land uses this makes little difference. Traditional Brazilian pasture, for instance, provides only 11 days of employment a hectare per year. But rubber agroforestry, intensive cocoa, and intensive palm oil provide about 100 days of employment, at roughly $1.50 a day. Counting a portion of this as a cost would somewhat increase the cost of conserving carbon.

One way of looking at these calculations is to ask whether society should incur these costs. Are they justified by the benefits from mitigating climate change? Making this assessment requires assigning a value to abating emissions. Yohe, Andronova, and Schlesinger (2004) suggest that to mitigate climate change, the global community needs to value carbon abatement at $10 a ton now (and rising over time based on the interest rate). At that value, converting forest to intensive cocoa barely breaks even from a social viewpoint—though from a private viewpoint it is the most profitable land use shown in figure 4.2.

Efforts are under way to scale up estimates of this type to the global level. These estimates must be considered tentative, because comprehensive information on land use systems is lacking. Still, the estimates are useful for assessing the potential scale of the contribution of land management to carbon abatement. Sathaye and others (forthcoming) estimate the potential contribution of avoided deforestation to carbon abatement for different levels and trends of carbon prices. (Anticipating the discussion in chapter 7, imagine that per hectare monetary incentives are offered to nations if they reduce planned forest conversion.) Relatively modest carbon prices ($5–10 a ton in 2010, rising 5 percent a year) could, in principle, deter con-

Figure 4.2 Deforestation Would Be Unprofitable in Many Land Systems at Modest Carbon Prices

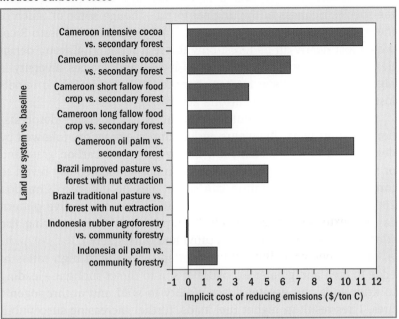

Source: Authors' calculations using data from Tomich and others 2005.

version of 1–2 million square kilometers of forest by 2050, preventing the release of 8–15 billion tons. A price of $100 per ton of carbon would induce conservation of 5 million square kilometers by 2050, abating the release of 47 billion tons.

Forest Loss—Sometimes Irreversible

In an uncertain world, it's good to have options. Even if an option isn't worth exercising today, there's a chance it may be worth a lot tomorrow. That possibility is enough to give the option real value today. The theory of options finds sophisticated application in financial markets and investment decision making. It also applies to forests.

A forest owner has two options: converting the forest to agriculture or maintaining it. In some cases conversion is irreversible, so individuals and nations need to exercise this option wisely.

Sometimes deforestation is reversible. Deforestation for extensive pasture, subsistence cropping, or perennial crops is often followed by field abandonment and spontaneous regrowth. Regenerated forests often recover their biomass and carbon content and the species richness of the original forest—though some or much of the original biodiversity may be lost. That happened in Puerto Rico, which lost nearly all its forest only to see it rebound. Carbon densities are now nearly at their original levels, and species diversity is high. But the set of species has changed, with some of the originals lost (Lamb, Erskine, and Parrotta 2005a).

But sometimes the outcome is the worst possible: deforestation for short-lived, low-value agriculture or extraction, followed by degradation to a persistent, low-biodiversity, low-carbon grassland or shrubland. These degraded lands do not spontaneously revert to forest, though regeneration can sometimes be induced (Chazdon 2003; Lamb, Erskine, and Parrotta 2005). This destructive pattern can result from "vicious circles"—especially those involving fire (Cochrane and others 1999; Nepstad and others 2001).

Deforestation results in fragmented forests with high ratios of edge to area and greater exposure of soil to direct sunlight—leading to drier soils and greater susceptibility to wild and anthropogenic fires. Fires result in higher fuel loads, further increasing susceptibility. Repeated fires favor the growth of grass and inhibit forest regeneration. Smoke may also inhibit rainfall, further drying out the soil and increasing flammability (Nepstad and others 2001). The result, in Latin America, southern Africa, and Southeast Asia, is a relatively stable grassland system with no tendency to revert to forest (Lamb, Erskine, and Parrotta 2005a). Another vicious-circle mechanism involves loss of mammals that disperse large seeds. In Madagascar, for instance, lemurs are important seed dispersers. Fragmented forests support fewer lemurs; fewer lemurs means less dispersal of tree seedlings and hence more fragmentation of forests.

These degraded areas cover an appreciable portion of the Earth's surface. *Imperata* grasslands in Southeast Asia are estimated to cover about 350,000 square kilometers (Garrity and others 1996), a bit less than the area of Paraguay. Degraded areas are thought to be large in parts of Latin America. For instance, in long-settled parts of the eastern Amazon, extensive tracts are reported abandoned but unused and appear to be the degraded remains of former forests.

Ecologists have identified risk factors for persistent degradation (Chazdon 2003; Lamb, Erskine, and Parrotta 2005a). Geographic risks include areas with poor soil fertility and high susceptibility to erosion, due to soil or slopes. Risks are also related to the cause and conduct of deforestation. Soil compaction from bulldozing or cattle is an important risk. So are repeated fires. Large expanses of deforestation contribute to irreversibility, because natural reseeding is vigorous only within 100 meters of existing forest. Low-productivity pastures—characterized by fire use, compaction, and large clearings—may be at particular risk of irreversibility. They represent a particularly bad bargain: low and temporary returns, little employment generation, large environmental damage, and high probability of irreversibility.

Summary

Environmental externalities associated with forests are diverse, unevenly distributed, and understood with varying degrees of scientific consensus and precision. Table 4.1 arranges environmental externalities in rough order of scale of impact, from global to local. It shows that, carbon aside, most externalities are generated by distinctive and often narrow places and circumstances, ruling out one-size-fits-all responses. Most cases involve different people at the sending and receiving ends of the externalities. Mosaiclands are a hotbed of externality-generating forests, reflecting their rapid deforestation and the close interaction between forests, agriculture, and people in these areas.

Carbon emissions and extinction risk rank at the top of the list of globally important externalities. Returning to the example that opened this chapter, this opens a path for the global beneficiaries of forest conservation to compensate those who bear its costs. For instance, a serious global commitment to implementing the Framework Convention on Climate Change—which calls for stabilizing greenhouse gases in the atmosphere—would imply benefits for forest conservation that exceed the profits of most current forest conversion processes. Chapter 7 explores the implications of the forest-carbon connection for global policy.

The hydrological impacts of deforestation are extremely sensitive to local conditions. In the past, policy was influenced by hydrological myths, such as the one that forests generate water. Reliance on these myths has led to reforestation with perverse outcomes and may have undermined efforts to mainstream forest protection.

Current knowledge suggests that the highest payoff to watershed management occurs within small watersheds, in small steep basins

Table 4.1   Externalities of Deforestation Vary by Location of Source and Impact

Type of damage	Location of deforestation	Burden/location of impact
Global climate change	All deforesting locations; higher per hectare damages come from dense humid forests	Global
Imminent risk of globally significant biodiversity loss	Specific areas in mosaiclands and nonremote frontier forests	Global, but especially on high-income populations and future generations
Long-term risk of globally significant biodiversity loss	Frontier and transfrontier forests	Global, but especially on high-income populations and future generations
Local and regional climate change	Unclear, possibly widespread	Unclear, possibly widespread
Smoke and smog from forest fires	Most areas of rapid deforestation	Populated areas downwind of large, rapid deforestation
Local flooding, erosion, and diminished dry season flows	Small, steep upper watersheds in mosaiclands, nonremote frontier forests, and short littoral watersheds	Small, steep lower watersheds in mosaiclands; coral reefs
Reduced water quality for drinking and irrigation	Small, steep watersheds near cities and reservoirs	Downstream cities and reservoirs
Loss of pollination, pest control, and other biological services	Mosaiclands; high-density frontier forests	Fields near deforesting locations; possible far-field effects

from which cities draw their water, or along the erodible margins of rivers. Fine-tuning the behavior of a watershed requires attention not just to the presence or absence of trees but also to their placement, to agricultural activities, and especially to road placement and maintenance. Native trees will not necessarily be superior to agroforestry or other kinds of vegetation in achieving hydrological benefits. So biodiversity conservation may not be the best way to achieve hydrological benefits. On the other hand, forest conservation motivated primarily by biodiversity could pay dividends in hydrological benefits—perhaps even in large river basins.

Nonetheless, scientific understanding of hydrological processes is incomplete. Large-scale deforestation could affect regional climate in some circumstances. And the extent to which deforestation could lead to reduced dry-season flows is debated. More scientific and economic research is needed to pinpoint situations where deforestation poses these risks.

This is also true for other externalities in table 4.1. Because these externalities can be both subtle and important, solid demonstrations of their magnitude will be needed to motivate policy makers and their constituencies to take action to correct them.

Endnotes

1. This point is an adaptation of Hamilton and King's (1983) metaphor: "roots may be more appropriately labelled a pump rather than a sponge," quoted in Bruijnzeel (2004).

2. The map does not distinguish areas prone to shallow landslides, argued above to be most sensitive to loss of forest cover.

3. This term means that, in the absence of intervention, the habitat has a low to medium probability of surviving over the next 15 years. But the WWF classification does not necessarily imply the complete loss of trees, as the simulations assume.

Dantanpalli village is inhabited by the Gond tribal group and is part of the Andhra Pradesh (India) Community Forestry Project. In this meeting, the village community and Forest Department staff discuss forest management plans for the coming year.

Grant Milne / World Bank.

PART II

Institutional and Policy Responses

Villagers in East Cameroon carrying drinkable water from a facility constructed with funds from forest royalties.

© WWF-Canon / Olivier VanBogaert.

Inhabitants of this village, near the Lobeke National Park in East Cameroon, usually clear forested land to plant plantains, cocoa and manioc.

© WWFCARPO / Peter Ngea.

CHAPTER 5

Improving Forest Governance

Emerging from the first part of this report are two overarching public policy issues that affect equity, incomes, and the environment: forest ownership and environmental externalities. Finding institutions to grapple with these issues is at the core of better forest governance.

Who Should Have Rights over Forests? Which Rights?

Much of the world's tropical forest is under nominal state ownership—ownership sometimes disputed by indigenous groups and other forest dwellers. But even forests under community and private ownership are typically subject to some restrictions on timber extraction or against forest clearance. At stake is a vast amount of real estate, considerable timber wealth, and other assets including minerals, genetic information, and carbon rights. The public policy question is how to equitably adjudicate and efficiently defend these rights.

How Should Society Balance Environmental Services against Production of Food, Fiber, and Wood?

At all scales of land management, from the farmer's plot to the planet, there are trade-offs and complementarities between production of food and maintenance of environmental services. Consider a simplified example (with just one environmental service) that

Figure 5.1   Optimizing the Mix of Agricultural Output and Biodiversity

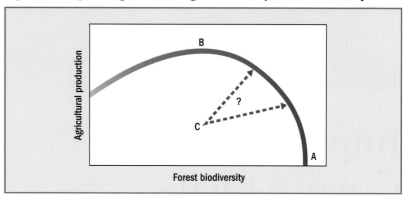

Source: Authors.

can be applied to all scales (figure 5.1). This production-possibility curve shows different combinations of agricultural production and biodiversity conservation arising from different ways of managing land. The curve shows the ultimate technical and biological trade-offs: the maximum production consistent with a given level of biodiversity. At point A all land is devoted to undisturbed forest. Movement along the curve upward and to the left represents conversion of forest to agriculture. At first, production is gained with little loss of biodiversity—for instance, by substituting forest gardens for native forest.

As more forest is affected, the trade-off becomes steeper. Increasingly marginal land is brought into production, increasingly critical habitats are disturbed, and more intensive production results in pollution from agrochemicals. Eventually at point B, further conversion to agriculture results in so much environmental damage that agricultural production suffers.

What combination of production and biodiversity should society pursue? A society that did not value biodiversity would choose point B, the point of maximum production. A society that valued biodiversity would choose some point along the curve between B and A. The precise point would depend on preferences for agricultural production relative to biodiversity. But in real life, societies have incomplete control over landholder behavior and are likely to end up at point C—inefficient for both agricultural production and biodiversity. The policy challenge is to reach societal consensus on a target point between A and B, and then use carrots and sticks to urge land managers toward that target.

This challenge occurs at all scales. At the continental and global scale, scientists have worked on prioritizing the world's most unique spots for conservation, seeking a portfolio of locations that occupies little area but contains as many different species, ecosystems, and ecological processes as possible (Rodrigues and others 2004; Ceballos and others 2005; Burgess and others 2006). This is a search for the flat part of the curve to the right of point B, where major increases in biodiversity are secured for negligible opportunity costs in forgone agricultural production.

At the national level, agroecological zoning efforts follow a similar logic, seeking to allocate the most productive lands to agriculture while restricting agricultural uses on land that is marginal for agriculture and crucial for biodiversity. Decisions on regional development, such as road placement, also determine where a society ends up on the production-possibility curve. And at the local level, many interventions in community management of natural resources and in diffusion of land management technologies can be seen as seeking ways to push landholders away from inefficient points such as C.

Balancing Interests while Enforcing Commitments

To address these two big issues, society has to find fair ways to balance opposing interests, forge agreements, and commit to those agreements. This is the essence of dealing with environmental externalities (see chapter 4)—a problem particularly salient in less remote mosaiclands. The second problem is fair allocation of property rights. As the frontier expands into the forest, undefended trees, land, and environmental services take on value, and people scramble to claim them. Who should get the rights to these goods? Who or what will guarantee those rights? The same questions arise when communities challenge nominal ownership of forests by governments.

These are essentially institutional problems, and they are difficult to address due to imbalances of power, lack of information, and lack of checks and balances. With environmental externalities, typically a relatively few people benefit a great deal from logging or agricultural conversion. Those people are typically influential—often a wealthy elite of loggers or ranchers with close ties to politicians, with continuing deforestation at the top of their agendas.

The losers from deforestation—those who bear the burden of environmental externalities—are a large, diffuse, unorganized group. They may not be well informed about the losses because it is difficult to monitor forests, and the environmental impacts of deforestation are hard to track. And even if this group suffers large losses, deforestation may not be at the top of the agenda for each member of the group. These asymmetries of power, information, cohesion, and priority create hurdles to collective action. The hurdles may be even greater when there is a contest for resources between the powerful and the voiceless.

Institutions exist to mediate these interests and implement agreements: forest codes, zoning laws, logging regulations, courts, and forest services. But sometimes these institutions appear hopelessly broken. With wealth to be made in forests, regulators can become captured by powerful interests or powerless to intervene. The voices and interests of forest dwellers, far off and disconnected, are not heard. Constituencies for conservation are dispersed and difficult to organize. In many forests remoteness and poor communications have cloaked resource grabs, conflicts, and inequities.

Catalytic Innovations in Institutions and Technology

A combination of institutional and technological innovations has started to offer some hope for correcting this situation. These new approaches seek to catalyze change by organizing dispersed constituencies, improving transparency and information flows, and marshaling new counterweights against resource seizures. None of them is, by itself, a panacea. But together they provide an expanded portfolio of tools for addressing what have been almost intractable problems.

How Can Institutions Mobilize Domestic Constituencies?

In 1995–97 the World Values Survey asked people in 43 countries if they actively participated in an environmental organization (Steinberg 2005). The top-ranking countries were Nigeria (12.3 percent participation) and Ghana (11.5 percent). Environmental participation rates in these and 13 other developing countries surpassed those in Finland, Germany, Norway, Spain, and Sweden. Other surveys reinforce this finding: the developed world does not have a monopoly on environmental concern (Steinberg 2005).

A tougher question is whether the public is concerned specifically about forest conservation. Urban residents may be more concerned about local environmental issues such as air pollution, while rural dwellers may favor forest exploitation over conservation. Some insight is provided by an opinion survey conducted in connection with Indonesia Forest and Media (INFORM), a campaign to promote conservation (Insan Hitawasana Sejahtera 2003). A purposive, stratified sample of three forested provinces and metropolitan Jakarta was evenly split by gender and location (urban or rural). Two-thirds of the 926 respondents were community leaders, the remainder high school and college students. Nearly all agreed that "Indonesian forests are mostly destroyed," and 90 percent considered local individuals and businesses responsible. At least 90 percent agreed that deforestation was linked to floods, fires, landslides, droughts, higher temperatures, and biodiversity losses. Respondents expressed strong opposition to forest burning and were inclined to oppose logging by local governments to raise local revenue (figure 5.2).

The group was mildly inclined to permit forest clearance for agriculture, with stronger support in the forested provinces. And despite the publicity attached to corruption in forestry, respondents overwhelmingly supported government control of forests. Less than 15 percent would make forest corruption their first choice for a media campaign. About half said they were willing to sign a petition opposing forest destruction, half said they would boycott products of forest-destroying companies, and a third said they would be willing to participate in a demonstration. These proportions were lower but not negligible in the forested provinces. In sum, local Indonesian opinion leaders are aware of forest loss, concerned about the environmental impacts of forest fires, and often support restrictions on clearing and especially logging.

To be heard, though, environmental interests must extend their bases and mobilize political resources. Environmental education is important. One subtle but perhaps catalytic intervention has been the creation of local-language guides to animals and plants. Appreciation of the importance of biodiversity conservation is difficult if people do not know what is at risk. The World Bank has sponsored about 100 of these field guides. One way that they may be effective is by increasing both the local demand for ecotourism and the supply of nature guides.

Another way to mobilize public support is through individuals and organizations that can frame environmental issues. Steinberg (2001) describes how "policy entrepreneurs" and "coupling" institutions catalyzed path-breaking environmental policy innovations in

Figure 5.2   Indonesians Favor Some Restrictions on Forest Exploitation

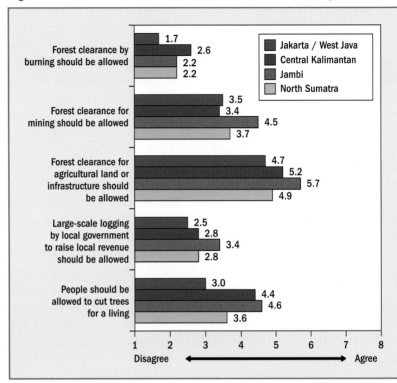

Source: Insan Hitawasana Sejahtera 2003.

Bolivia and Costa Rica. (A similar argument could be made for Brazil.) Internationally linked scientific research organizations served as incubators of expertise and action. They fostered the development of local capacity in ecology, created networks of domestic and foreign scientists and environmentalists, and fostered a nonpartisan atmosphere where policy entrepreneurs could draw on scientific findings to formulate locally relevant proposals. The results? Skyrocketing local appreciation of conservation—and a long list of globally influential local policy innovations in environmental finance and management.

Forging links between civil society and government is another way to mobilize environmental constituencies. One expression of this is the rapid rise in the number and prominence of environmental and other nongovernmental organizations (NGOs) over the past decade (Steinberg 2005).

Another way to mobilize is by incorporating civil society input into government activities. In the Philippines provincial and local multisector forest protection committees were created as part of a World Bank environmental adjustment loan (Cruz and Tapia 2006). The committees, which included participation by civil society groups and the National Resources Department, were charged primarily with monitoring forests but also with evaluating policies and operations and conducting information campaigns. Credited with reducing illegal logging, there were 314 such committees in 1999, when the loan closed. But many subsequently collapsed when funding ended, raising questions about the depth of popular support.

Brazil's local environmental councils offer an interesting view on the links between civil society and government. Local governments in Brazil, urban and rural, are organized around the country's more than 5,000 *municipios* governed by locally elected mayors and municipal councils. Municipal government also allows for advisory councils focused on certain sectors, including environment. Because Brazil presents continental-level variation among *municipios* in average income, education, size, rurality, and environmental conditions— while holding constant national laws and institutions—it provides an opportunity to look for evidence on the determinants and impacts of local environmental institutions.

The presence of an active environmental council is strongly related to income and education. (An active council is defined here as one that meets at least once a year, and at least half of whose members are from civil society.) Assume that the presence of an active municipal environmental council indicates environmental participation. About 14 percent of Brazil's 5,500 *municipios* meet this description. Councils are far more common in wealthier, better-educated *municipios* (29 percent) than in the poorest, least-educated *municipios* (6 percent). Multivariate analysis confirms that this is not merely because rich *municipios* are larger and thus have a larger pool of recruits. Although size and urbanization affect the likelihood of an active environmental council, mean income and education have a strong independent effect.

It is difficult to determine whether active environmental councils are effective in bringing forest-related environmental issues to the attention of local governments. One problem is forest and land fires. Used for forest conversion and pasture management, fires can create serious problems when they get out of control, damaging neighboring fields, fences, and woods (Nepstad and others 2001). Among *municípios* that experienced fires (based on remote sensing data), a substantially higher share of those with active environmental coun¹ cils reported a fire problem (28 percent versus 18 percent) and a smoke problem (23 percent versus 15 percent). Ongoing research is examining whether the council has a causal impact in prompting recognition of these problems.

Revolutions in Monitoring Have Raised Awareness and Accountability

For a long time forests have been invisible and their dwellers inaudible. It has not been easy for the public and the law to detect deforestation, logging, or mining deep in the forest. The scope of forest destruction and private appropriation of public property has gone unnoticed. So too has the extent to which public agencies charged with protecting forests have done their jobs. For most large forested nations in the developing world, reliable data on deforestation are lacking even at the aggregate level—let alone the provincial or regional level.

All that is changing due to synergistic developments in institutions and technology. These have the potential to drastically cut the cost of monitoring forest activities and to empower civil society to use this information to more fairly balance forest interests.

The first revolution involves remote sensing. Satellite images can detect deforestation and logging. Since the debut of Landsat in 1972, image quality and frequency have improved while the costs of acquiring, interpreting, and using images have plummeted. For detailed monitoring of particular sites, it is now possible to order snapshots with 1 meter resolution. For monitoring of global forests, MODIS images cover the entire world daily, can detect land cover changes as small as 25 hectares, and are available free of charge. The costs of hardware and software for analyzing and using images have also plummeted, placing them within reach of small NGOs.

The social and political impacts of this technology are becoming evident. In the developing world, Brazil has led the way in technology and applications. Its National Institute of Space Research (INPE) has long published annual or biannual reports on Amazônian deforestation by state. These reports have helped focus national and international attention on Amazônian deforestation. More recently, INPE has started publishing on the Internet real-time images of fire locations and detailed (30-meter resolution) maps of annual deforestation. It also provides South Americans with free data from CBERS2, the Sino-Brazilian satellite. These data are used by government agencies to enforce land regulation and by local NGOs to draw attention to forest issues and galvanize public support.

Land and forest fire monitoring uses an even more accessible technology, providing nearly real-time results that can be used for fire prevention and control. CONABIO, Mexico's National Biodiversity Commission, began monitoring after the disastrous fires of 1998. Indonesia's space agency also provides nearly real-time information on fire occurrences and risks.

Monitoring information of this kind can become much more valuable when combined with information on forest ownership and control. A complementary technological revolution—geographic positioning systems—makes it possible to identify the boundaries of properties and concessions at minimal cost. A third revolution—cheap geographic information systems—makes it easy to overlay maps of deforestation on maps of property boundaries. This technology enables government enforcement agencies to do their jobs better, and civil society to make sure that they're doing their jobs.

For instance, prosecutors can use remote sensing images as evidence of illegal deforestation. The Brazilian state of Mato Grosso has set up a system that registers the location of large properties and uses remote sensing to track their compliance with land use regulations. In Cameroon NGOs are using remote sensing to correlate the construction of new logging roads with logging concessionaires' reports of timber extraction (Global Forest Watch 2005). Mismatches may indicate mischief. Roads without logs may mean that producers are evading taxes. Logs without roads suggest timber laundering—for instance, taking timber from a protected area but claiming it comes from a legal concession. In neither case has official enforcement been entirely successful. But the ability of outside groups to monitor the behavior of private parties and government may put pressure on both to comply with laws.

As information gets better and cheaper, new possibilities emerge. Several groups are working on ways to use MODIS to cheaply detect large-scale deforestation, at an annual frequency or better, for entire nations or even the world. At the global level this would be a quantum leap in tracking deforestation. Among developing countries only Brazil and India regularly report remote sensing information on forest cover, though Indonesia is creating such a system.

At the national level such a monitoring system could detect hot-spots of deforestation rapidly enough to trigger action. It could be used, for instance, to track the impacts of new road construction or macroeconomic policy changes. It could also be used to direct higher-resolution monitoring for enforcement purposes. Technologies to detect hidden logging have been demonstrated by Asner and others (2005), and progress is being made in the use of satellite-based cloud-piercing radar.

Complementing the use of remote sensing is the rapidly growing potential for participatory, ground-based observations by citizens. These observations could be used to help interpret satellite images and to provide information unavailable from the sky. The Confluence project (www.confluence.org) provides a hint of the possibilities. It has asked for volunteer observations of the world's latitude and longitude intersections, at 1-degree intervals. The map is rapidly filling in. The explosive growth of cell phone coverage is rapidly putting a lot of mosaic forest within instant communication and reporting range. Already, about a quarter of the world's "imminent extinction spots" (see map 1.8) are covered by GSM cell phones.[1]

Weak State Institutions Can Be Aided by Better Checks and Balances and Transparency

Institutions charged with enforcing forest laws are often ineffective. Even worse, they may be captured by the interests they're supposed to regulate. This is a grave risk when large amounts of money are at stake—as when state agencies allocate land or forest concessions or are charged with ensuring that industrial loggers and large land-owners comply with environmental regulations. Corrupt officials, legislators, and military officers can form alliances with large actors (including timber companies, pulp mills, ranchers, and plantation owners) to allocate land and forests for exploitation. The result is private appropriation of wealth that belongs to the public or local communities, conflict with forest dwellers, and unregulated forest destruction.

In response, an efflorescence of institutional innovations have been created to bolster the performance and accountability of government agencies and the interests they oversee. It is possible to strengthen a system from within. Akella and Cannon (2004) explain why forest law enforcement often fails. Landowners are deterred from illegal deforestation or logging only if they perceive a significant probability of a significant penalty. In a system that relies on criminal penalties, a long chain of events must occur before a miscreant is punished: detection of the legal violation, citation, prosecution, conviction, and execution of the penalty. If landholders perceive low probabilities of progressing from any link in this chain to the next, the level of deterrence is low.

Links may be weak by design or for lack of capacity. Palmer (2005) describes how Indonesian logging regulations motivate enforcers to seek bribes from log smugglers, rather than prosecute them. On the other hand, Brito, Barreto, and Rothman (2005), in a review of Brazilian environmental crime law enforcement, identify fixable logistical problems as an impediment to prosecution.

Against a global backdrop of failed systems of internal checks and balances, Brazil's Public Ministry provides an interesting model for a possible solution. The ministry, which exists at both state and federal levels, is a prosecutorial agency charged with ensuring legal compliance by both citizens and the executive branch. A meritocratic institution, its staff are selected through competitive exams that only a few percentage of applicants pass. As a result it attracts extremely qualified and idealistic staff, many of whom are interested in environmental issues. Prosecutors have considerable autonomy in choosing cases to pursue. This promotes independence but impedes focus. Typically the ministry seeks to resolve problems through negotiations, holding the threat of prosecution in reserve. Brito, Barreto, and Rothman (2005) call the Public Ministry the most powerful institutional force for environmental protection in Brazil.

A new institution of independent monitors stands at the boundary between strengthening internal controls and enabling external ones. The governments of Cambodia and Cameroon, under international and domestic pressure to strengthen oversight of forest resources, have employed donor-funded independent monitors of forest law enforcement. A concern in both cases was that timber wealth was being nontransparently and inequitably allocated, and that loggers were not adequately supporting the sustainability of forest resources.

In Cameroon a monitor observed the conduct of concession auctions, spurring an increase in bids and better application of technical standards for prequalifying bidders. In both countries monitors examined logging operations and enforcement actions. A review of these and similar experiments by Brown (2004) found strong positive impacts on transparency, but questioned the sustainability of the monitoring institutions. The fundamental issue is whether there is a domestic constituency that values and demands the information provided by the monitors.

A variant of public disclosure policies from the field of industrial pollution control may offer lessons. Indonesia's PROPER program rates the pollution control efforts of industrial firms. The program was set up by the country's environmental protection agency in response to difficulties in enforcing pollution laws. Based on audited self-reports, it classifies firms on a five-point scale: completely non-compliant and making no effort to comply, some environmental effort but inadequate to meet standards, minimally compliant, good practice, and best practice. These ratings are easily understood by the public and have induced firms to improve their performance. The ratings' interesting feature, relative to current practice in forest law, is the recognition that PROPER gives to better-performing firms. This may help defuse opposition to the program.

Voluntary certification systems share similarities with public disclosure systems. From a policy perspective, certification systems are appealing because they can encourage better forest management even where local institutions are ineffective at enforcing regulations. Like public disclosure systems, they seek to reward good performers—though usually only on a pass/fail basis, without the finer distinctions made by PROPER. The best-known examples are for forest management, where the Forest Stewardship Council and other standards-setting organizations have developed standards for responsible, sustainable forest management. These standards include compliance with national laws, respect for indigenous rights, conservation of biodiversity, and establishment of and compliance with a management plan. Systems have also been proposed to certify that commodities such as beef and soybeans are produced without illegal deforestation. Certification is conducted under contract by accredited private, third-party certifiers. The integrity of the certification process rests on the desire of the certifiers to maintain their reputations.

Can certification make a big difference in forest management? The main question is whether forest owners will find it worthwhile to seek certification. Certification imposes substantial direct and indirect costs. Because there are direct fixed costs associated with filling out paperwork and paying for a certifier's visit, community forests and other small producers are at a serious disadvantage.

Indirect costs are those associated with compliant behaviors—such as refraining from cutting timber on slopes. These costs can be substantial, depending on the stringency of regulations and the nature of the forest. The most widely cited benefit for forest owners is increased access to export markets, possibly with a price premium for certified products. Skeptics doubt whether this benefit is wide enough and deep enough to motivate widespread change in forest management. Demand for certified products is only a small (but rapidly growing) portion of export markets, accounting for 12 percent of wood production in Africa and 18 percent in Asia.

Moreover, it is controversial whether there is any price premium for certified wood. A survey in the U.K. market finds price premiums of 2–3 percent for some tropical woods—and premiums of 20 percent in thin markets where demand at such prices may be lacking (Robinson 2006). But if passed back to the producer, even a small retail or wholesale premium can translate into a large stumpage premium, and certification may be important for certain markets. Still, questions remain on whether certification can be expected to influence producer behavior on a large scale.

But certification may change firms' behavior through another mechanism. Because certification criteria are consistent with risk and liability reduction and with the existence of good internal management controls, certified loggers and landowners may find it easier to obtain insurance and financing. For the same reason certification—seen as a proxy for good management and low risks—may increase the value of a forest concession or property, or of a logging company. This avenue may prove to be a stronger incentive than a consumer price premium. And there could be indirect effects through local politics, as certified companies seek to ensure that uncertified competitors also comply with local regulations.[2]

Finally, anti–money laundering laws are beginning to attract attention as a tool against illegal logging and forest conversion. Intergovernmental bodies—the Financial Action Task Force and associated regional bodies—have offered recommendations on these laws, which designate certain crimes as "predicate" crimes. Disguising the movement of gains from predicate crimes is a money laundering offense.

Indonesia has explicitly designated illegal logging as a predicate crime; in many other countries violations of forest or land use laws could be interpreted as predicate crimes. What this might mean is that a much broader net can be cast for violators of forest law. Domestic law enforcement agencies have another tool at their disposal: money laundering crimes may be easier to detect and prosecute than forest law violations. Money laundering crimes require domestic banks to exert closer scrutiny of their clients, deterring crime. Foreign banks must scrutinize their correspondent banks as well as deposits by offshore clients. But application of money laundering laws to forest law enforcement is still at an early, speculative stage.

Summary

This chapter looked upstream of the policy process. If societies are to maintain environmental services in the face of strong pressures for forest degradation, there must be vocal and effective constituencies for such services. And if societies are to fairly allocate and defend rights to forest resources, they must prevent powerful elites from seizing them. New institutions and technologies for transparency, monitoring, and incentives can help address these challenges. With this context, the next chapter examines successes and failures of policies affecting forest management and protection.

Endnotes

1. Authors' calculation based on 2005 coverage data.

2. The contrary is also possible. As pressures for certification increase on large companies, they may transfer forest assets to small companies that evade certification or are subject to laxer standards.

Road building and agricultural development projects triggered forest clearance in Santa Cruz, Bolivia.

UNEP / GRID-Sioux Falls.

Most of Mexico's forest is owned by communities, and many have developed viable commercial forest enterprises.

Heriberto Rodriguez.

Local and National Policies: Framing Rights and Incentives for Forest Management

We turn now to twin governance challenges introduced in chapter 5. These challenges revolve around the assignment and enforcement of rights:

- In frontier and transfrontier areas much of the forest is nominally owned by the state—but the reach of government and the rule of law are weak and property rights insecure. Who should control these vast tracts and receive revenues from them? And as demands on these areas increase, how can large-scale environmental disruption be prevented?

- Within mosaiclands, how can land and forest be managed productively and equitably? For instance, how should society balance landowners' desire to exploit rich riverfront soil against downstream neighbors' interest in maintaining riverrine forests as a bulwark against sediment?

This chapter examines ways of improving forest outcomes, such as:

- Sorting out who has rights to use forests for different purposes, and how stringently to regulate those rights in the interests of sustainability and environmental benefits.

- Making sustainable forest management more financially attractive relative to agricultural conversion.

- Coordinating regional development and agricultural policies.

The chapter first reviews the challenge of forest conflict, then assesses zoning and land use allocation mechanisms at the national and regional scales. After that it analyzes the pros and cons of various property rights schemes—government management, community management, private management—under different circumstances, and for each examines ways of making forest management more attractive. Finally, the chapter considers how to manage road building and other development policies to take into account their impacts on forest management.

The Challenge of Forest Conflict

Violent conflicts are endemic to forests. According to the FAO (2005, p. 117), over the past 20 years at least 26 tropical countries have experienced armed conflicts in forested areas; another 4 experienced "substantial social violence." Some of these have been civil wars, reflecting failed states. Many rebels and insurgents have used forests as a base of operations and timber sales to finance fighting. Resolving these disputes involves governance issues far beyond the forest agenda.

In stronger states conflicts can erupt in frontier areas over access to land and timber. In an analysis of violence in Brazilian Amazônia, Alston, Libecap, and Mueller (2000) illustrate some basic challenges in allocating property rights at the frontier. During the 1990s there were frequent clashes as landless groups and large landholders disputed property ownership. According to the authors, these clashes stemmed from legal ambiguity. One set of laws guaranteed land ownership to the property holders, while another allowed redistribution of "underutilized" land (including forest) to landless people.

The authors asked why this dilemma leads to conflict in some places and not others. They concluded that clashes are more likely when land is valuable and there is uncertainty about which laws will prevail. It's not worth fighting over valueless land, and it's not worth fighting for a lost cause. Good laws and good judges are the basis for property rights at the frontier. But this maxim, easily enunciated, is hard to put into practice.

Forest Rights and Restrictions—A Range of Possibilities

"Who owns the world's forests?" asked White and Martin (2002) in a seminal piece. Appendix table A.3, drawn from International Tropical Timber Organization (ITTO) (2006) and United Nations Food and Agriculture Organization (FAO) (2005), updates their answer, but reaches many of the same conclusions.

First, much of the world's tropical forest is under insecure state ownership and much is managed unsustainably—or not at all. Governments own almost all forest in Africa and Asia and most in Latin America. Some 3.5 million square kilometers of forest in ITTO member countries is zoned for timber production, with about half under government concession. But only 7 percent is under sustainable management, and only 3 percent is under certified management. Another 4.6 million square kilometers of ITTO forest is zoned for protection (some on private lands), but just 4 percent is under some kind of management plan.

Second, a large and growing portion of the forest estate is owned or managed by communities. Local and indigenous groups own most forests in Fiji, Mexico, and Papua New Guinea; own large tracts in Bolivia, Brazil, Colombia, Ecuador, Guyana, Panama, and Peru; and co-manage forest in Guatemala, India, and the Philippines. In Southeast Asia communities manage 10 percent of publicly owned forest and have limited user rights to another 54 percent (Romano and Reeb 2006).

But forest ownership and management rights are almost always restricted, and restrictions on ownership and use define alternative tenure systems (table 6.1). These two dimensions mirror the two main challenges identified in chapter 5—assigning ownership and recognizing environmental externalities. The balance of rights can be tilted strongly toward society, in the form of publicly owned, strictly protected areas. Or state ownership and management can be retained, but with sustainable timber extraction allowed. Much of the world's tropical forest falls into this second category, under either direct (often ineffective) state supervision or concessions. But community participation in forest ownership and management is also growing quickly, though still with restrictions on extraction and conversion.

In contrast, most or all forest rights—including to conversion—can be allocated to private owners, as in many mosaiclands. In such

Table 6.1   Examples of Forest Ownership and Use Restrictions

Allowed forest uses	Ownership or management type		
	State	**Community**	**Private**
Any, including full conversion	—	—	Many mosaiclands
Limited permanent conversion permitted; remainder must be managed sustainably	Zoned areas for conversion (Indonesia)	—	Brazil, Paraguay
Conversion prohibited; sustainable management for commercial forest products permitted	Direct state management (often ineffective) and industrial timber concessions; includes a lot of Asian and African forests	Community concessions (Guatemala), Joint Forest Management (India), community forests (Mexico), indigenous lands (Papua New Guinea)	Regulated private forests
Limited or no extractive uses permitted	Strictly protected areas	Some indigenous areas	Private reserves and conservation easements

Source: Authors.

cases society must compensate landholders to get them to mitigate carbon emissions, sedimentation, and other consequences of deforestation. Where conversion rights are limited, the rights of private forestholders are circumscribed so that they share with society the costs of environmental protection. In Brazil and Paraguay, for instance, landholders must keep a proportion of their property under forest cover. Making this obligation tradable could, however, reduce the costs of achieving environmental goals. Finally, in some places landholders retain only a few rights to forest use, such as establishing a residence or conducting ecotourism. Examples include private reserves such as Brazil's Reserva Particular do Patrimônio Natural (RPPN).

Choices among these tenure systems will reflect an area's history, the relative power of different interest groups, the efficiency of different groups in managing forests, the importance of environmental protection relative to agriculture, and societal attitudes about private and social interests. The next few sections discuss mechanisms for making those choices and examine issues related to implementing these alternative systems.

Zoning Has Technical Appeal but Poses Practical Difficulties

Zoning has a sensible premise: efficient land allocation and management. Some land is suited to agriculture, with flat terrain, fertile soils, favorable climates, and available water. Some is terrible for agriculture, as on erosion-prone hillsides. Similarly, some areas have unique animal or plant species or play a crucial role in moderating water flows. So land use planners suggest dedicating good agricultural land to farming, keeping crops and cows away from easily degraded lands and protecting areas of high biodiversity.

Sophisticated land use planning methodologies have been developed, at scales ranging from continent to nation to province to watershed. There are at least two strands of technical planning, though in practice they may be combined. One is rooted in agricultural science and forestry. Information on topography and soils is used, together with crop modeling, to indicate the "vocation" of the soil—that is, the recommended land uses. Data on forest cover and distributions of tree species and human populations are also used to indicate areas for sustainable timber management. This approach is common in Latin America and was also used in Malaysia.

The second approach comes from systematic conservation planning (Margules and Pressey 2000; Cowling and others 2003; Stoms, Chomitz, and Davis 2004). This highly technical approach is framed as a mathematical optimization problem: finding the landscape configuration that achieves specific environmental goals at minimum cost. For instance, given a set of potential reserve sites in a region, a planner may try to identify the smallest number containing all of the region's threatened species. More sophisticated formulations try to ensure that there is enough contiguous habitat to ensure the long-term survival of those species and to maintain broader ecological processes.

The resulting zoning plans can be indicative or prescriptive. Indicative plans can be used by landholders to choose appropriate land uses, or by governments to decide on road placement, establishment of protected areas, granting of permits for mines and plantations, and other regional development issues. Prescriptive plans dictate which land uses are permitted or prohibited at each spot on the landscape. When environmental externalities are the motivation, plans are often prescriptive, identifying specific hillsides, floodplains, biodiversity corridors, and wildlife habitats for protection or restrictions on use.

The promise of prescriptive zoning is also its pitfall: to achieve its social and environmental goals, it must restrict the rights of current or prospective landholders to use the land or forest. The legitimacy and effectiveness of zoning are thus closely linked to land tenure and depend on securing landholder consent and cooperation. Poor people can suffer if zoning is imposed on them without consent or compensation, while wealthier or more powerful interests may flout the rules with impunity—or there may be no political will to impose zoning on anyone.

For this reason, implementation of zoning has been problematic at the national level (Hoare 2006):

- In Suharto-era Indonesia, the government asserted claims to a forest domain encompassing about three-quarters of the country, superseding the rights of traditional communities to their forests. A large-scale zoning plan delineated areas for protection, timber management, and conversion. But the plan was often disregarded or manipulated. Communities were denied rights to agroforests they had created, and the plan did not prevent deforestation of protected areas. Either because of poor planning or subsequent deforestation, 40 million Indonesians live in areas zoned for forest but lacking trees—areas where agriculture is not allowed.

- In Brazil two expensive World Bank–funded exercises developed zoning plans for the states of Rondônia and Mato Grosso. The plans were devised without much popular participation or political buy-in. Because they placed significant areas off-limits to powerful ranching and timber interests, they failed to gain widespread support and apparently did not have much effect on land use (though no rigorous evaluation has been conducted). A revised plan is being implemented in Rondônia (Mahar 2000; World Bank 2003).

- Agroecological zoning has been undertaken at the provincial or state level in several Latin American countries, often with support or methodology from the FAO. These include large exercises in Bolivia and Peru and regional or local exercises in Chile, Colombia, Costa

Rica, Nicaragua, and Paraguay. No formal evaluations of these exercises have been produced.

- Conservation science has produced a number of elaborate land use plans that try to reconcile biodiversity, agricultural, and commercial forestry goals, such as one for Papua New Guinea (Faith, Walker, and Margules 2001). Yet according to Faith and others (2003 p. 313), "In spite of a decade or more of work on reserve selection methods, no complete set of areas produced by such computer algorithms, to our knowledge, has been implemented anywhere in real-world regional biodiversity planning."[1]

In sum, these plans have failed because they did not muster popular support and did not consider how people with claims or designs on forests would react.

Zoning with a Human Face?

It is not enough to draw up a rational zoning map at 1:250,000 scale. Planners must also induce land users to conform to the map—but how? They can try exhortation, which may work if the maps provide novel information about agricultural suitability or if the target audience is a tight-knit group with strong social controls. They can try legal compulsion, which requires public consensus on means and ends if it is to be legitimate and effective. They can provide incentives for compliance, including compensation for accepting restrictions. And perhaps most important, they can draw on popular participation when shaping plans and negotiating the land rights that often underlie them. That means adjusting the map to recognize reality on the ground, rather than vice versa.

An example is Cameroon, which has zoned its permanent forest estate to reflect land use patterns. The 1994 forest code mandated reserving 30 percent of the country as permanent forest estate for conservation and sustainable timber production. A preliminary zoning plan achieved that goal largely by reserving areas with dense forest and few people. Although the permanent estate is state property, communities inside it can manage local forests, are entitled to half the revenue from nearby timber concessions, and can challenge and redraw the boundaries of those concessions.

The zoning plan is thought to have deterred agricultural conversion in the permanent forest estate, though no formal evaluations exist and pressures may be low. But critics say that the plan was insufficiently participatory, did not adequately recognize the needs of indigenous forest dwellers, sometimes deprived communities of traditional rights, and was sometimes treated as immutable rather than subject to objection and renegotiation (Hoare 2006). Oyono (2005), however, suggests that the zoning plan and associated legal changes are improvements over the previous de facto rights regime.

Another approach is more systematically participatory. It starts, as do the technical exercises, with maps of the landscape and its resources. Thanks to new technology, such maps are becoming relatively cheap and easy to assemble. They may vary in sophistication from simple paper maps to complex geographic information systems with decision support software. Residents and claimants review the maps, delineate historical claims, negotiate boundaries, and discuss issues that require coordination. Mediation and conflict resolution are important parts of the exercise.

There has been an efflorescence of this participatory land use planning. It is often used to help demarcate indigenous lands. For instance, it is being used to resolve conflicts between forest dwellers and plantation interests in Papua province, Indonesia, and to delineate community boundaries in Vietnam. Successful applications have also been reported in Cameroon (Lescuyer and others 2001) and Madagascar (Cowles and others 2001).

Over the past decade Australia has instituted 10 regional forest agreements to zone public forests with commercial timber potential (Hoare 2006). The agreements set conservation goals that try to achieve a "comprehensive, adequate, and representative reserve system" (www.rfa.gov.au). To realize conservation goals while also taking into account the interests of forest dwellers, indigenous people, and forest industry groups, the agreements were created through extensive consultations. The process started with substantial investment in gathering and mapping information on social and environmental values of forests. This information was gathered in a participatory fashion and provided the basis for stakeholder negotiations. Hoare (2006) cites studies (published before 2000) that credit the regional forest agreements with increasing the nation's reserve network and increasing stakeholder involvement, especially of indigenous people. But she concludes that stakeholder participation could be further improved and final decision making on forest allocations made more transparent.

While participatory land use plans are promising, they face two implementation challenges. The first is legitimacy. Who participates in the participation, and who do they represent? If local governments are deemed unrepresentative, what alternatives are better? How can capture by elites be avoided? Is there a solid legal basis for land right allocations and restrictions?

The second challenge involves commitment and enforcement. How will agreements be enforced, and how will future disputes be negotiated? Actions such as physically marking boundaries can help prevent disputes. But if there is a disagreement between local communities and powerful industrial groups, what will keep the powerful from capturing the machinery for dispute resolution? There are no easy answers to these questions. For a while, anyway, participatory land use planning will remain a novel endeavor—one from which it is essential to quickly learn lessons.

Public Management of Forests: Protected Areas and Concessions

Publicly owned forests are often poorly regulated and administered. This section examines the two most prominent approaches to public administration of forests: protected areas and regulated concessions. The next section considers an alternative: devolving ownership or some management responsibilities to communities.

Protected Areas Are Expanding Quickly

Protected areas represent, in extent and financing, the largest policy intervention for conservation and active management of tropical forests. FAO (2001b) estimates that 3.46 million square kilometers of tropical and subtropical forest have protected status—about a seventh of the world's forest and approximately equivalent in area to India. Over the past 20 years the number of protected areas and the area under protection have grown rapidly (figure 6.1).

A full accounting on spending to establish protected areas in tropical forests is unavailable. But during 1992–2002 the Global Environment Facility financed $3.6 billion in projects for protected areas, covering about a quarter of the world's protected areas. Across the developing world, total annual spending (including recurrent spending) on protected areas is roughly $800 million.

161

Figure 6.1   Protected Areas Have Grown Rapidly in Tropical and Subtropical Forests

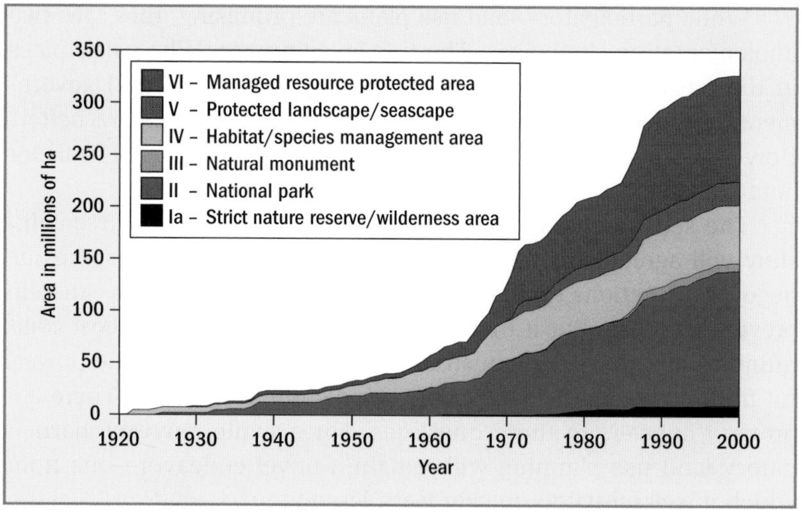

Source: Kloss 2006.
Note: Excludes areas for which establishment dates are not available.

Are Protected Areas Protected?

Though sometimes denigrated as "paper parks" because of their poor funding or management, protected areas may be more effective than is commonly thought. Remarkably, despite their flagship role in conservation, there is little quantitative analysis of their effectiveness in protecting biodiversity. But some remote sensing studies suggest that protected areas may deter deforestation. Nepstad and others (2006) compare deforestation inside and outside the boundaries of protected areas in Brazil. (This is a clever way of controlling for differences in soils, market access, and other confounding factors.) The authors consistently find much higher deforestation rates outside, suggesting a strong protective effect.

A similar study of Costa Rica also found a strong differential (Sanchez-Azofeifa and others 2003). Remote sensing images such as those of Laporte show intact protected areas surrounded by a sea of agriculture.[2] Many of the spatial analyses reviewed in chapter 2 also find that deforestation is lower in protected areas, holding constant accessibility, agroclimatic conditions, and other factors. Gorenflo and others (2006), for instance, find that even in Madagascar's weak institutional setting, parks appear to reduce conversion.

But against this generally positive view of park effectiveness, there are examples of ineffectiveness. Curran and others (2004) document rapid, massive deforestation in the protected areas of Kalimantan, Indonesia. Moreover, biodiversity can be damaged in ways that are undetectable by remote sensing—as with hunting of large mammals.

Only a couple studies explore reasons for variations in the effectiveness of protected areas. Bruner and others (2001) and Dudley and others (2005) survey such areas, correlating management practices with self-reported measures of park conditions. The clearest result is a correlation between staffing and effectiveness, suggesting that guards are an important part of the transformation between "paper parks" and working parks, though staff may also be important in working with local residents.

Can Protected Forests Sustain Livelihoods?

Park creation has sometimes been associated with reduced forest access for local people (see chapter 3). In response, there has been a trend to actively engage local and indigenous populations in comanagement and sustainable use of protected areas. Kloss (2006) shows that new protected areas are less likely to have strict protection (World Conservation Union categories I–III) than to allow multiple uses (IV–VI; see figure 6.1). The 1990s saw striking growth in category VI, which is land managed not just for biodiversity but also for "a sustainable flow of natural products and services to meet community needs," according to the IUCN (1994, p. 23) definition.

There has also been an extensive—but largely unevaluated—effort to seek win-win outcomes through integrated conservation-development projects (ICDPs). These projects aim to boost development in forest communities, often those in or near protected areas. Development of an ICDP is often based on several premises: that poor people are the main agents of forest degradation, that provision of higher incomes or alternative income sources will reduce deforestation by poor people, that project-based interventions can stimulate long-term sustainable improvements in livelihoods, and that communities can credibly commit to relinquish future use of a forest in exchange for current compensation. All these premises are subject to debate (Fisher and others 2005).

First, ICDPs won't reduce deforestation if targeted communities are not to blame for deforestation. A review of Indonesian ICDPs found that local communities were bystanders to ongoing deforestation by wealthy timber and plantation interests (Khan and others

1999). Second, there is no strong reason to expect that unconditional provision of alternative livelihoods will automatically reduce a community's pressure on forests and other natural resources. Chapter 2 shows that higher incomes and increased agricultural productivity often increase deforestation, not retard it. Third, while ecotourism and nontimber forest products can motivate conservation and raise incomes, it can be difficult to set up these businesses. Some researchers have concluded that ICDPs can succeed only if there is a specific quid pro quo bargain—such as periodic payments to communities based on measured conservation outcomes (Ferraro and Kiss 2002).

A recent review by the Global Environment Facility supports these propositions (GEF 2006). The review examined the impact on local incomes of 88 biodiversity projects, mostly in protected areas (but not all forests). Less than half of projects for which information was available succeeded in boosting incomes (table 6.2). Not surprisingly, alternative income generating programs often failed when they were not financially viable. Moreover, financial success did not guarantee environmental success when the new business was unrelated to the natural resource at risk.

Ecotourism ventures were more likely to prosper in areas with tourism infrastructure. Such ventures required sophisticated skills and often benefited wealthier community members. Forests, with their shy and elusive wildlife, tend to offer less spectacular tourism experiences than savannas with large mammals. Projects based

Table 6.2   Integrated Conservation-Development Project Interventions Have a Mixed Record

Outcome	Type of intervention		
	Alternative income generating activities	Ecotourism	Sustainable resource use
Success in boosting incomes	17	21	11
Failure	19	25	22[a]
No information	15	23	
Not applicable	37	19	55

Source: GEF 2006.
Note: Shows the results of an evaluation of 88 biodiversity projects. Some projects supported more than one type of intervention.
a. Breakdown between "failure" and "no information" not provided.

on sustainable resource management were successful when they built capacity to care for attractive common property. For instance, a Ugandan project supported regulated beekeeping in the forest and so motivated the community to prevent forest fires. Elsewhere, strict park regulations were often an insuperable legal barrier to sustainable resource use. Overall, though, the evidence on ICDP impacts is weak, reflecting a lack of systematic monitoring and evaluation (Agrawal and Redford 2006).

Protecting Additional Areas Is Difficult—And Other Options Exist

What is the scope for creating additional protected areas? Where are they most appropriately situated? From a conservation viewpoint—the demand side—the need is most urgent where unique biodiversity (species, ecosystems) is under threat and fares poorly in human-dominated landscapes. Gap analysis points to places with these characteristics. Many are in nonremote areas where economic pressures on forests are likely high. (Though Brandon and others [2005] argue that opportunity costs are low in "gap" areas in Mexico, which is rich in biodiversity.)

On the supply side, protected areas have traditionally been created in remote areas where economic demands on the land have been weakest. This trend has not changed over the past three decades (figure 6.2). While sometimes considered opportunistic, protecting large remote forests under low current threat may be a far-sighted and cost-effective way of averting their long-run fragmentation and degradation. In addition, maintaining large forest blocs provides an important hedge against climate change, because large contiguous blocs allow plants and animals to migrate in response to temperature or precipitation changes.

But in both remote and nonremote areas, the economic and social costs of creating new protected areas must be weighed against those of other forms of ownership and management. In mosaiclands and nonremote frontiers, where land values are high and tenure relatively well defined, protected areas are likely to be small and have to be purchased from landowners and managed against encroachment by fairly high-density populations. Since protected areas are already poorly funded, acquiring such areas may be difficult. Environmental service payment systems are a potential alternative (see below). In remote transfrontier areas creating new protected areas on public lands must address the potential claims of indigenous

Figure 6.2   Recent Decades Have Seen Little Change in the Remoteness of New Protected Areas

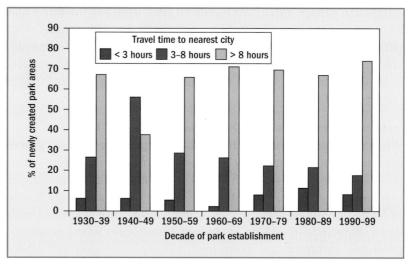

Source: Kloss 2006.

people, whose rights are increasingly recognized and supported (for instance, through the International Labour Organization's Convention 169 on Indigenous and Tribal Peoples). In such places comanagement of protected areas (Redford and Painter 2006) and transfer to indigenous ownership are alternative management forms.

Forest Revenues, Concessions, and Regulations

The owners of a forest—whether a nation, community, or indigenous group—may find it politically or economically infeasible to conserve it without any revenue (point A in figure 5.1). Sustainable timber extraction represents a move up and to the left on the curve of figure 5.1. Although revenue comes at an environmental cost, the damages associated with logging are typically much smaller than those with clearing for permanent agriculture. In some cases sustainable logging may provide more income than agriculture; in others it lowers the opportunity cost of forgoing agriculture. In short, forest management potentially provides a mechanism that can defend against pressure to convert forests to agriculture. And for many forest communities, it is the main source of income.

Many forest owners, both governments and communities, lack the technical skills or inclination to undertake commercial forest management directly. When they look for a logger to do it for them, they face a problem with contracting and supervision: how to maximize the extraction of rent (that is, profit from timber sales) while maintaining the quality of the resource (for instance, avoiding damage to the forest as a result of sloppy logging, poaching of rare animals, or follow-on invasions of farmers) and meeting social goals. This is a difficult problem. Unregulated, a logger will not have strong incentive to log sustainably or responsibly. It is hard to monitor and supervise loggers in the expansive depths of the forest. It's difficult to know how much to charge them for the right to log. And public or community officials may collude with loggers, awarding cheap contracts, failing to enforce regulations, and sharing the resulting gains.

The traditional approach to logging concessions involves high transactions costs and is conducive to corruption. It relies for revenue on taxes per cubic meter of extracted timber, sometimes differentiated by species. These fees are difficult to set and don't reflect variations in profitability associated with different road access. Collecting these fees requires monitoring the flow of logs over the landscape—a massive task that lends itself to petty corruption by inspectors. Forest laws may require complex management plans to regulate logging and protect resources. Stringent on paper, these regulations tend to be unenforced. Monitoring and inspection are costly, and inspectors are easily bribed.

An emerging approach strives for efficient regulation, combined with transparency and public disclosure. Instead of trying to tax each log, it auctions concession rights by the hectare. If the auction can be made competitive, that extracts more revenue for the forest owner, and the revenue is easy to collect. Efficient regulation of logging looks carefully at the enforceability of regulations, preferring imperfect but easily monitorable criteria to ideal but unenforceable ones. For instance, it can use remote sensing or ground verification to check requirements such as maintaining forests on slopes and proper siting and construction of logging roads. Above all, the emerging approach relies on transparent information to enlist public oversight of loggers and officials. This new approach is exemplified in Cameroon (box 6.1), in an experiment that will be of wide interest for nations and communities with forest resources.

Box 6.1   Cameroon: A Nexus of Institutional Reform

Cameroon's forest experience over the past 10 years exemplifies a central theme of this report: How can diffuse public interests in forest conservation and in a broad allocation of forest wealth counterbalance narrow vested interests in forest exploitation? Cameroon has set up far-reaching, complementary institutional and policy innovations that try to do that. These innovations illustrate many of the policy and institutional issues discussed in this chapter and chapter 5: zoning, mobilization of the public interest, promotion of community forestry, efficient design of concession contracts, and checks and balances.

The emergence of reform

In the 1980s Cameroon was rich in timber, but timber concessions and revenues were allocated opaquely, based on political patronage. Concessions were awarded for only five years, so concessionaires had no incentive to care for forests. Meanwhile, agriculture-driven deforestation threatened the country's rich biodiversity.

The economy fell into crisis in 1986 due to a fall in prices of the country's main exports: oil, coffee, and cocoa. As a condition of ongoing World Bank and International Monetary Fund (IMF) assistance, in 1994 the government adopted a new forest policy allowing for the award of timber concessions by auction. When the auctions failed to meet the standards embodied in the reform, additional institutional reforms were made a condition of a 1998 World Bank structural adjustment loan. Another external catalyst was the listing

of Cameroon by Transparency International in 1998 as the most corrupt of 85 countries surveyed. These catalysts arguably helped induce change partly because they provided leverage for domestic reformers.

Reform elements

- *Allocation of forest concessions by transparent auctions.* This approach replaced discretionary procedures and awarded concessions based on competitive bidding for area-based fees.

- *Appointment of an independent observer.* The initial auctions resulted in concession awards that were inconsistent with the rules. In response to pressure from the World Bank and others, an independent observer began reporting on subsequent auctions.

- *Forest tax reform.* A new forest tax system prominently relied on the auction-determined area tax. Independent of production volumes, this tax is predictable and easily administered. Reforms also simplified the tax system, slashing export taxes and using harvesting and factory entry taxes to help monitor forestry and reduce waste.

- *Allocation of timber rents to communities.* The law requires that 40 percent of timber royalties go to rural councils (municipalities) and 10 percent to local communities. In theory, this should promote local political support for the reforms.

- *Concession management plans required, with another independent observer.* Concession-

Box 6.1   (*continued*)

aires are now required to create and follow management plans. A second independent observer's office monitors enforcement of these plans, taking missions with and independently from government authorities. In addition, remote sensing is used to monitor logging activity.

- *Definition of the forest estate and provision for community forests.* A forest zoning plan identified and provided preliminary boundaries for conservation and production forests. Outside the permanent forest estate, it provided for community forests that could be managed for timber or converted to non-forest uses based on local needs and preferences. The law allowed forest communities to challenge and redraw the provisional zoning boundaries.

Outcomes
- *Transparency and monitoring.* The independent observers' offices have greatly increased public scrutiny of concession operators and the government. One important consequence was an increase in auction bids above the floor price after the creation of the independent observer. The precedent for transparency and oversight may spill over into other parts of government.

- *Greater potential control over large-scale logging.* With the introduction of better monitoring and a performance bond requirement, there has been a reported reduction in illegal logging by large-scale concessionaires.

Illegal logging by the informal sector has reportedly increased, reflecting a scarcity of legally cut timber for local markets.

- *Effect on government revenue.* The new auction and tax system mitigated what would otherwise have been a severe drop in government revenues due to a ban on log exports introduced in 2000. The reduction in tax revenues since the reforms should be viewed against the improvements in sector governance and reductions in areas under logging and annual volumes harvested. Vincent, Gibson, and Boscolo (2003) note the unique character of Cameroon's system, which fixes area-based taxes for a long-term (15-year) contract. According to the authors, the lack of adjustments for timber price volatility exposes concessionaires to risk and may depress bids relative to a system indexing taxes to international timber prices.

- *Effect on local incomes and capacity.* By 2004 a total of $53 million in forest royalties had been distributed to communities, and additional money went to community forests. There were no such distributions before the forest tax reform. Annual audits of these funds are produced with donor support. Oyono (2005) gives a mixed but mostly disappointing account of the use of these funds. Positive impacts include stimulating community organization, growing recognition of Pygmy rights, some productive social investments, and retention of youth in rural areas. Negative impacts revolve

(continued on next page)

Box 6.1 (continued)

around the emergence of elites that control forest revenues sent to locally elected bodies and communities. These elites conflict with traditional authorities and are poorly supervised. The result is social conflict and misappropriation of funds, according to Oyono.

Further insight is provided by official audits on what may be an evolving situation as institutions mature (Ndjanyou and Majerowitz 2004). There are strong efforts to impose transparency on the system, starting with public transfer of royalty checks to local officials. As a result the share of verifiable expenditures by rural councils rose from 49 percent in 2003 to 72 percent in 2004. About a quarter of this revenue went to recurrent expenses, half of it salaries. Of investment expenditures, about 60 percent went to municipal buildings and vehicles,

13 percent to roads, and 10 percent to education and health. There is less accountability at the community level, where only about half of expenditures could be tracked. Education, housing, water management, and culture and sport were spending priorities.

- *Industry impacts.* About 15 companies changed ownership, with a trend toward more efficient and law-abiding companies and increased domestic ownership.

- *Environmental impacts.* There have been no studies on how the zoning of the forest estate and other reforms have affected deforestation or forest degradation.

Source: Vincent, Gibson, and Boscolo 2003; World Bank staff.

Efficient regulation also calls for a reexamination of logging rules. Stringent rules appear to favor sustainability, but they also have disadvantages. Increasingly stringent rules provide smaller and smaller environmental benefits at escalating costs to forest owners. Boscolo and Vincent (2000) use a bioeconomic model to examine the costs and benefits of logging regulations in Malaysia. They find that shifting from unregulated to regulated logging, with a 40-centimeter minimum cutting limit, reduces the net present value of the timber stand by $510 a hectare (12 percent) but conserves carbon and biodiversity. Raising the minimum cutting limit from 40 to 60 centimeters reduces the value of the stand by another $1,223 a hectare and yields only a modest additional benefit for carbon and biodiversity conservation.

Because stringent regulations impose large burdens on loggers and forest owners, and because they are more difficult and expensive to enforce, compliance is likely to be low. Burdensome and unenforceable laws spawn evasion, illegality, and corruption. A distressing example of a lose-lose consequence occurs when it is easier to get a permit for forest conversion than for forest management—reportedly the case in Brazil, Indonesia (FWI and GFW 2002), and elsewhere. This leads loggers to clear-cut and abandon plots that they would have been content to harvest selectively.

Community Control of Forests—Balancing Rights and Responsibilities

Centralized control of forests is increasingly considered untenable. Central authorities have difficulty defending forests against residents with little incentive to maintain someone else's resource. Central authorities are also viewed as being subject to capture by loggers and other vested interests.

Devolving forest control into local hands is seen as having equity dimensions—locals get a larger share of resource rents and efficiency benefits—with tenure, and locals are more likely to manage the resource for long-term yields. In addition, locals have a deep understanding of local forest resources.[3] Finally, indigenous and local people may hold traditional rights to these forests.

On the other hand, there are potential trade-offs in devolving forests to local management. Devolution processes may be imperfect, with national authorities relinquishing poor-quality forests but maintaining control over rich ones. Moreover, local residents often lack management capacity. Local elites may wrest forest control away from the poorest, and local leaders may be as susceptible to corruption and capture as agents of the national government. Although communities may have an incentive to maintain local environmental goods, such as watershed protection, they cannot necessarily be expected to take into account regional, national, and international externalities such as biodiversity loss and carbon emissions. Communities also might not be expected to engage in sustainable management of resources, such as old-growth timber or rare animals, that fetch high prices but reproduce slowly.

This section discusses several types of decentralization and devolution, following a spectrum of increasing rights transfer and drawing in part on a recent review by Shyamsundar, Araral, and Weeraratne (2005).

Indigenous Populations Seem to Limit Deforestation

Devolution to indigenous communities is a case of special importance. The International Labour Organization's Convention 169
(on Indigenous and Tribal Peoples), which went into force in 1991,
reflects the growing attention paid to indigenous rights and issues.
The convention stresses the central importance of land to such populations, and requires that "the rights of ownership and possession
of the peoples concerned over the lands which they traditionally
occupy shall be recognized." But the convention has only been rati-
fied by 17 countries. The convention has had particular resonance
in Latin America, where it has been associated with shifts toward
devolution in Bolivia, Brazil, Colombia, Costa Rica, Panama, Paraguay, and Peru (Roldan Ortega 2004). As noted, indigenous land
rights have also been recognized in a number of nonsignatory
countries.

Limited evidence suggests that, other things being equal, indigenous forest ownership can be associated with significantly lower
deforestation. The reason is debated. It could be that national governments treat indigenous areas as if they were protected, guarding
them against encroachment by outsiders but also restricting conversion and degradation by residents. It could also be that indigenous
people place a higher value on forest maintenance than outside
colonists, use more benign and appropriate technologies for land
and forest management, or have less contact with markets. Or indigenous lands may simply have extremely low population densities,
and indigenous people may be unwilling (or not permitted) to sell
or rent their land to others.

The Brazilian study by Nepstad and others (2006) shows that
indigenous areas have much lower deforestation rates than surround-
ing areas. The protective effect of these areas shows up clearly in
maps of fire incidence, which show, in effect, flames lapping at edges
of reserves. The authors show that the protective effect of indigenous
reserves declines with increasing population density and increasing time that indigenous groups have been in contact with Western
society—but remains significant even for higher population densities
and longer contact times. Stocks, McMahan, and Taber (2006) argue
that in Nicaragua, indigenous people have different and more forest-
friendly land use technologies than do colonists and can defend their
land from colonists even in the absence of state support.

Decentralization to Local Governments Has Mixed Results

Some countries are moving forest management authority from central to local governments, often as part of broader decentralization programs. Examples include Bolivia, Guatemala, Honduras, Indonesia, Malawi, and Zimbabwe. Results are mixed, especially for forest conservation. Given the chance, local populations may prefer to rapidly exploit forest resources if returns are high (Pacheco 2002; Colchester 2006). And local governments may be as incapable, or as subject to elite capture, as national ones.

Andersson (2003) examined 50 Bolivian *municipios* with the mandate and funding to administer local forests. He found that the governments were much more likely to pay attention to forest administration if pressured by central government oversight, nongovernmental organizations (NGOs), or communities. But forestry issues ranked low on community priorities, so such pressures were typically not exerted. Early accounts of Indonesian decentralization paint a picture of local officials with little accountability to their constituency, resulting in increased logging (Larson 2004). A more recent study paints a much brighter picture, showing a tremendous increase in the proportion of community members who benefit from logging (Palmer and Engel 2006).

Community Forests Vary a Lot in Structure and Outcomes

In a recent trend, some countries are sharing responsibility for administration of state-owned forests with local communities—or have transferred ownership outright. This represents a transfer of management of a significant portion of the Earth's surface. Although some prominent examples provide a sense of the achievements and shortcomings, rigorous evaluation data are almost entirely lacking.

The largest and best-known example is probably India's Joint Forest Management program—a complex experience that eludes easy summary. Although there were precursors, nationwide adoption of the program grew out of the National Forest Policy of 1988. By 2005 Joint Forest Management covered 27 percent of the national forest area across 27 states (17.3 million hectares) and included more than 8 million families—half belonging to scheduled tribes and castes. Although program rules differ by state, they give communities access to forests for fuelwood, fodder, and other extractive products and grant them a proportion of revenue from commercial timber sales. But more degraded, less commercially valuable forests are the most likely to be put under the program.

One review paper found that Joint Forestry Management improves forest regeneration in these settings (Murali, Murthy, and Ravindranath 2002). Several papers suggest that it has a positive impact on livelihoods (Sarin and others 1998; Shyamsundar and Bandyopadhyay 2004; Köhlin and Amacher 2005). A recent study suggested institutional reforms that might increase the program's benefits for communities—suggestions that might apply even outside India (World Bank 2005). These include providing longer-term, more secure tenure arrangements, giving communities a larger share of revenue from commercial forest products, and strengthening the legal basis for the program, which in many states is based on a mutable executive order rather than legislation.

Nepal's community forestry arrangements give more control to communities. Gautam, Shivakoti, and Webb (2004) studied the Nepalese experience over 1976–2000. They found that the highest net improvement and gain in forest cover occurred in semigovernment forests (area legally under the forest department but with de facto control and ownership claims by local communities or municipalities), followed by formalized community forests (including leasehold), with government-run forests faring least well. Schweik, Nagendra, and Sinha (2003) similarly found that community management explained the persistence of forests in areas that would otherwise be under deforestation pressure. Somanathan, Prabhakar, and Metha (2005), studying an unusual Indian setting akin to Nepal's, found that community-run forests fared much better than open-access forests and as well as government-run forests, despite being much cheaper to administer. But Malla (2000) shows that after implementation of community forestry, poor Nepalese lost their privileged access to forest products (such as fuelwood) because the forest user group shared those products equally among all households. This observation is common among observers of community devolution and highlights the reality of intracommunity political and economic inequality.

In Mexico about 80 percent of forests are owned by indigenous communities and by nonindigenous communities called *ejidos*. Each forest is owned as common property by the formal members of the communities. Although ownership dates to the early 20th century or before, the Mexican government has transferred substantial management authority to the communities only over the past two decades. By 2002 more than a quarter of the 8,500 communities with forests were engaged in formally recognized commercial forestry, with lack of technical skills impeding its wider diffusion (International Tropical Timber Council 2005). But Antinori and Bray (2005) report that some communities have mastered a progression of skills, moving from sales of standing timber to felled logs to sawn wood to wood products.

Despite these successes, deforestation remains high in the forest communities, at about 1.7 percent a year over 1993–2000 (Fernandez and Munoz 2006). Most deforestation results from conversion to pasture or cropland, not from timber extraction. In many cases this reflects a failure of communities to restrict activities by people who are fellow residents but not formal community members and thus difficult to control.

During the 1990s Guatemala placed almost 500,000 hectares of forest in the Petén region under 13 community-managed concessions, with substantial donor funding (Nittler and Tschinkel 2005). Although corruption and incapacity have been a problem in this remote region lacking strong community organization, these enterprises are profitable—often highly so, due to valuable stands of mahogany. Almost all the enterprises are certified by the Forest Stewardship Council (FSC), although the mahogany extraction rate may not be fully sustainable. A striking impact is that deforestation within the concession areas appears to be much lower than outside them or in protected areas.

In highly degraded areas of Tanzania, new government policies and law reforms enabled local villagers to redevelop their *ngitili* (fodder and grazing reserves; Monela and others 2004). As a result fuelwood collection times fell by two to six hours a day per household, fodder and wood availability increased (including for poor people), flora and fauna became more abundant, and local income and investment rose significantly. WRI (2005) cautions, however, that tenure insecurity could threaten the program's long-term sustainability.

Finally, Papua New Guinea presents a warning that formal legal tenure is insufficient to guarantee favorable outcomes. All the country's land is held by indigenous communities, who are permitted to grant industrial loggers access under what are supposed to be highly regulated conditions. But a summary of government-commissioned, independent reviews found poor enforcement of and compliance with regulations (Forest Trends 2006). None of the loggers secured informed consent from landowners, and none set up a sustainable timber harvest system. Cash royalties are not equitably or transparently distributed and are not being invested for community welfare. Moreover, promised infrastructure is generally not fully delivered.

Community Forest Management Presents Challenges

Timber is, for the most part, the most valuable resource available to forest communities. But even if communities have rights to that timber, they face hurdles if it is to both provide income and motivate forest conservation.

The first hurdle involves geography and markets, which determine the value of the resource and the cost of defending it. In frontier and transfrontier areas, big and valuable trees remain, but it may be difficult to get them to market or protect them against poachers. Some places are blessed with precious woods such as mahogany, or with high densities of less valuable but still marketable trees. But many tropical forests are a heterogeneous mix of species without established markets. Markets are closer in mosaiclands, boosting timber values, but forests are more depleted and conversion to crops or plantations is a greater threat (or opportunity).

Second, the community has to prefer sustainable management—and not everyone shares that preference (see chapter 2). Discount rates in developing countries are typically 25 percent or more (GEF 2006), while logged-over forests tend to grow in value more slowly. So rather than spare seed trees or small trees from the axe, forest dwellers may prefer to liquidate these resources, using the proceeds to finance their children's education, migration, or other higher-return investments. But communities with abundant forest, or strong cultural and subsistence ties to it, may be content to manage it sustainably for a wide range of benefits.

Third, communities need people with management and marketing skills. If communities decide to sell stumpage to outside loggers, they need legal and negotiating skills. If they manage their forests themselves, and especially if they set up sawmills or other processing facilities, they need sophisticated technical and financial skills. These capabilities are often lacking in remote forest areas with poor access to education.

Finally, communities need effective and equitable ways of organizing themselves. They need to set rules for accessing forests and sharing benefits, and monitor and enforce compliance (Ostrom 1990; Baland and Platteau 1996; Agrawal 2001; Gibson, Williams, and Ostrom 2005). While some forest communities have centuries-old traditions to draw on, others are communities in name only—assemblages of recent migrants who face greater challenges in building the needed trust and internal organization. Elite capture is a grave risk in both settings. It is inevitable that wealthier, better educated, more politically connected community members will exercise disproportionate control over forests, but this control can be more or less benign. In the worst cases, corrupt leaders sell or seize community resources for private gain, often in collusion with outside interests.

But as discussed, some communities have surmounted these obstacles. While a community's social capital appears to play a deep role in its success, public policies can help. Scherr, White, and Kaimowitz (2003) provide a detailed overview of options. Provision of secure forest rights is a basic prerequisite. Through training, governments and aid agencies can build technical capacity for forest management. There could be a public role in marketing. For instance, popularizing less-known tree species can increase the value of forests. Reducing transport costs can also make forestry more profitable, though it could tip landholders toward agriculture.

Improving forest governance at the local and national levels is also crucial (Ribot 2002, 2003). This could involve interventions at the community level to deter elite capture by making local leaders downwardly and upwardly accountable. A thicker web of reporting, transparency, and accountability relationships is presumed to help, as is local democracy. Again, the forest agenda merges with the broader governance agenda.

Regulating community forests poses special challenges. Colchester (2006) shows how onerous regulations can burden communities. In Bolivia complying with logging regulations can cost a community $20,000 to start and $8,000 a year after that. Avoiding such regulations imposes costs, either in limited marketing opportunities or bribes to officials. An obvious answer is to minimize the burden on communities through simpler rules. Contreras and Peter (2006) provide examples from Guatemala, The Gambia, and elsewhere. But when community forests are near more heavily regulated industrial concessions, it can lead to "leakage" of industrial logging into community forests.

Why should communities be subject to any kind of forest regulation? Regulation could be justified as protecting community forests against exploitation by outsiders or community elites. Or it could be a protection against myopia—a public decision that people should not allow their high discount rates to induce them to sacrifice future production for current consumption. Or sustainability restrictions could reflect a decision that communities should bear part of the social cost of providing the environmental benefits of forest. These rationales, and the trade-offs among social protection, environmental protection, and income potential require careful consideration in framing restrictions on the ability of communities to use their forests.

Private Property—Especially in Mosaiclands

Rights to land are not the same as rights to trees. Landowners, in mosaiclands and beyond, may have secure tenure but still face restrictions on tree cutting, for the public good. For instance, there is a strong environmental rationale for maintaining vegetation near rivers and streams and on steep hillsides (see chapter 4). Many countries limit landowners' rights to clear riverrine or hillside vegetation, and may require permits or management plans for any kind of tree cutting (table 6.3). But these restrictions are often poorly enforced.

Carrots often work better than sticks—if you can afford the carrots. A wide range of programs and policies seek to change landholders' incentives for forest maintenance over degradation by

Table 6.3   Latin American Countries Impose Varying Restrictions on Deforestation of Private Property

Country	Width of protected buffer around watercourses (meters)	Degree of protected slopes	Size of property requiring forestry plan
Argentina	100	> 20	No information
Brazil	30–500	> 45	No information
Bolivia	10–100	> 45	> 3 hectares
Chile	100–200	> 45	20–1,000 hectares
Costa Rica	10–50	n.a.	> 2 hectares
Ecuador	50	n.a.	All properties
Peru	50	n.a.	All properties

Source: Environmental Law Institute 2003, p. 32.
Note: n.a. = not applicable

offering them money or technical assistance. This section discusses two such approaches:

- Promotion of greener agricultural technologies to make mosaiclands more like forests.

- Environmental service payments and other payments to landholders conditioned on forest status or environmental conditions.

Greener Agriculture: A Technical Fix?

Can farmers benefit by enhancing the amount of biodiversity on their lands? And if so, are they aware of it? This debate often gets muddled by the ambiguity of the term biodiversity. Farmers can benefit from having larger portfolios of cultivated biodiversity. Rice crops become more profitable, for instance, when different strains are mixed together.

Less clear is whether there is an advantage to having more "wild" biodiversity. Some people (Rosenzweig 2001; McNeely and Scherr 2003) argue, plausibly, that some agricultural technologies favor wild biodiversity while also promoting farm profitability or reducing risk. It's further plausible that market forces might not, unassisted, spur the invention and diffusion of these technologies. If so, policy might fill these gaps. To return to figure 5.1, the goal is to improve over point C.

Although systematic evidence is lacking, there are indications that these win-win technologies exist. But policies might be needed to overcome barriers to their adoption. Vosti, Gockowski, and Tomich (2005) contrast a land use system in the Sumatran forest with a potential alternative. Sumatrans have long practiced rubber agroforestry, enriching secondary forest with rubber trees. This maintains far higher biodiversity than in monoculture oil palm, a competing land use. But returns to land planted with traditional rubber material are low. Improved rubber clones could drastically boost the profitability of rubber agroforestry, allowing it to compete with oil palm plantations. But problems in creating markets for seedlings, together with credit market failures, are blamed for the failure of this model to take off.

The pastures of Central and South America provide another example. Pastures are poor in biodiversity and carbon storage relative to the forests they replace. Yet there is more biodiversity in them than meets the eye. Farmers plant trees as living fences, allow them to persist on hillsides, and suffer a few to remain in pasture. Harvey and others (2005) have found that these trees harbor substantial bird life while providing shade that improves the health of livestock. Pagiola and others (2004) hypothesize that silvopastoral systems (which involve planting more trees in pasture) could improve ranch profits, sustainability, and labor demand by providing fodder, fruit, nutrients, and nitrogen fixation. But ranchers—facing large upfront costs of planting, a four-year wait for the trees to mature, and uncertainty about the viability of the systems—see mediocre investment returns and substantial risk. The Regional Integrated Silvopastoral Ecosystem Management Project (RISEMP), discussed below, is testing whether one-time payments to adopt these systems will lead to their retention and diffusion. The hypothesis is that once the trees are in place, the higher income they produce will ensure that they are maintained.

Integrated pest management is another win-win technology that faces barriers to adoption. Using pesticides in forest-agriculture mosaiclands not only damages biodiversity, it also sickens and kills farmers. Integrated pest management is an appealing alternative. It uses natural antagonists to get rid of pests—at low cost and with a substantial reduction in pesticide use. But adoption has been slow. One problem is coordination: it is nearly useless to be the only farmer in a neighborhood using integrated pest management. Neighbors' pesticides will kill your beneficial bugs. Everyone has to adopt at the same time. The need for collective action is a hurdle that not all communities can surmount. (One way of reducing that hurdle would be to ensure that prices of pesticides and herbicides fully reflect their societal costs.)

In sum, there could be a range of win-win technologies that improve incomes and environmental outcomes, especially in agriculture-forest mosaiclands. There is inadequate investment in research, development, and diffusion of these technologies, because they could be difficult to protect through patents or other means. (Genetically engineered plants could be an exception.) Much more research is needed to compile, develop, and test such technologies.

Economic Instruments and Markets for Environmental Services Provide Alternatives to Command and Control

The starting point for an approach to conservation based on direct incentives assumes that landholders have some rights to modify or cut their trees. It is then up to others—perhaps downstream residents, perhaps society as a whole—to provide incentives for the landholders to manage their land and trees in a way that provides benefits (or reduces costs) to others in society. For instance:

- Urban residents may pay upstream farmers to reduce sediment in drinking water sources, to lower costs of water treatment.

- Society may compensate landholders for maintaining or improving biodiversity-friendly habitats.

- Firms required to reduce carbon emissions may pay landholders to reduce emissions from deforestation or to sequester carbon in regenerating forests.

- "Run of river" hydroelectric plant owners may pay landowners to maintain forests in a way that promotes stable water flows.

These incentive-based or economic instrument strategies could yield more efficient land management than do command-and-control approaches. They do so by eliciting information from landholders on the true value of land under alternative uses, then motivating conservation only if the value to society of doing so is more than the value to landholders of putting the land into agriculture. If society has flexibility in meeting its environmental goals, economic instruments can reduce the cost of meeting them.

Because the use of economic instruments for land management is still new in the developing world, reviewing some actual and proposed examples will help ground the discussion of their potential implementation.

Transferable Forest Protection Obligations in Brazil[4]

An emerging topic of policy discussion in Brazil is the possibility of shifting from a command and control system of forest regulation to an economic system of tradable rights found in other environmental spheres, such as fishing management and pollution regulation. For more than 70 years Brazilian landholders have been obliged to maintain a portion of each rural property under natural vegetation. This requirement is 20 percent in southern states and 80 percent in Amazônian forest. The legal reserve requirement supplements a separate requirement to maintain riverrine and hillside forest.

But the reserve requirement has not been strictly enforced. In many agriculturally dynamic locales aggregate forest cover has dropped well below 20 percent. These areas now face increasing pressure to enforce the regulation. But compliance will be expensive if landholders are required to abandon valuable plantings. And on heavily farmed properties with little remaining natural vegetation, the rate and quality of natural regeneration might be extremely slow, so biodiversity gains might be minimal. On the other hand, forests and woodlands—often with high biodiversity values—remain in more remote and less favorable regions. Yet deforestation continues there, often for low-value extensive pasture, with charcoal as a by-product from clearing. In many of these forests, deforestation remains legal down to the reserve requirement.

As enforcement pressure increased in the 1990s, it occurred to many people that the property-wise legal reserve requirement, while well motivated, was neither economically nor environmentally efficient. Why not allow out-of-compliance landholders to meet their obligations by protecting land of more biodiversity value but less agricultural value? Landholders with more than 20 percent forest cover could be rewarded with the right to sell legal reserve services (equivalent to development rights) from their "excess" forest.

Chomitz, Thomas, and Brandao (2005) simulated the impact of such a plan for the state of Minas Gerais. They found that relative to command and control rules, a tradable rights scheme would cut compliance costs by up to two-thirds and protect up to one-third more forest designated as being a high conservation priority. Gains were greater when the ambit of permitted trades widened from microwatershed to river basin to biome.

Could this kind of tradable obligation system be widely adopted? In Brazil, where other states are examining this approach, the long history of the legal reserve obligation is an important contributing factor. Other countries might start with long-standing but sporadically enforced prohibitions on tree cutting. Relaxing and making flexible these obligations might be welcomed as an improvement by landholders and lead to preferred environmental outcomes. A point in favor of the approach is that it represents a social compromise between the extremes of assigning landholders complete rights to their trees versus none.

Examples of Environmental Service Programs

In contrast, payments for environmental service programs take as their starting point landholders' full rights—in fact or in law—to plant, maintain, or cut trees on their property. People affected by those decisions offer conditional payments for maintaining trees. An environmental rationale for these programs distinguishes them from the more frequent, well-funded practice of subsidizing plantation forestry as an industrial or development strategy.

A diverse set of environmental service programs are under way in the developing world. A few snapshots:

- Costa Rica's pathbreaking system is probably the most famous (Chomitz, Brenes, and Constantino 1999; Pagiola 2005). It grew out of a 1996 forestry law that recognized forest environmental services such as carbon sequestration, biodiversity, hydrological regulation, and provision of scenic beauty. Landholders volunteer to participate; those selected receive about $45 a hectare per year to maintain forests. FONAFIFO, a government agency, funds the program from a variety of sources. Some of these conform to the model of paying for environmental service: a grant from the Global Environment Facility to conserve biodiversity and payments from hydropower plants to maintain watersheds. But a national fuel tax provides most of the funding. About 240,000 hectares are under contract.

- Mexico introduced payments for hydrological environmental services in 2003 (Muñoz-Piña and others 2005). Similar to the Costa Rican program, but motivated by concerns about water scarcity and quality, it rewards landholders for forest conservation, paying $27 a hectare per year to conserve cloud forest and $18 for other types. The program was initially funded by an $18 million earmark on water fees.

- China's sloping land program is one of the world's largest environmental service payment programs (Xu and others 2004; Bennett 2005). The program, initiated in 1999, was motivated by concern over severe sedimentation: sloping farmlands generate 1.3 billion tons of sediment a year in the Yangtze and Yellow rivers, which was believed to have been a major cause of the Yangtze floods of 1998. The program offers seedlings, cash, and grain to farmers who retire marginal or steep, erosion-prone farmland, replanting it with grass, fruit-bearing trees, or trees for timber. Nominal per-hectare incentives are two to three times the mean value of payments in the analogous U.S. program (Conservation Reserve Program), though a survey found shortfalls in payments (Xu and others 2004). More than 7 million hectares were enrolled in the program's first five years, with another 7 million planned.

- RISEMP, which began in 2002 in Colombia, Costa Rica, and Nicaragua, is testing whether payments for environmental services can catalyze permanent adoption of silvopastoral systems (see above; Pagiola and others 2004, 2006). The project pays landholders for environmentally beneficial changes in land cover. An ecological index establishes a point value for each type of land cover based on a rough assessment of its significance for biodiversity and carbon storage. For instance, degraded pasture is worth 0 points a hectare, native pasture without trees 0.2, native pasture with trees 1.0, and young secondary vegetation 1.4 points. Landholders receive $75 a point per year for changes, for up to four years. After two years the share of the project area considered to be improved "pasture with high tree density" had tripled from its initial 5 percent. In addition, the ecological index for the area rose 42 percent.

These, and a host of smaller programs worldwide, are pioneering efforts to solve the complex questions of collective action running through this chapter. Their early successes and shortcomings offer lessons for current and would-be designers of systems providing payments for environmental services.

Designing Environmental Service Payments

Three sets of design issues shape the feasibility and impact of a system to provide payments for environmental services:

- *Financing:* is there demand for the environmental service, and can people organize themselves to pay for it?

- *Structuring the payments:* who is eligible, for how much, and under what conditions?

- *Logistics:* is it possible to cost-effectively collect funds, make payments and monitor compliance with conditions for payment?

Financing. Ultimately, buyers have to believe in the services they are buying. The case for domestically funded payments, as the examples suggest, is largely based on the promise of hydrological benefits. Sensible enough: clean, plentiful water commands a large constituency. But the link between tree protection and water benefits can be tenuous. Systems predicated on questionable assumptions—for instance, that forest maintenance will increase water flows—could backfire if they fail to deliver promised services. Monitoring, modeling, learning, and adjusting the system are essential if programs based on subtle services are to succeed.

Suppose people are convinced that they will benefit from an environmental service. They still might not be willing to pay for it if they think it is possible to free ride. For instance, all the residents of a broad plain can enjoy scenic vistas of a forested mountainside, even if they individually fail to contribute to forest conservation. To overcome this obstacle, beneficiaries need to organize themselves and commit to sharing the costs.

Sometimes there will be a ready-made institutional solution. When the New York City Water Authority buys water on behalf of its clients, it can build the cost of watershed protection into the rates it charges. Often government is a natural choice for financing the public good, especially one whose benefits are widely enjoyed. But where internal controls are weak, government administration can be problematic.

Structuring the payments. Defining payment rules for a government-coordinated environmental services payment program can entail a struggle between technical efficiency and political viability. Economic efficiency requires keeping forest on properties whose environmental value exceeds their value as cropland. Fiscal efficiency requires minimizing payments to landholders who would have maintained their services in any case. Both kinds of efficiency can be approached through auctions. For instance, in the U.S. Conservation Reserve Program, landholders submit bids specifying the environmental services they can provide and the lowest rate they will accept. The government ranks the bids by cost-effectiveness, funding from the top of the list until the budget is exhausted (box 6.2).

But efficiency doesn't always win support. A focus on efficiency directs attention to special spots—those with the most threatened species or highest erosion rates. If these places are in the minority, there will be pressure to extend the benefits more broadly. There

---

Box 6.2   Self-assembling Biodiversity Corridors: Reconciling Voluntary Participation Decisions with Landscape-level Goals

Biodiversity survival depends on connected habitat (box 4.1). But what kind of policies can induce landholders to create these connections? Conservation planners have developed sophisticated methods for laying out biodiversity corridors and reserve networks that allow thriving wildlife populations. But it is difficult to make landholders comply with such plans. Even if funding is available for compensation, an obstinate landholder could block the formation of a planned corridor. Programs that make payments for environmental services, in contrast, have the virtue of voluntarism. But how can uncoordinated responses result in a connected, viable corridor?

A simulation by Chomitz and others (2006) suggests that this might be easier than it seems in conditions typical of biodiversity hotspots. The simulation addressed conservation in the Atlantic forest of Bahia, Brazil—a place with high species richness and endemism and extreme fragmentation. The authors introduced flexibility into the conservation problem by specifying a biological goal: increase the number and geographic diversity of connected forest patches large enough to support a viable population of primates.

They proposed a hypothetical, auction-based system to make payments for environmental services, modeled after the U.S. Conservation Reserve Program and Australia's BushTender (Stoneham and others 2003). In this system, a conservation agency solicits offers from landowners. The landowners name a price at which they would be willing to accept a conservation contract for their property, retaining ownership but protecting existing forest and promoting forest regrowth. Their property is also rated, on a point system, for environmental benefits. The agency then ranks the landowners' bids on the basis of environmental benefit points per dollar, funding the highest ranked bid until its budget is exhausted.

Chomitz and others (2006) found that relatively modest budgets could theoretically elicit the formation of self-assembling biodiversity corridors, as contracted properties coalesced into viable, connected forest patches. The reason is that in Bahia, which has suffered substantial deforestation, remaining forest is often a marker for plots with low land value. Because of isolation or poor soil quality, such places occur in clumps. By focusing on goals (viable habitats) rather than means (a prespecified corridor plan), it might be possible to reconcile voluntarism with conservation planning.

Source: Chomitz and others 2006.

---

will be strong temptation to use the program to meet social goals such as poverty alleviation and strong pressure to direct it toward elites and well-connected groups.

Another targeting dilemma is related to moral hazard. Payments will be most effective in delivering services if they focus on areas most at risk of deforestation. This tends to exclude landholders who, out of conviction or by default, have preserved their forests. Finally, auction systems and targeting systems result in differentiated payments. Some landholders get more money, either because they are providing more services or because their opportunity costs are higher. But despite firm economic justification, differentiated payments may be perceived as inequitable, nontransparent, costly to administer, or subject to manipulation.

The tension between implementation and efficiency issues was evident in the initial design of Mexico's payment program for hydrological services (Muñoz-Piña and others 2005; Alix-Garcia and others 2005) and Costa Rica's (Chomitz, Brenes, and Constantino 1999). Although the Mexican program's rationale emphasized protecting forests in recharge areas of water-scarce basins, at least 85 percent of payments went to basins known to be underexploited (Alix-Garcia and others 2005). Both countries used simple flat payment systems rather than auctions or highly differentiated payments. Flat payments might be expected to result in adverse selection, attracting landholders with no intention or opportunity to convert their land to agriculture. In fact, only about 10 percent of the Mexican contracts went to the 20 percent of areas with the highest predicted risk of deforestation. There is evidence of similar outcomes in Costa Rica. In both countries demand for payments far exceeds supply.

Logistics and administration. Although the logistics of environmental payment systems are daunting, Costa Rica and other countries have shown that it is possible to create such systems. A basic remaining problem is reducing transactions costs. There are fixed costs associated with drawing up contracts, making payments, and verifying compliance. Consequently, it is cheaper to enroll large properties. Zbinden and Lee (2004) show that such properties are overrepresented in Costa Rica's program.

There are two related ways to cut these costs. One is to explore the tradeoffs involved in detailed specification of management plans and payment criteria—do gains from theoretical efficiency outweigh added transactions costs? RISEMP considers this issue, assessing the benefits of tying payments to detailed measurements of carbon and biodiversity benefits. Many more such experiments are needed.

The second way to reduce costs is by using modern technologies. Mato Grosso's SLAPR program (see "Setting the Stage" after the Overview) used Global Positioning System (GPS) technology to map the locations of enrolled properties, and satellite monitoring to check compliance with forest obligations. The original program design envisioned public disclosure of enrollment and monitoring information. Failure to use such oversight may have contributed to the program's problems.

The three design questions—finance, structure of payments, logistics—all bear on the implications of such payment programs for poor people (Pagiola, Arcenas, and Platais 2005). It would be inequitable to ask the poor to finance these programs if wealthier people were the source of the externality in question. In that case there may be an argument for government to finance the services from general revenue, as a means of improving poor people's income or decreasing their vulnerability. Poor people can also benefit as service providers. Pagiola, Arcenas, and Platais (2005) argue convincingly that environmental services, not poverty, must be the basis for payments. Otherwise a program could fail to provide the services it promises. The challenge is to reduce barriers to participation by qualified poor people. Those include information barriers and economies of scale in participation. Community groups can help solve those problems.

Mexico's program provides an interesting example of reduced transactions costs and possibly of the spatial coincidence of poverty and environmental services. As noted, most forests in Mexico are owned by communities, and for these forests the program paid entire communities—lowering transactions costs relative to dealing with many smallholders. Although early suggestions to make poverty an explicit criterion for payments were rejected, 83 percent of contracts (weighted by enrolled area) went to communities with high or very high marginalization (Alix-Garcia and others 2005). But it is not yet clear whether poor communities are more likely to provide real services—that is, an actual reduction in deforestation combined with a real link between forest cover and hydrological services.

Other Development Policies with Forest Spillovers

Often policies conceived outside the confines of forestry have important implications for land use and for the incomes of forest dwellers.

Road Planning Can Ease Poverty-Environment Tradeoffs

Planning and regulating rural roads may present a trade-off between poverty alleviation and conservation. Building roads in forest areas can lead to deforestation. It also accelerates deforestation, as new roads branch out from old ones.

Yet roads also stimulate agricultural production and can alleviate poverty. Roads are favorite investments for local communities and politicians, especially in remote areas. Consider Papua, Indonesia, a forest-rich province with few people and few roads. After fiscal reforms in 1999, the province was flush with cash from increased revenue sharing and rents from oil and mining operations. The province devoted more than a fifth of its development spending to roads, extending its paved network by 20 percent in just three years.

Grappling with this trade-off requires political decisions at levels corresponding to the road under consideration. Building new or improved roads through forest areas can profoundly affect regional development and the environment by triggering follow-on offshoots of roads in forests. These roads could set the world's few large, relatively undisturbed tracts of tropical forest on a trajectory toward long-term fragmentation and loss. Examples of such roads under discussion or planning include BR163 in Brazil and trans-Kalimantan highways in Indonesia. In the Democratic Republic of Congo rehabilitation of the collapsed road infrastructure is sure to be part of the long-run development strategy. Elsewhere, mining and logging can open new roads in trackless areas. And it is important to remember von Thünen's lesson: that road improvements near markets or ports are transmitted through the entire network, affecting deforestation hundreds of miles away (see chapter 2).

Now is the time for long-term planning, including road planning, for remaining transfrontier areas. This planning should steer conversion pressures toward areas with higher agricultural potential and away from areas with unique biodiversity or environmental characteristics. If planning starts now, it may be possible to develop a rational, widely shared vision of a forest region's potential and to build constituencies for conservation and sustainable use. But if planning is delayed, it may be too late. After colonists arrive, and after forestlands begin to offer significant rents, strong political constituencies form for deforestation. It is easier to clarify ownership while the forest still has negligible value, before disputes arise.

In frontier areas there may be opportunities to tie road construction or upgrades to changes in forest tenure or protection (Ledec and Posas 2006). A good example is the construction of the San José–Guápiles Highway in Costa Rica. Planned when deforestation was high, this major road had the potential to trigger it on hydrologically sensitive slopes. But establishment of the Braulio Carrillo National Park, before the road was constructed, has protected the area.

In mosaiclands road construction may tend to target remaining forest stands because doing so requires less disturbance of fields and settlements. Here a possible solution is to apply compensatory rules, requiring set-asides or regeneration of sites equivalent to (or larger than) the forest to be cleared.

Can Local Development Reduce Local Forest Pressure?

As a rule, development and deforestation propagate outward from towns and intensive agricultural areas. But as with many rules, there are possible exceptions. Local development could attract workers away from nearby marginal forestlands. If local people maintain reasonably secure tenure over those lands or there are barriers to migration, it could result in abandonment of farming in the marginal forestlands.

There are indications of such processes at work in Southeast Asia. Shively and Pagiola (2004) describe an interesting natural experiment in southern Palawan, a forest frontier of the Philippines, using panel data on household income and activities. There, upland dwellers at the forest margin live within commuting distance of lowland populations in fertile, deforested river valleys. Between 1995 and 1999 nearly all the lowland farms were converted to irrigated rice production, enabling a shift to multicropping. As a result lowland farmers nearly tripled their employment of uplanders. The uplanders, now better employed, reduced by about half their rate of forest clearance and intensified production on their plots. At last report there was not a compensating influx of immigrants to augment forest clearing on the upland frontier.

Müller and Zeller (2002) report similar dynamics for two districts of the Central Highlands of Vietnam, using remote sensing data on land cover. There too there was paddy rice production in valleys, surrounded by shifting cultivation in hillsides and uplands. From 1975–92 paddy and shifting cultivation expanded at the expense of open forest. During the 1990s substantial investments in roads, irrigation, and rice technologies led to a tripling of the rice yield. In addition, new crops were introduced. Shifting cultivation apparently gave way to permanent cropping. Grasslands reverted to secondary forest. Müller and Zeller attribute these developments to the labor-absorbing impact of intensified production techniques, despite population growth. But the authors note that this outcome contrasted with continued deforestation in nearby districts, where soils were better suited to high-value crops such as coffee and pepper. This pattern underscores the lesson that increased agricultural productivity reduces deforestation only where the labor supply or commodity demand is rather limited.

Policies Affecting Agricultural Prices

Macroeconomic policy making involves balancing interests between sectors and between producers and consumers. Because of the macroeconomy's complexity, it can be difficult to trace the repercussions of policy shocks. Perhaps the easiest to trace, and most relevant to this report, are those that affect the prices of forest-competing commodities.

Higher prices for forest-competing commodities should increase pressure for deforestation, unless those prices attract deforesters away from yet more forest-damaging activities. These effects should be most evident at the forest frontier, because a small change in prices at an urban port or market translates into a large proportional change at the frontier. Consider again the example of Brazilian Amazônia (see figure 2.1). Deforestation rates were much higher near markets, where beef fetches up to 800 reais a ton, than at the frontier, where it commands only 400 reais a ton because of transport costs. At 400 reais a ton, farmers barely break even (Arima, Barreto, and Brito 2006). If the price of beef rises by 80 reais a ton at the market, profits of periurban farmers increase 20 percent. Transmitted down to the frontier, this increase transforms worthless (for agriculture) transfrontier forest into land worth ranching. Arima, Barreto, and Brito (2006) calculate that a 10 percent increase in the urban price would extend the frontier of cattle ranching by 260,000 square kilometers. And it would increase the area of high profitability and high deforestation (where the farmgate price of beef exceeds 600 reais a ton) by almost 600,000 square kilometers.

In Brazil—the only tropical country with good annual data on deforestation—this prediction is consistent with recent macroeconomic and price changes. A substantial devaluation at the beginning of 1999 was followed by increases in world prices of three important export commodities: beef, soybeans, and pig iron (which in Brazil is produced, in part, using forest charcoal rather than mineral coke). At the same time, hoof and mouth disease restrictions on Amazônian cattle movement have been eased (Kaimowitz and others 2004). Together these changes greatly increased incentives for deforestation, with annual deforestation rates rising from 18,000 square kilometers in 1999 to more than 26,000 square kilometers in 2003–04.[5]

Wunder and Sunderlin (2004), using less rigorous data, tell the converse story for Gabon—where currency overvaluation, the result of oil revenue, has made agriculture and deforestation relatively unattractive. Similarly, they describe how a Venezuelan oil boom over 1930–50 resulted in pasture abandonment and forest regrowth as agriculture became unattractive. Later, though, Venezuelan investments of oil revenue in frontier roads and transport subsidies led to renewed deforestation. But Jensen, Robinson, and Tarp (2004) warn that changes in exchange rate can have counterintuitive effects due to intersectoral shifts.

Wunder and Sunderlin's account of Cameroon's volatile economy bears out this point. During 1978–85, when high prices for oil, coffee, and cocoa created a boom, the net effect was an urban bias that accelerated rural-urban migration and slowed deforestation. After 1986 low prices for oil and cash crops, combined with a fixed and overvalued exchange rate, precipitated a crisis. That reversed the migration and significantly increased deforestation for crop production, more than offsetting a decline in clearing for export crops.

Madagascar also shows how changes in agricultural prices can affect deforestation and welfare. The country's southwest region experienced a boom in maize exports when European subsidies stimulated hog production on nearby Reunion Island—until Argentina's devaluation made it a lower-cost supplier of hog feed (Moser, Barrett, and Minten 2005; Minten and Méral 2005). The maize boom accounted for about a fifth of deforestation in Madagascar's southwest region; deforestation there is thought to lead to irreversible land degradation and abandonment after a few years. The boom may have contributed, at least temporarily, to higher incomes in this extremely poor region.

These examples suggest that price levers put deforestation and poverty alleviation at odds. A look at Madagascar's main staple crop, however, intimates the possibility of a nearly win-win combination, at least in theory. Even though 60 percent of the households grow rice, most of them buy more than they sell, and the country is a net rice importer (Minten and Dabat 2005). A tariff protects rice growers. Reducing the tariff would reduce the price of rice with little effect on the purely subsistence population, but it would benefit the larger part of the population who are net buyers. A lower price and more imports would ease pressures for expanding the area under rice cultivation. Although net sellers of rice would tend to lose, some ameliorative options are available. Large areas of Madagascar are constrained by transaction costs from participating in the national rice market (Dorosh and Minten 2005). Improving the country's dilapidated roads and mitigating other market failures could boost the farmgate price for growers in degraded areas (Moser, Barrett, and Minten 2005).

Summary

Managing forests is difficult because it requires balancing weak and powerful interests, concentrated and diffuse interests, and today's certainties and tomorrow's possibilities. Creating institutions that do this fairly and efficiently requires mobilizing constituencies for conservation and sustainable land management and giving voice to poor and indigenous groups. As communications and monitoring become cheaper, these groups can be empowered with information and may be able to resist resource grabs by large actors at the forest frontier. Placing frontier and transfrontier forests under clear and guaranteed stewardship—of indigenous groups, other local populations, protected area managers, or regulated concessions—is necessary but insufficient. It is essential to recognize that the steward's interests may not be perfectly aligned with the wider public interest, making some form of regulation or incentive necessary to align interests. Efficient regulation can minimize burdens on forestholders as well as costs of monitoring and enforcement.

Within the frontier, it is necessary to arrive at a workable balance between landholders' rights and responsibilities. Attempts at complete regulation of tree and forest management are unworkable. But it may be equitable and efficient to enforce some land management responsibilities on some groups of forestholders. Domestically financed payments for environmental services must be tightly focused on clearly demonstrable, locally valued services, because the ability to raise domestic funds will be limited. Turning to an international arena, however, can create new possibilities.

Endnotes

1. An emerging exception may be conservation plans for the Cape region of South Africa, which compensate landowners for reserving areas.

2. http://www.whrc.org/africa/INFORMS/study_sites/Kasyoha_Kalinzu.htm

3. Ostrom 1999; Ribot 2002; Molnar, Scherr, and Khare 2004; Colfer and Capistrano 2005; Ribot and Larson 2005.

4. This section is based on Chomitz, Thomas, and Brandao (2005).

5. Data are from INPE (http://www.obt.inpe.br/prodes/).

Clearance of tropical forest for agriculture is a major source of CO_2 emissions, contributing to global warming, and also causes local air pollution. This satellite photo shows vegetation burning near an oil palm plantation in eastern Sumatra.

Image acquired and processed by CRISP, National University of Singapore IKONOS image © CRISP 2005.

CHAPTER 7

Mobilizing Global Interests for Forest Conservation

T wo rationales for forest conservation attract a large, wealthy, worldwide constituency. All forests store carbon, so preventing deforestation can mitigate global damages from climate change. In addition, some forests harbor unique biodiversity whose survival is threatened by deforestation. The challenge for international policy is to find ways to tap these global interests to finance forest conservation, using approaches acceptable to forested countries.

Forest Carbon Finance: An Ungrasped Opportunity

Chapter 4 presented a paradox. Throughout the developing world, farmers fell trees for sometimes small and ephemeral gains, creating croplands and pastures worth perhaps a couple hundred dollars a hectare. As those trees burn and rot, they release carbon dioxide (CO_2) to the atmosphere—perhaps 500 tons a hectare in dense rainforests. Meanwhile, the European Union (EU) market values CO_2 abatement at $20 a ton.[1] In other words, farmers are destroying a $10,000 asset to create one worth $200. (While the $20 price is highly volatile, the disparity would remain even if prices plummeted. And the sum doesn't include the value of biodiversity and other environmental attributes.)

There seems to be a great opportunity for arbitrage here. Industrial countries could pay the poor farmers for forest conservation, at some amount between $200 and $10,000 a hectare, and both parties would gain. That would be a good deal for the farmers even if industrial countries' willingness to pay were at the modest price of

$2.70 a ton suggested by Yohe, Andronova, and Schlesinger (2004) as a target for global policy. Yet this opportunity remains ungrasped. Why? What are the obstacles? And can they be overcome?

Why Carbon Finance Makes Sense for Climate

The United Nations Framework Convention on Climate Change, signed by 189 countries, aims to stabilize the amount of greenhouse gases (GHGs) in the atmosphere. Greenhouse gases are increasing largely because people are burning more fuel. Thus stabilization requires a long-term shift to cleaner energy. Halting all deforestation, even if possible, would not by itself achieve the convention's goal.

But no single line of action will be sufficient to achieve that goal. Pacala and Socolow (2004) outline 15 options for reducing CO_2 emissions over the next half-century. Each option would cut emissions by about 25 billion tons during this period. Seven to ten activities of this magnitude would be required to stabilize GHGs in the atmosphere (that is, hold atmospheric concentrations of CO_2 to 500 parts per million). Reduced deforestation and increased reforestation are one option. So while containing forest carbon is no panacea for climate change, it could be part of the solution.

And it could be an important part if it is cheap. Cheapness is a virtue. We don't know how much it will cost to mitigate climate change. And we don't know how much mitigation is needed. More stringent targets for atmospheric CO_2 concentrations provide better insurance against catastrophic climate changes, but each part per million reduction will cost more than the last. Because the risks are difficult to quantify, it is hard to achieve global agreement on how much to spend and how to split the bill. Thus anything that reduces the cost of a global mitigation strategy will increase the chance that the strategy is embraced.

Why Carbon Finance Makes Sense for Forests and Rural Development

Forests may play a relatively small role in mitigating climate change, but climate change mitigation could play a large role in financing forest maintenance. Among the potential environmental services of forests, carbon sequestration has the widest applicability. That is because any action that keeps a ton of carbon out of the atmosphere has the same climatic impact no matter where it occurs. In contrast, many of the environmental services enumerated by the Millennium Ecosystem Assessment are location-specific and idiosyncratic: eco-tourism, hydrological regulation, or maintenance of globally significant biodiversity.

Carbon payments might provide significant benefits to tropical countries. Sathaye and others (forthcoming) find that over 40 years, paying $10 per ton of carbon (rising with the interest rate) would have a net present value of $150 billion in payments to developing countries for avoided deforestation. Containing forest carbon would also provide local and global benefits that would otherwise be difficult to finance—including conservation of globally significant biodiversity and of forests with spiritual or other values that are difficult to monetize. Forest carbon control might also help finance agroforestry and agricultural intensification in unforested areas.

Financing Avoided Deforestation: Problems and Solutions

The UN Framework Convention on Climate Change is responding to a submission by Costa Rica and Papua New Guinea to examine options for providing countries with incentives to avoid deforestation through forest carbon. To gain acceptance, these options will have to address, in practical ways, the objections that kept deforestation out of the Kyoto Protocol. This section lists the main concerns—and ways to deal with them. (The discussion here draws on and expands Chomitz 2002.)

"Forest Carbon Makes Mitigation Too Cheap"

Problem: At first glance this objection is hard to understand. Cheapness, as noted, is a virtue. Getting people, firms, and countries to take actions for global benefit is easier if those actions are cheaper. What drives this objection is a fear that introducing forest carbon into the Kyoto Protocol would swamp the emerging carbon market—driving prices toward zero and reducing industrial countries' incentives to shift to clean energy.

But that outcome would arise not from overly cheap mitigation. Rather, it would be the result of a timid, ineffective mitigation goal. The Kyoto Protocol currently places only moderate limits on greenhouse gas emissions from participating industrial countries. The limits for 2008–12 are perhaps a billion tons a year (CO_2 equivalent) less than would be emitted in the absence of the agreement.

Countries can try to reduce their emissions by this amount, or they can buy offsetting emission reductions abroad. Either way, the total Kyoto limit is still met. Developing countries can reduce CO_2 emissions, for instance, by switching from coal to wind power—then sell the reductions. This approach creates a market for emission reductions. The Kyoto emission limits determine the demand for these reductions, and opportunities for switching fuels and increasing efficiency in the developing world largely determine the supply.

The Kyoto Protocol doesn't allow developing countries to create emission reductions from avoided deforestation. But suppose it did and that countries could instantly create the institutions needed to reduce deforestation and that the protocol did not change its limits on total CO_2 emissions. In this unlikely set of contingencies, the supply of emission reductions would increase and their price would fall. The Kyoto emission limits would still be satisfied, and the cost of meeting them would be reduced. But the resulting low prices for CO_2 reductions would provide little benefit to developing countries and little stimulus for energy research and development.

But because the Kyoto limits are so slack, this scenario is not very relevant to policy. As it stands, Kyoto is just a pilot program. If all industrial countries (currently participating or not) met the negotiated Kyoto limits, it would merely delay the buildup of greenhouse gases by a few years. To limit CO_2 buildup to prudent levels, reductions of tens of billions of tons a year are needed by mid-century. To attempt meaningful mitigation of climate change, the protocol would have to drastically limit emission allowances. But doing so might drive the price of compliance so high that countries would refuse to sign on.

Solution: This is where cheapness comes in. By incorporating avoided deforestation into the global climate strategy, the world could afford to set a more ambitious goal for reducing CO_2 buildup. In the Kyoto context that would mean tightening emission allowances while allowing avoided deforestation as a source of emission reductions. By increasing both demand and supply, the price can stay around acceptable levels for all parties, but the climate impact is greater.

"Deforestation Avoidance Has to Be Permanent to Be Useful—but It Is Impossible to Secure Permanence"

Problem: Buyers of forest carbon want permanent agreements, while sellers want temporary ones. For buyers the problem is this. Because mitigating climate change requires stabilizing CO_2 concentrations, many people assume that every project to reduce CO_2 emissions must have a permanent effect.

Many energy projects do have permanent effects. Replacing a diesel generator with a windmill today means that less fuel will be burned this year. Even if the windmill breaks and the generator is put back in service next year, CO_2 emissions will have been reduced—the atmosphere is a little cleaner than it would have been without the windmill. But forest conservation is riskier. Forests can burn. Climate change may imperil tropical forests if temperatures rise and rainfall decreases. And drastic changes in politics or markets may lead the heirs of today's forest owners to repudiate decades-old conservation commitments. Given these risks, buyers worry that it is impossible to sign an agreement today that securely guarantees carbon sequestration into the distant future. And without such a guarantee, they see no benefit from sequestration or reduced deforestation.

Sellers, on the other hand, may not want to sign such an agreement precisely because it closes off future options. Agricultural technologies and markets change rapidly, and expanded transport networks can transform development possibilities for once remote regions. So forest owners may not want to commit to conservation forever.

Solution: Recognize that avoided deforestation is valuable even without a guarantee of permanence. Carbon sequestration doesn't have to be permanent to be part of a climate change mitigation program. There are three ways that temporary commitments to carbon sequestration buy time to act on climate change:

- Temporary sequestration buys insurance against catastrophe in the face of uncertainty. The climate system is unstable. Small changes can trigger large and irreversible impacts, such as those that apparently shifted the Sahara from being heavily vegetated to desert (Foley and others 2003; Schneider 2004). There's a fear that too much CO_2 in the atmosphere, or too rapid a rise in CO_2, could have the same kind of catastrophic effect. But we don't know the thresholds beyond which such a catastrophe could occur. In the face of such ignorance, it is prudent to buy insurance—that is, to try to keep CO_2 levels low and rising slowly.

  Gitz, Hourcade, and Ciais (2006) show that forest carbon could be a crucial, cost-effective part of a long-term climate change mitigation program. In their model, inexpensive forest carbon offers insurance over the next few decades—after which the world may be better able to assess the risk of catastrophe. If a dangerous threshold is then imminent, the world could continue to rely on forests as a carbon sink, or step up investments in geological carbon sequestration.

- Temporary sequestration could be a bridge to a clean energy future. Under Kyoto rules, industrial countries need to meet limits on total carbon emissions. They can park their carbon in trees temporarily, but when their storage contracts are up, they need to put that carbon someplace else—or reduce emissions someplace else. This strategy will work nicely if, at the end of the contract term, there are new, cheaper opportunities for storing carbon or reducing emissions.

  Translated from the project to global scale, this suggests that a temporary, renewable decision to protect forests could buy time for technological advance. The strategy would be to protect threatened forests with low opportunity costs. Over time those costs might rise if there is pressure for agricultural expansion. Development of emissions-reducing technologies would then allow the option of substituting emission reductions for continued forest maintenance. (But, as the next section suggests, forestholders at that time might choose not to exercise that option.)

  For the global community it makes sense to approach climate change mitigation through a program that uses not-necessarily-permanent avoidance of deforestation as one way to buy time for more effective investments in energy research and development. There is no need to tie the two approaches at a project level, but rather to move toward simultaneous global implementation of avoided deforestation and more vigorous research and development. The faster that cheap emissions-reducing technologies are developed, the less time has to be bought through temporary sequestration—potentially allowing forest owners to exercise their option of forest conversion.

- Temporary sequestration could become permanent.
  However, the history of the forest transition suggests that
  "temporary" sequestration could bridge the trough of the
  transition and end up being permanent. Many places face
  temporary pressures to convert forests for small gains.
  A 20- to 40-year effort to halt deforestation would not
  involve large opportunity costs, so equitable compensation
  could be arranged. At the end of that period, rising wages
  and appreciation of biodiversity values could prompt a
  reevaluation of the desirability of forest conversion. The
  forest owner and the host country may not want to exercise their option for conversion at that time. Thus temporary efforts to avoid deforestation provide a valuable
  climatic service and may end up being permanent.

"If You Protect One Forest, Someone Will Just Cut Down Another"

Problem: Does it really do any good to protect a forest plot from conversion to agriculture, or to reforest a working pasture? Won't market pressures just push someone else to deforest some other plot, to
meet demands for food and employment?

This problem is called leakage or slippage, and it occurs in many
contexts where a project acts locally but has distant repercussions.
It's a concern in policies that seek to retire farmland to in order
to prevent erosion or shore up commodity prices—do the farmers
retire one field and open another? It also occurs in projects intended
to reduce energy use and associated carbon emissions: switching a
city from coal to wind power nudges down the price of coal slightly.
Elsewhere, millions of people respond by increasing their coal consumption a bit. Such effects can add up to a large proportional dimi-
nution of the putative gains at the project site.

Solution: Leakage from forest protection isn't necessarily hectare for hectare (Chomitz 2002), as a naïve view would suggest. Suppose that a forested property is about to be converted to pasture, but
is protected instead. The immediate effect is to drive up the price of
beef a scintilla and to send a small amount of capital and a smaller
amount of labor looking for other opportunities. One possibility is
that the cowboys and ranchers move to an adjacent forest plot and
set up a ranch there. But it is also possible that another ranch, possibly a distant one, intensifies a bit, adding a few animals and farm-

hands. This is especially likely if the protected forest would have been used for low-intensity grazing. In addition, the slight upward pressure on beef prices may nudge some consumers toward chicken. In sum, leakage will be smaller if other parts of the economy can intensify production and absorb the freed capital and labor; and if consumers are sensitive to the price of beef (or whatever commodity is affected by the forest project).

Leakage can be moderate even without any effort to control it. The U.S. Conservation Reserve Program pays farmers to revegetate erosion-prone land. Wu (2000) found leakage of about 20 percent in terms of area and 9–14 percent for erosion prevention. In other words, for every 5 hectares of land put into the program, 1 hectare of forest was converted to agriculture outside it. But the newly converted land was less erosion-prone than the protected land.

Murray, McCarl, and Lee (2004) simulate the impacts of a hypothetical U.S. program that would protect forestland from agricultural conversion, putting it under sustainable timber management instead. Depending on where the program was implemented, carbon leakage ranged from –4 percent (implying a gain in carbon sequestration outside the program) to 73 percent. The different outcomes could be due to differences in whether the system responds through extensification (land conversion) or intensification (higher productivity).

The solution to leakage, then, is to neutralize it by encouraging sustainable agricultural intensification in nonforest areas—intensification that soaks up the workers, commodity supply, and capital diverted by forest protection. And of course it is important to seek intensified systems that do not produce environmental burdens such as agrotoxic or nitrogen emissions.

"It's Too Expensive to Monitor Carbon"

Problem: It takes a fair amount of effort to measure the amount of carbon in a tree, let alone on a farm. Measuring changes over time makes things even more complex. Is it affordable to gauge the impact of carbon sequestration efforts?

Solution: Measuring forest carbon, in a district or a nation, involves two steps (to oversimplify a bit). The first is estimating how much carbon there is in a tree of a given size, based on its volume and characteristics. The second involves counting the number of trees of different sizes and multiplying by the amount of carbon in each tree. The second step could be done by tallying every tree—difficult even in a small forest. But technology is making this approach cheaper. For instance, it is possible to take aerial pictures and have computers recognize trees and estimate their volumes. Still, the cost per tree or hectare is significant, as the airplane must cover the countryside in many low-altitude swaths.

Statistical techniques offer potentially huge economies of scale in carbon measurement (Chomitz 2002). Statistics can be used to estimate the number or volume of trees based on a sample. And statistical methods have a remarkable property, familiar from household surveys: the accuracy of an estimate depends on the size and representativeness of the sample, not the size of the population being sampled. With 2,000 interviews it is possible to accurately assess mean household income—for a city, province, or nation. Hence there are huge economies of scale, in costs per ton, of measuring changes in carbon stocks at a national rather than project level. Although the statistical issues in drawing appropriate samples can get complicated, the principle is clear: enlisting a few statisticians can drastically reduce the number of fieldworkers or aircraft needed to measure carbon.

Implementing Incentives for Avoided Deforestation

The solutions to these concerns about forest carbon are mutually supportive. They strongly suggest working at a national level, to incorporate leakage-neutralizing policies and drastically cut the costs of carbon monitoring. Potential steps toward avoiding deforestation in developing countries include:

- Agreement by some industrial countries to provide incentive payments for developing countries to reduce deforestation.

- Development of national systems for forest and carbon monitoring, including win-win steps to reduce excessive deforestation.

- Elaboration of the forest carbon infrastructure into national programs for deforestation avoidance. These programs would use the international incentive payments to fund deforestation reduction activities.

- Emphasis on neutralizing emissions though sustainable agricultural development.

- Incentive payments would be "pay as you go"—based on annual reductions against a reference level.

Fostering Sources of Global Finance for Avoided Deforestation and Supporting Research and Development on Emissions

Programs for avoided deforestation in developing countries will require global finance. There are different ways to provide it. One is within a Kyoto framework: some countries accept a cap on emissions but can meet that cap by purchasing emission reductions abroad, including from averted deforestation. This approach could lead to a market for emission reductions based on forest carbon, with pricing based on supply and demand.

Developing National Forest Carbon Infrastructure

To manage and use incentive payments, investments must first be made in building capacity and creating needed physical and institutional infrastructure. These investments, supported by donor financing, would include win-win investments that reduce deforestation pressure in any case.

At the core of the system are institutions and hardware for monitoring forest cover, forest and land fires, and carbon. Initially the system could track land cover—providing rapid, indicative measures of change. Later it could become a more comprehensive and accurate carbon monitoring system, combining new remote sensing technologies (such as MODIS) with ground-based observations.

Such a system can do far more than provide the carbon readings needed for incentive payments. It could aid in land use planning, forest fire prevention, and forest law enforcement. To facilitate this, the monitoring system would map the boundaries of protected areas, forest concessions, indigenous areas, and large private properties. Authorities could then use this information to help enforce forest laws and improve management of public forestlands. Public disclosure of these data would raise awareness of the issues and might help build constituencies for enforcement of laws against illegal forest conversion and logging.

Creating National Programs to Reduce Deforestation

The next step is to develop a blueprint for a program of domestic institutions, policies, and initiatives to reduce emissions from deforestation and, probably, increase carbon storage in agricultural and forest landscapes. This program would translate international incentive payments for reduced deforestation into incentives for forest owners to contribute to the achievement of these reductions.

One approach would be through direct pass-through of incentive payments to individual property owners. But this approach has disadvantages. It doesn't address illegal deforestation or deforestation on public land. It doesn't facilitate government policies that can affect entire landscapes. It fails to recognize the contribution of agricultural intensification in reducing leakage and facilitating emission reductions. And measurement, monitoring, and transactions costs are prohibitively high at the property level, especially for small properties.

An alternative is to delink incentives to the nation from incentives to individuals and firms. The national government can use incentive payments to fund diverse interventions in different sectors and locations. These interventions might cover the range of options discussed earlier in this report, such as:

- Paying communities for reduced deforestation or natural regeneration.

- Funding fire prevention programs.

- Improving tenure security.

- Enforcing regulations against illegal deforestation and logging.

- Setting up taxation of large-scale land clearance.

- Promoting off-farm employment.

- Intensifying agriculture in favorable areas to attract or divert workers from marginal lands at the forest fringe.

- Implementing strategic planning of road improvements.

- Supporting community forestry where it deters conversion to agriculture.

These programs might then be certified for participation in a globally financed incentive program. Certification could facilitate grants or loans from donors or international financial institutions to invest in the programs. To be certified, programs would have to meet some basic criteria. For instance, the monitoring system would have to eliminate any perverse incentives to replace natural forests with planted ones.

There are strong benefits to combining forest protection programs with agricultural and silvicultural intensification programs.

First, the latter neutralize leakage. For instance, road improvements in less-forested areas can lead to agricultural intensification and increased demand for labor, reducing migration to the forest frontier. Second, the combination creates a broad constituency of beneficiaries who can support program implementation.

How Should National Incentives Be Set?

Funders and recipients of incentive payments will be keenly interested in how prices and quantities are set. The framework envisions a negotiated reference level (*RL*) of emissions or net emissions. Incentives would be offered for reductions below that level. (This is different from offering an incentive based on total forest area.) The key terms to be negotiated are how to set the reference level, how much to reward reductions below it, and whether and how to discourage emissions above it.

First, if the reference level is set above the unobservable baseline (business as usual) of emissions, the country will receive rents—pure transfers unrelated to emission reductions. If these rents are too large, funders may decline to participate. But if the reference level is set too far below the baseline, deforesting countries may decline to participate. Reference levels could be set at historical emission levels, but these may be difficult to assess if data are lacking, or may reflect market conditions that no longer exist. Setting reference levels at current emission levels would introduce moral hazard because countries might be tempted to increase deforestation to obtain a higher target.

An alternative is to compute a normative reference level. The normative estimate would be based on a standardized estimate of the rate of increase in agricultural production, adjusted for an estimate of the rate of increase in agricultural productivity as well as the mean carbon content of forestland at the agricultural margin. Separate estimates could be made for logging-related emissions and the rate of abandonment of current lands. A normative reference level would tend to reward countries already trying to reduce deforestation, without introducing perverse incentives to increase deforestation to get more credits.

Second, what is the reward for reducing emissions below the reference level, and should the temporary nature of the reductions be dealt with? For simplicity, suppose that the reductions result from national incentives and are not tied to the Kyoto Protocol's carbon market or a successor. In that case funders and recipients could negotiate a payment amount per period per ton-year. The calculations would be made as follows. Reductions in year t would be calculated as:

$$R_t = RL - E_t,$$

where E_t is measured net emissions. R could be positive (meaning a reduction relative to the reference level) or negative (implying emissions above the reference level). The payment at time T would be:

$$\max(0, P\sum_{t=1}^{T} R_t),$$

where P is the price per ton-year and $t = 1$ marks the beginning of the program. This formula is cumulative because it focuses attention on carbon storage. Each year, the country is rewarded if its actual carbon storage is greater than the baseline implied by the emissions scenario. The price P can be thought of as a storage fee, paid per ton per year. Suppose the country protects two hectares from deforestation in year 1, and an additional hectare in year 2, and suppose that each hectare would release 100 tons of CO_2 if deforested. Then $R_1 = 200$, $R_2 = 100$; the country would receive $200P$ in year 1, and $300P$ in year 2. Suppose however, that in year 2, no additional hectares were protected, and in fact one of the previous year's protected hectares was deforested, so that $R_2 = -100$. Then only $100P$ would be paid in year 2.

How should the price P be set? Ton-years have value because delaying emissions is valuable and because there is a significant chance of unintended permanence. But these values, while real, are difficult to compute on the basis of available information. So P would have to be decided by negotiation. A natural reference point would be the current interest rate times the market or normative price of a carbon allowance. This is the rental value of a permanent allowance. For example, under the EU Emissions Trading Scheme (ETS) a ton of CO_2 abatement is currently priced at about $20. At 6 percent annual interest, this implies a payment of $1.20 a ton per year. At that rate, averting deforestation of a hectare of moist rainforest might return a few hundred dollars a year. But even a price based on 6 percent of $3 per ton of CO_2 might still return an amount comparable to the annual payment rate in Costa Rica's payment for environmental services program (see chapter 6).

This approach could be made Kyoto-compatible by setting an exchange rate between ton-years and permanent tons. There is a long, inconclusive history of discussion on the proper exchange rate for ton-years. Again, setting it at, say, 6 percent of a permanent reduction might be a starting point for discussion.

Though the obstacles to setting up avoided deforestation programs are considerable, so are the potential benefits. Moreover, solutions to those obstacles might be self-reinforcing (table 7.1).

The policies discussed here require fairly sophisticated institutional capabilities and so may not be immediately applicable to all forested countries. But countries could proceed in steps—starting by creating forest carbon infrastructure and proceeding to pilot tests of national-to-individual incentives. These early stages might be rewarding to participating countries and beneficial to the global climate, while providing information that would improve the design of international incentives.

Table 7.1 Policies to Reward Avoided Deforestation Can Have Synergistic Effects

Policy	Permanence/ contribution to long-run climate mitigation	Acceptability to host country	Leakage	Monitoring
Bundle with commitment to research and development	X			
Invest in agricultural intensification	X	X	X	
Set national baselines			X	X
Secure temporary commitments from host country		X		
Focus on marginal areas with ephemeral pressure or risk of irreversibility	X	X		
Catalyze technology diffusions	X	X		

Related Opportunities for Biodiversity Conservation

The emergence of global carbon markets may blaze a trail for new approaches to global biodiversity finance. A precondition would be mobilization of significant funding. This might be achieved through biodiversity offset requirements (ten Kate, Bishop, and Bayon 2004). For instance, large mines might be encouraged or required to offset any nonmitigatable habitat destruction by buying offsets—protection of areas elsewhere of equivalent or greater biodiversity or environmental importance.

Offsets could be done by putting an equivalent domestic area under protection or by contributing to a fund for conservation of globally significant biodiversity. Such funds could solicit contracts with landholding individuals, communities, and local or national governments. Would-be participants could submit bids specifying the services to be provided and the compensation requested, and the bids could be ranked by cost-effectiveness—as in the U.S. Conservation Reserve Program and Australia's BushTender. Geographic criteria might include the combination of temporary threat and likely irreversible degradation in the absence of action. A side benefit of this approach is that it might stimulate investments in better surveying the condition and geographic distribution of biodiversity, using new technologies such as genetic bar coding. That in turn could catalyze renewed, more sophisticated, and more productive markets for bioprospecting from which developing countries and communities could benefit.

Summary

Carbon storage and biodiversity conservation are forest services that benefit large but diffuse global constituencies. Mobilizing those constituencies to finance forest maintenance and negotiating and implementing agreements with forestholders pose institutional challenges of planetary magnitude. Still, the potential gains to all parties are big enough to motivate such efforts.

Endnote

1. Based on pointcarbon.com, August 31, 2006.

Juan Pablo Moreiras / Fauna & Flora International / Comisión Centroamericana de Ambiente y Desarrollo photo archive.

CHAPTER 8

Conclusions and Recommendations

Are development and the environment at loggerheads in tropical forests? This report has shown that trade-offs sometimes exist between the two. Poverty and deforestation are not closely linked at the local level, so we shouldn't expect fixing one problem to automatically solve the other. Indeed, some deforestation contributes a lot to development, poverty alleviation, or both. And when poor people deforest for paltry gains, it's often because the alternatives—including forest maintenance—are less attractive. The vast environmental benefits of forests have been difficult to tap in ways that motivate forest conservation while improving livelihoods.

Moreover, forest poverty and deforestation are difficult problems to solve. They revolve around the allocation and enforcement of rights. Strong, equitable institutions are needed to resolve these problems—but such institutions are in short supply in many developing countries.

Still, there are grounds for hope. Technological and institutional innovations create possibilities for catalyzing change and for minimizing or transcending trade-offs. But problems must be properly diagnosed. Challenges for poverty, equity, and the environment are systematically different in areas in and beyond the agricultural frontier, and different kinds of management institutions are needed at the international, national, and local levels. Various policy and institutional interventions could help reduce poverty, ease environmental damage, and make allocations of wealth more equitable (box 8.1).

Box 8.1   This Report's Recommendations

International level

- Mobilize carbon finance to reduce deforestation and promote sustainable agriculture.
- Mobilize finance for conservation of globally significant biodiversity.
- Finance national and global efforts to monitor forests and evaluate the impacts of forest projects and policies—including devolution of forest control.
- Foster the development of national-level research and evaluation organizations through twinning with established foreign partners.

National level

- Create systems for monitoring forest conditions and forest dwellers' welfare, make land and forest allocations and regulations more transparent, and support civil society organizations that monitor regulatory compliance by government, landholders, and forest concessionaires. The prospect of carbon finance can help motivate these efforts.
- Make forest and land use regulations more efficient, reformulating them to minimize monitoring, enforcement, and compliance costs. Economic instruments can help.

Areas beyond the frontier

- Avert disruptive races for property rights by equitably assigning ownership, use rights, and stewardship of these lands.
- Options for forest conservation include combinations of indigenous and community rights, protected areas, and forest concessions. Still, some forest may be converted

to agriculture where doing so offers high, sustainable returns and does not threaten irreplaceable environmental assets.

- Plan for rational, regulated expansion of road networks—including designation of roadless areas.
- Experiment with new ways of providing services and infrastructure to low-density populations.

Frontier areas

- Equitably assign and enforce property rights.
- Plan and control road network expansion.
- Discourage conversion in areas with hydrological hazards, or encourage community management of these watersheds.
- Use remote sensing, enhanced communication networks, and independent observers to monitor logging concessionaires and protect forestholders against encroachers.
- Consider using carbon finance to support government and community efforts to assign and enforce property rights.
- Encourage markets for environmental services in community-owned forests.

Disputed areas

- Where forest control is transferred to local communities, build local institutions with upward and downward accountability.
- Where community rights are secure and markets are feasible, provide technical assistance for community forestry.
- Make landholder rights more secure in "forests without trees."

Box 8.1 *(continued)*

- When forest tenure is secure, use carbon markets to promote forest regeneration and maintenance.

Mosaiclands
- Reform regulations so that they don't penalize tree growing.
- Promote greener agriculture—such as integrated pest management and silvopastoral systems—through research and development, extension efforts, community organization, and reform of agriculture and forest regulations.
- Develop a wide range of markets for environmental services—carbon, biodiversity, water regulation, recreation, pest control— to support more productive, sustainable land management.

International Level

Two areas stand out for international cooperation.

Financing Forest Environmental Services

Internationally financed incentives for avoiding deforestation and stimulating forest regrowth could catalyze global forest conservation and agricultural development while cutting the costs of mitigating climate change. Any serious effort to grapple with global climate change must place an explicit or implicit charge on carbon dioxide (CO_2) emissions. And at any reasonable charge on CO_2 emissions, there are huge dividends to engaging in more intensive, labor-absorbing agriculture on degraded lands—instead of deforestation that yields trifling, ephemeral gains.

That substitution, which would also provide domestic benefits, won't happen automatically because private incentives work against it. But sharing the global dividends of CO_2 reduction could provide the funds and motivation for needed national-level efforts. The UN Framework Convention on Climate Change, whose 189 signatories have agreed to the goal of stabilizing greenhouse gas concentrations in the atmosphere, provides a natural venue for negotiating financing for international incentives.

These efforts would have to be coordinated with research, development, and diffusion of environmentally friendly agricultural technologies and practices. Some approaches to agricultural intensification can create or exacerbate environmental problems, including eutrophication, pesticide pollution, and emergence of new pathogens related to animal husbandry. New technologies—such as integrated pest management and other landscape management techniques—could mitigate the potential side effects of intensification.

The international community could also provide direct incentives for global biodiversity conservation. Financing sources might include industries dependent on biodiversity, such as agriculture based on plants with wild relatives in forests. Financing could be funneled through national programs for environmental service payments.

Addressing Monitoring and Information Needs

The international community could undertake monitoring efforts that would have immediate payoffs while contributing to these long-term financing goals. A priority is to fund and coordinate basic monitoring on the rate, location, and causes of global deforestation and forest poverty and the impacts of project and policy interventions. Without this information, policy makers are flying blind, and interest groups lack a solid basis for dialogue. For instance:

- Despite intense concerns about deforestation, among developing countries only Brazil and India report forest cover on a regular basis. (Indonesia is developing a system.) For Africa, estimates of deforestation vary by a factor of 10.

- Despite billions of dollars spent setting up and running protected areas, there has been little analysis of their conservation and development impacts and of how these are related to their funding, management strategies, and context. Similarly, there has been little monitoring and analysis of the impacts of the massive transfers in forest tenure of recent years.

- Despite hopes for securing support for forest conservation based on local environmental services such as hydrological benefits, there are few studies and tools for quantifying those benefits and relating them to specific interventions in specific places. And measurements of weather and rivers, the foundation for such studies, are increasingly difficult because meteorological and gauging stations are being abandoned.

- Despite concerns about forest poverty, information is spotty on the numbers and conditions of people in two distinct poverty situations: deep forest (highly forest-dependent people in remote areas) and mosaiclands (who get a small but significant share of their income from forests).

- Despite concerns about global biodiversity loss, information on the global distribution of biodiversity is inadequate. Conservation scientists have made great strides in organizing available data, but systematic sampling is lacking.

With the possible exception of the last, these information gaps are relatively easy to remedy. New remote sensing technologies make it feasible and affordable to identify hotspots of deforestation. Ridder (2006) estimates that it would cost $12 million to create a global network for forest monitoring that could produce annual, medium-resolution estimates of deforestation. That price tag includes support for building local capacity to acquire and interpret remote sensing data. A World Bank–WWF survey tool for managing protected areas (Stolton and others 2003), already in use by the Global Environment Facility (GEF), could be applied more widely and integrated with quantitative indicators of biodiversity status. Household survey instruments could be adjusted to better account for forest income. In addition, collaborative research institutes—twinning staff from industrial and developing countries—could conduct monitoring and evaluation studies from a policy perspective, as well as research and development on land and forest management. Such efforts would build capacity and generate analytic and research results and could nurture the development of policy entrepreneurs as described in Steinberg (2001).

National Level

At the national level, strengthening the voice and influence of diffuse interests—for environment and for poverty—is essential to institutional reforms. Environmental councils might be one way to mobilize people affected by forest externalities. There may be a virtuous circle between mobilizing these interests and generating better information on forest conditions: interest groups demand information, which empowers them to negotiate better outcomes. The critical factor is local demand for forest regulation, which external sources of finance (such as for carbon) could help spark.

National monitoring of forests is increasingly easy thanks to improvements in remote sensing and communications. A national forest monitoring program—combined with mapping of indigenous areas, protected areas, forest concessions, and other tenure zones—can form the basis for better forest law enforcement and fire control, and for certification or rating of large logging firms and landowners. Public disclosure of this information is important for encouraging enforcement. Internationally financed incentives for forest carbon could be a powerful inducement for countries to set up national monitoring.

Within countries, this report's policy recommendations are differentiated by three forest regions: beyond the frontier, at the frontier and in disputed areas, and within the frontier.

Areas beyond the Frontier

A few countries have large, remote forests beyond the range of most agriculture or timber extraction. Pressures to exploit those forest resources will likely eventually arise—in some places chainsaws are already almost within earshot. In other, more remote forests such pressures may be decades off and will result from technological changes. For instance, the development of productive, forest-competing biofuel crops could greatly increase global land demands and pressures for forest conversion.

Now—before those pressures arise and stakeholders are entrenched—is the time to think about how to manage those forests, accounting for their unique ecological values. This process entails recognizing and enforcing indigenous land claims where applicable and demarcating and institutionalizing protected areas. Indigenous and protected areas have been relatively successful in deterring deforestation, though the determinants of their effectiveness and their impacts on livelihoods are poorly understood. Now is also the time to think about long-term planning of road networks in areas beyond the frontier. Strong technical methodologies exist for planning roads and protected areas, but must be exercised in a context that mediates between competing interests.

Poverty is often high in transfrontier areas, as is the proportion of indigenous people. Protecting rights and building capacity can help empower these isolated people. In addition, innovative technologies—such as satellite communications—can lower the cost of providing services such as health and education to low-density populations.

Frontier and Disputed Areas

Governance at the frontier and in disputed areas requires equitable, secure assignment of land and forest rights. There is no easy prescription for achieving that, since forests are subject to elite capture as they take on value. Although models of participatory zoning and conflict resolution exist for small areas, challenges remain in scaling them up to legitimately disentangle forest claims at the provincial and national levels. A special challenge is rationalizing tenure in "forests without trees"—areas where agriculture is legally prohibited but forest has been severely degraded.

Many forests are nominally owned by governments, but poorly administered. Devolving nationally owned forests to local ownership and control might result in a more equitable allocation of forest rents and better management. But local ownership and management are no panacea, because communities face their own institutional issues, including elite capture. Where markets are accessible, building capacity, providing marketing assistance, and streamlining regulations could help community forestry.

In some contexts, putting forests under regulated logging concessions could provide income to the forest owner (whether state or community) while maintaining environmental values. New tools—including auctions and independent monitoring—are available for ensuring that concession awards and operations contribute to the public good.

Shifting the balance from forest degradation toward forest maintenance could require technical assistance in production, management, and marketing. But neither concessionaires nor local communities have strong incentives to manage forests for national or global environmental benefits. So regulations or incentives (or both) will be needed to secure those benefits. Efficient regulation focuses on the flexible achievement of clear environmental goals, uses criteria that are cheap and easy to monitor, does not lend itself to petty rent seeking by enforcers, and imposes low opportunity costs on those who comply.

Because roads are an important driver of deforestation in frontier areas, some control should be exercised over the expansion of road networks—especially discouraging road extensions into areas

217

with low agricultural potential. In other places clarification of forest tenure should precede road extension.

Mosaiclands

Within the frontier, high-density mixes of people and forest fragments generally lead to both stronger pressures for deforestation and greater incidence of environmental benefits. But this is a heterogeneous region, presenting a range of challenges. Where marginal uplands are near agriculturally favorable lowlands, intensification of the latter might ease pressure on hillside forests.

Elsewhere, balancing environmental externalities against pressures for forest conversion or exploitation will require a variety of interventions. There is scope for exploring technological and institutional innovations for greener management of agriculture and forest mosaiclands. Again, efficient regulation is needed, placing on landholders only restrictions and responsibilities that provide clear external benefits, are easy to monitor and enforce, and do not burden poor people.

Areas within the frontier have the greatest scope for developing payment systems for environmental services. But if they are to be effective in delivering the promised services, these systems must be tightly focused on efficiency. International finance for forest carbon or threatened biodiversity could be important in these areas, which are likely to be home to threatened species.

Accelerating the Forest Transition

As development progresses at the national level, rising wages attract farmers to urban employment and away from low-return farming at the forest fringe (see box 2.1). In some countries a demographic transition—with shrinking youth populations—will intensify this trend, driving up wages and reducing the number of people willing to live hard lives at the frontier. Many developing countries are at the cusp of another demographic transition, with their rural populations poised to decline (figure 8.1).[1] In much of Sub-Saharan Africa, however, this transition is distant.

The prospect of a forest transition isn't cause for complacency. True, industrial countries have seen a remarkable rebound in forest cover. For instance, despite its high population and economic densities, Japan is about two-thirds forest.

But the quality and nature of regenerated forest may be quite different from the original. This risk is profound in tropical forests,

Figure 8.1   Some Forested Countries Will See Shrinking Rural Populations

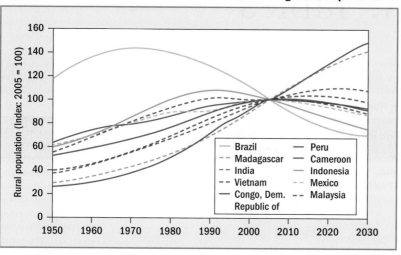

Source: UN Population Division 2004.

where ecologies are far richer and more complex than in temperate regions, and where soils are poorer and more degradable. The danger is that, for ecological reasons, the pulse of tropical forest clearance over the next few decades will often yield paltry benefits and leave behind not a renaissance of the original forest but a degraded landscape where biodiversity and carbon storage have been permanently impaired.

At the global level, pro-poor growth, the creation of sustainable cities, and the development of agricultural technologies that are intensive, labor-absorbing, and environmentally benign can help accelerate the forest transition. Incentives for carbon storage and biodiversity conservation can help countries maintain these assets, bridging the trough of the transition. It is in this important sense that poverty alleviation, development, and forest conservation are fully aligned.

Endnote

1. However, the figure shows a cautionary lesson from Brazil. There, market forces and road building drove deforestation even as the rural population declined.

Appendix A: Tables

Table A.1　Findings of Studies Assessing How Road Proximity Affects Deforestation

Study	Location, square kilometers, year(s)	Variable capturing road effect	Impact on deforestation
Andersen and Reis (1997)	Brazilian Amazônia, ~5 million, 1970 to 1985	Road length	+***
Andersen and others (2002)	Brazilian Amazônia, ~5 million, 1980 to 1985	Unpaved road density	– (at least **)
		Unpaved road × cleared land	+ (at least **)
		Paved road density	n.s.
	1985 to 1995	Paved road density	+ (at least **)
		Unpaved roads density	+ (at least **)
		Paved roads × cleared land	– (at least **)
		Unpaved road × cleared land	+ n.s.
Bray and others (2004)	Mexico, 7,300, 1976 to 1984 and 1984 to 2000	Distance to roads	n.s. (1976–84) –*** (1984–2000)
Chomitz and Gray (1996)	Belize, 11,712, 1989–92	Distance to market	–***
Chomitz and Thomas (2003)	Brazilian Amazônia, 4.86 million, 1970 to 1985	Proportion of land within 50 km from main federal roads	+***
		Distance to cities with populations > 25,000	–***
		Distance to cities with populations > 100,000	– (n.r.)
Cropper, Griffiths, and Mani (1999)	Thailand, 514,000, 1976 to 1989	Road density	+***

Control for spatial auto-correlation?	Control for endogeneity?	Control variables (impact on deforestation)		
		Soil quality	Slope	Altitude
Yes	No	n.i.	n.i.	n.i.
No	Yes	n.i.	n.i.	n.i.
No	Yes	n.i.	n.i.	n.i.
Yes	Yes	n.i.	n.i.	n.i.
Yes	Yes	+***	±	n.i.
No	Yes	n.r.	n.i.	n.i.
n.a.	Yes	+	–***	n.a.

(continued)

Table A.1 (*continued*)

Study	Location, square kilometers, year(s)	Variable capturing road effect	Impact on deforestation
Cropper, Puri, and Griffiths (2001)	Northern Thailand, area not reported, 1986	Cost to nearest market	−***
Deininger and Minten (2002)	Mexico, 160,000, 1980–90	Distance to nearest paved road	−***
Etter and others (2006)	Colombia, 1.1 million, 1998	Distance to roads, town	−***
Geoghegan and others (2001)	Mexico, 22,000, 1988 to 1992 and 1992 to 1995	Distance to roads	−*** (1988–92) −*** (1992–95)
		Distance to market	+** (1988–92) +*** (1992–95)
		Distance to village	+*** (1988–92) −*** (1992–95)
Kirby and others (2006)	Brazilian Amazônia, 5 million, 1999	Distance to roads	−**
McConnell, Sweeney, and Mulley (2004)	Madagascar, 940, 1957 to 2000	Distance from village	− n.r.
Mertens and others (2002)	Pará, Brazil, 56,300, 1986 to 1992	Distance to main road	−*** (planned colonization, 1) +*** (small-scale colonization, 2) −*** (medium-size colonization, 3) −*** (large *fazendas,* 4)
		Distance to secondary road	−** (1) −*** (2) +* (3) + n.s. (4)
		Distance to village	+** (1) −*** (2) +*** (3, 4)
	1992 to 1999	Distance to main road	− *** (1) +*** (2, 3) + n.s. (4)
		Distance to secondary road	−*** (1, 2, 3, 4)
		Distance to village	−*** (1, 2, 3, 4)

Control for spatial auto-correlation?	Control for endogeneity?	Control variables (impact on deforestation)		
		Soil quality	Slope	Altitude
Yes	No	+***	_***	_***
No	No	+*	_***	_***
No	No	+***	±	n.i.
No	No	+***	+***	_***
Yes	No	n.s.	n.i.	n.i.
Yes	No	n.i.	– n.r.	– n.r.
Yes	Yes	n.i.	n.i.	±
Yes	Yes	n.i.	n.i.	±

(continued)

Table A.1 (*continued*)

Study	Location, square kilometers, year(s)	Variable capturing road effect	Impact on deforestation
Mertens and others (2004)	Bolivia, 364,000, <1989 and 1989 to 1994	Distance to roads and to Santa Cruz	−***
Müller and Munroe (2005)	Vietnam, ~1,390, 2000	Distance to long-established road network	+ n.s. (sample includes only less-remote areas)
Müller and Zeller (2002)	Vietnam, ~2,390, 1975 to 1992 and 1992 to 2000	Distance to nearest all-year road	−*** (1975–92) −*** (1992–2000)
		Distance to district capital	+*** (1992–2000) n.i. (1975–92)
		Travel time to all-year road	+*** (1992–2000; n.s. for paddy) +*** (1975–2000; n.s. for mixed agriculture)
Munroe, Southworth, and Tucker (2004)	Honduras, 1,015, 1987 to 1996	Distance to nearest village	−***
		Distance out of region	− n.s.
Naidoo and Adamowicz (2006)	Paraguay, 2,920, 1991 to 2004	Distance to unpaved roads	−* (smallholders) − n.s. (ranchers) + n.s. (soybeans)
		Distance to paved roads	−***(smallholders) − n.s. (ranchers, soybeans)
		Distance to towns	− n.s. (all groups)
Nelson and Hellerstein (1997)	Mexico, area not reported, 1973	Cost to nearest road or village	−**
		Cost to large population center	+ n.s.
Nelson, Harris, and Stone (2001)	Panama, 15,995, 1987 to 1997	Cost to border	− (n.s.)
		Cost to port	+***
		Cost to village	−***
		Cost to nearest town	−***

Control for spatial auto-correlation?	Control for endogeneity?	Control variables (impact on deforestation)		
		Soil quality	Slope	Altitude
Yes	Yes	±	n.i.	n.i.
Yes	Yes	+***	±	±
Yes	Yes	+***	–***	–***
Yes	No	n.i.	+***	–***
Yes	No	+***	–***	±
Yes	No	n.s.	–***	–***
Yes	Yes	+***	–***	–***

(continued)

Table A.1 (*continued*)

Study	Location, square kilometers, year(s)	Variable capturing road effect	Impact on deforestation
Nelson and others (2004)	Panama, 16,100, 1987 to 1997	Cost of transporting wood to market (by road or river)	− n.r.
Osgood (1994)	Indonesia, area not reported, 1972 to 1988	Extension of roads	+ n.s.
Panayotou and Sungsuwan (1994)	Northeast Thailand, 169,000, 1973 to 1982	Rural roads extension	+*
		Distance to Bangkok	−***
Pender and others (2004)	Uganda, area not reported, 1990 to 1999	Change in distance to tarmac roads	−**
		Change in distance to market	− n.s.
Pendleton and Howe (2002)	Bolivia, area not reported, clearance during 1995	Walking time to roads	−** (primary forest) + n.s. (secondary forest)
		Walking time to closest market	+*** (primary forest) +** (secondary forest)
Pfaff (1999)	Brazilian Amazônia, area not reported, 1975 to 1988	Density of unpaved roads	+***
		Density of paved roads	− n.s.
Pichón (1997)	Ecuador, ~70,000, 1990	Distance to roads, nearest market	−***
Reis and Guzmán (1994)	Brazilian Amazônia, 5 million, 1983–87	Extension of unpaved roads	+**
		Extension of paved roads	+ n.s.
		Distance to state capital	− n.s.

Control for spatial auto-correlation?	Control for endogeneity?	Control variables (impact on deforestation)		
		Soil quality	Slope	Altitude
Yes	Yes	n.i.	n.i.	n.i.
n.a.	No	n.i.	n.i.	n.i.
n.a.	No	n.i.	n.i.	n.i.
No	Yes	n.i.	n.i.	n.i.
No	No	n.i.	n.i.	n.i.
Yes	Yes	+***	n.i.	n.i.
n.a.	Yes	+***	–***	n.i.
Yes	Yes	n.i.	n.i.	n.i.

(continued)

Table A.1 (*continued*)

Study	Location, square kilometers, year(s)	Variable capturing road effect	Impact on deforestation
Serneels and Lambin (2001)	Kenya, 10,694, 1975 to 1985 and 1985 to 1995		*Mechanized agriculture*
		Squared distance to roads	–*** (1975–85) –*** (1985–95)
		Distance to roads	+*** (1975–85) +*** (1985–95)
		Distance to village	–*** (1975–85) +*** (1985–95)
		Distance to Narok (district seat)	–*** (1975–85) –*** (1985–95)
			Smallholders (1975–85 model only):
		Distance to roads (log)	–***
		Distance to village (log)	–***
		Distance to Narok	+***
Southworth and others (2004)	Honduras, 1,015, 1987 to 2000	Distance to roads and regional market	–**
Tucker and others (2005)	Guatemala, 1,053, 1987 to 1996	Distance to nearest town/local market	–**
		Distance out of region (capital city or regional market)	+** also increases probability of forest regrowth
Vance and Geoghegan (2002)	Yucatan, 22,000, 1984–87 and 1994–97	Distance to market	–***
Wilson and others (2005)	Chile, 42,000, 1995–96	Distance to roads and town	–***

Note: Years x–y indicates a single cross-section analysis based on composite forest cover data for the period x–y; years x and y indicates separate cross-section analyses for years x and y; years x to y indicates an analysis of forest cover change between years x and y.

n.a. Not applicable; n.i. Variable not included; n.s. Not significant; n.r. Significance not reported; ± Effect differs for different land uses.

*, **, *** represent 10 percent, 5 percent, and 1 percent significance levels, respectively.

Control for spatial auto-correlation?	Control for endogeneity?	Control variables (impact on deforestation)		
		Soil quality	Slope	Altitude
Yes	No	+***	n.i.	−***
Yes	No	+***	n.i.	−***
No	No	n.i.	+*	−**
Yes	No	n.i.	−**	+**
No	No	+***	−***	−***
No	No	+**	−***	−***

Table A.2   Findings of Studies on How Roads Affect Development

Study	Location, year(s), and data level	Control for endogeneity?
Binswanger, Khandker, and Rosenzweig (1993)	India, 1960–82, district level	Yes
Buys, Deichmann, and Wheeler (2006)	Sub-Saharan Africa, 1999–2004, country level	Not applicable
De Castro (2002)	Brazil, 1970–96, municipal level	No
De Vreyer, Herrera, and Mesple-Somps (2002)	Peru, 1997–2001, household survey, geographic variables at district level	Yes
Dewi, Belcher, and Puntodewo (2005)	East Kalimantan, Indonesia, 1992–97, spatial data at village level	No
Escobal and Ponce (2002)	Peru, 1994–2000, household survey	Yes
Fan, Nyange, and Rao (2005)	Tanzania, 2000–01, household level	Yes
Fan and Chan-Kang (2004)	Uganda, 1999, household level	Yes
Fan, Hazell, and Haque (2000)	India, 1970–94, district level	Yes
Fan, Zhang, and Zhang. (2004)	China, 1978–2000, province level	Yes
Fan and Zhang (2004)	China, 1996–97, province level	Yes
Gibson and Rozelle (2003)	Papua New Guinea, 1996, household survey	Yes

Dependent variable	Road impact on dependent variable
Agricultural output	Elasticity (road length): 0.20***
Trade	Implementation of a $35 billion regional road improvement project would increase trade by $250 billion in 15 years
Agricultural output	Elasticity with respect to road density: 0.33***
Consumption growth	Road density and percentage of paved roads: n.s. Elasticity with respect to distance to provincial capital: −0.024*
Economic diversity index (heterogeneity of income sources)	Density of provincial and district road: +***
Income	Road improvements increased average income by 35% in villages with motorized roads
Poverty	Marginal effect of distance to public transportation facilities on probability of being poor: 0.0022–0.0033 per km depending on region. The coefficient was not significant in Lake Victoria and the southern coast. 30 people lifted out of poverty for each $1,000 invested in roads
Agricultural output	Returns to government investment in feeder roads: 600% (center—richest) 870% (east) 490% (north—poorest) 920% (west)
Poverty reduction	16 (center), 81 (east), 109 (north), and 46 (west) people lifted out of poverty for each $1,000 invested in feeder roads
Agricultural output	Elasticity (road density): 0.18** (irrigated). Of 13 rainfed zones, 6 display a negative elasticity but only 1 (most productive land) is significant: −0.28**. The other 7 rainfed zones display positive and significant elasticities, with the least productive land showing the highest magnitude: 0.082** to 1.38**
Poverty reduction	0.25 (irrigated areas) and 0.03–5.18 (rainfed areas) people lifted out of poverty for each $1,000 invested in roads
Agricultural output	Elasticity (road density): 0.099*
Poverty reduction	2.2 (coastal region), 6.9 (central), and 8.3 (western) people lifted out of poverty for each $1,000 invested in roads
Agricultural output	Elasticity (road density): 0.032**
Ln (region-specific poverty line)	Marginal effect of travel distance (hours) to nearest road: −0.04**. Expanding roads to be within a two-hour walk of everyone would reduce the number of poor people by 6–12%

(continued)

Table A.2 (*continued*)

Study	Location, year(s), and data level	Control for endogeneity?
Guimaraes and Uhl (1997)	Para, Brazil, 1994, household survey	No
Hettige (2006)	Indonesia, Philippines, and Sri Lanka, 1993–2001, household level	No
Instituto Cuanto (2005)	Peru, 1994–2004, household survey	Yes
Jacoby (2000)	Nepal, 1995–96, household level	Yes
Jalan and Ravallion (2002)	Four Chinese provinces, 1985–90, household, village, and county level	Yes
Lofgren, Thurlow, and Robinson (2004)	Zambia, 2001, household level	Yes
Minten (1999)	Madagascar, 2000–01, commune census data	No
Pender and others (2004)	Uganda, 1999–2000, community level	Yes
Renkow, Hallstrom, and Karanja (2004)	Kenya, 1999, household and village level	Not applicable

Dependent variable	Road impact on dependent variable
Transport costs	Road improvement: −
Travel time Access to electricity Increase in nonfarm income in the past five years	After road rehabilitation projects: Generally at least 50% shorter than in control villages 17% more households covered than in control villages 9% more households than in control villages
Travel time Freight transport costs Passenger transport costs Students registered Visits to health centers Male wages Female wages Children wages Poverty Quantity of agricultural land	Changes due to road (R) and track (T) rehabilitation (medium- to long-term effects): −61.8% (R and T) −5.7% (trucks) to −46.4% (minibuses) −8.8% (trucks) to −40.6% (minibuses) −0.4% (R), 14.1% (T) 45.6% (R), 25.4% (T) 20.6% (R), 6.5% (T) 2.4% (R), −10.6% (T) −21.3% (R), −9.0% (T) −4.1% (R), −5.7% (T) 15.8% (R), −39.0% (T); geographically, increase in farmed lands following road rehabilitation occurred mostly in the southern mountainous region and in the forest
Land value	Elasticity of land value with respect to "time to market center": −0.26***
Wage rate	Elasticity of wage with respect to "time to market center": −0.048***
Consumption growth	Elasticity with respect to of road density: 0.015***
Agricultural output	10% increase in feeder roads leads to 0.1 percentage point increase in agricultural GDP growth rate
Poverty	10% increase in roads leads to 3–4% decrease in rural poverty
Producer price of rice	Increase of $1.20 to $17.00 per ton per hour reduction in access time to paved road. (Mean price $389/ton)
Increase in nonfarm activities	Elasticity with respect to reduction in distance to tarmac road: 0.089***
Fixed transactions costs in the market for maize	Effect of distance to nearest village by truck (road): +***

(continued)

Table A.2   (*continued*)

Study	Location, year(s), and data level	Control for endogeneity?
Warr (2005)	Lao PDR, 1997–2003, household survey and district level	Yes
World Bank (2001)	Peru, 1994–2000, household survey	No
Zeller, Diagne, and Mataya (1998)	Malawi, 1993–95, household level	No
Zhang and Fan (2001)	India, 1971–94 district level	Yes

n.s. = Statistically not significant
Note: Where only the sign of the effect is reported, it either was not possible to give a meaningful interpretation of the coefficients in the study or no coefficient was reported.

Dependent variable	Road impact on dependent variable
Real per capita expenditure	District built road during 1997–2002 dummy: 0.188*. Providing all-weather road access to everyone would reduce by 7% the number of Lao PDR's rural poor (5.6% of its total population)
	Changes due to road (R) and track (T) rehabilitation (short-term effects):
Travel time	–33.3% (R and T)
Freight transport costs	–7.9% (trucks), –13.6% (buses)
Passenger transport costs	–14.3% (trucks), –41.1% (minibuses)
Students registered	0.2 (R), 6.9% (T)
Student dropouts	–9.0% (R), 24.7% (T)
Visits to health centers	4.1% (R), –2.9% (T)
Share of area cropped under new technologies (hybrid maize)	Elasticity with respect to travel costs to agricultural market: –0.276**
Agricultural productivity	Elasticity with respect to road density: 0.043**

Table A.3   Forest Management and Tenure
(thousands of hectares unless otherwise indicated)

Continent, country	Tropical forest area (millions of hectares)	Tropical closed natural forest	Permanent forest estate		
			Natural production	Planted production	Protection
Africa		208,581	70,461	825	39,271
Cameroon	13.3–23.8	19,985	8,840	17	3,900
Central African Rep.	22.9–29.3	4,826	3,500	3	300
Congo, Dem. Rep.	128.0–135.0	126,236	20,500	55	27,000
Congo, Rep.	20.3–22.1	22,000	18,400	72	2,860
Côte d'Ivoire	7.1–11.7	3,248	3,400	167	734
Gabon	25.8	21,800	10,600	25	2,700
Ghana	2.7–6.3	1,634	1,150	97	353
Liberia	3.5–5.7	4,124	1,310	n.d.	101
Nigeria	9.7–13.5	4,456	2,720	375	1,010
Togo	0.5–1.1	272	41	14	313
Asia		216,791	100,522	39,669	76,900
Cambodia	9.3–11.1	5,500	3,460	17	4,620
Fiji	0.8–0.9	747	0	113	241
India	*64.1–76.8*	22,500	*13,500*	*32,600*	*25,600*
Indonesia	105.0–120.0	100,382	46,000	2,500	22,500
Malaysia	19.3–19.5	19,148	11,200	183	3,210
Myanmar	34.4	32,700	9,700	710	3,300
Papua New Guinea	30.6	30,150	8,700	80	1,700
Philippines	5.4–7.2	5,288	4,700	274	1,540
Thailand	13.0–14.8	10,127	0	1,870	8,260
Vanuatu	0.9	442	117	2.1	8.37
Vietnam	19.0	12,307	3,145	1,320	5,921

Production forest management						Tenure		
Natural				Planted		Community owned or managed	Public forest (%)	Private forest (%)
License or concession	Management plan	Certified	Sustainably managed	Management plan	Certified			
44,049	10,016	1,480	4,303	488	0	n.d.	n.d.	n.d.
4,950	1,760	0	500	n.d.	0	M	100	0
2,920	650	0	186	n.d.	0	L	n.d.	n.d.
15,500	1,080	0	284	40	0	L	100	0
8,440	1,300	0	1,300	45	0	L	100	0
1,870	1,110	0	277	120	0	L	100	0
6,923	2,310	1,480	1,480	10	0	L	100	0
1,035	1,150	0	270	97	0	L	100	0
1,310	0	0	0	0	0	L	n.d.	n.d.
1,060	650	0	n.d.	175	0	L	100	0
41	5.5	0	5.5	1.2	0	M	27	73
75,045	55,060	4,914	14,397	11,456	184	n.d.	n.d.	n.d.
3,370	150	0	0	7	0	L	100	0
n.d.	n.d.	n.d.	n.d.	90	0	H	n.d.	n.d.
13,500	*9,720*	*0*	*4,800*	*8,150*	*0*	M	98	2
43,200	18,400	275	2,940	2,500	0.152	L	100	0
6,790	11,200	4,620	4,790	183	183	L	93	7
n.a.	9,700	0	291	0	0	L	100	0
5,600	4,980	19	1,500	n.d.	0	H	n.d.	<3
n.d.	910	0	76	274	0	H	89	11
n.d.	n.d.	n.d.	n.d.	250	1	L	87	13
n.d.	0	0	0	2.1	0	H	0	0
5,955	n.d.	n.d.	n.d.	n.d.	n.d.	M	56	18

(continued)

Table A.3 *(continued)*

Continent, country	Tropical forest area (millions of hectares)	Tropical closed natural forest	Permanent forest estate		
			Natural production	Planted production	Protection
Latin America and Caribbean		788,008	184,727	5,604	351,249
Bolivia	52.2–59.5	47,999	17,000	60	14,700
Brazil	*444.0–544.0*	489,515	98,100	3,810	271,000
Colombia	49.6–65.6	51,437	5,500	148	8,860
Ecuador	8.4–11.4	10,854	3,100	164	4,300
Guatemala	2.9–4.3	2,824	1,140	71	1,240
Guyana	16.9	16,916	5,450	12	980
Honduras	5.4	3,811	1,590	48	1,600
Mexico	*55.2–64.0*	33,120	7,880	100	5,600
Panama	2.9–3.5	3,052	350	56	1,580
Peru	65.2–86.4	64,204	24,600	250	16,300
Suriname	13.6–14.8	14,100	6,890	7	4,430
Trinidad and Tobago	0.2–0.3	250	127	15.4	59.1
R.B. de Venezuela	49.9–55.0	49,926	13,000	863	20,600
Total		1,213,380	355,710	46,098	467,420

n.d = No data.
Note: Data in italics are tropical and nontropical forests combined. L, M, and H indicate that community forests constitute a low, medium, or high proportion of the forest (based on authors' interpretations).
Public and private proportions of forest do not necessarily add to 100%; the remaining share may include community forests, or areas of undefined tenure.
Source: FAO 2005; ITTO 2006; Nguyen 2006.

Production forest management						Tenure		
Natural				Planted		Community owned or managed	Public forest (%)	Private forest (%)
License or concession	Management plan	Certified	Sustainably managed	Management plan	Certified			
34,651	31,174	4,150	6,468	2,371	1,589	n.d.	n.d.	n.d.
5,470	5,470	2,210	2,210	n.d.	0	M	85	10
n.d.	5,250	1,160	1,360	1,350	1,350	M	n.d.	n.d.
2,150	n.d.	0	200	80	58	M	n.d.	n.d.
n.d.	65	0	101	65	21.3	M	77	0
540	697	520	672	25	7.57	M	42	53
3,800	3,730	0	520	0	0	M	66	0
1,070	671	37	187	28	0	M	75	25
8,600	8,600	163	163	34	0	H	59	0
86	63	0	0	32	12.2	M	10	90
8,000	5,000	59.5	560	8	0	M	83	15
1,740	73	0	0	7	0	L		0
75	75	0	15	15.4	0	L	75	25
3,120	1,480	0	480	727	140	L	90	n.d.
153,745	96,250	10,544	25,168	14,315	1,773	n.d.	n.d.	n.d.

Appendix B: Data and Methods

This appendix briefly describes data and methods used for unpublished analyses in this report.

Global Data and Analyses (Chapter 1 and Figure 2.3)

Gridding

All mapped data were converted to a pantropical grid of 1 x 1 kilometer cells. Tables and figures in chapter 1 and figure 2.3 are based on this grid. Data scope included the tropical forest and savanna biomes, excluding Australia, Japan, and the United States.

Accessibility to Major Market

This index, constructed by Andrew Nelson, represents the notional time to travel to the nearest city of 100,000 or more people. It was constructed using standard Geographic Information System (GIS) methods, road information from the Digital Chart of the World (DCW), and assumed travel speeds for different road classes. Because the index is based on assumed rather than measured travel times, and because DCW maps are inconsistent and out of date, the imputed times should be considered only rough indexes.

This is especially the case for Africa, where travel in forest areas of the Democratic Republic Congo is probably much slower than represented by the maps and assumptions used for calculations. Elsewhere, some areas classified as very remote may in fact be relatively accessible due to recently constructed roads or rapidly growing towns.

Accessibility measures could not be computed for some areas, mostly in Asia. These include island portions of Indonesia and the Philippines, some island nations of the southwest Pacific, and for Taiwan, China. Populations and areas of these islands were included in table 1.3 based on judgments about remoteness but excluded from figures 1.3, 1.4, and 2.3.

Land Cover

The Global Land Cover 2000 (GLC2000) database (ECJRC 2003) was used for information about land use and forest cover throughout the tropics. This database is based on 1-kilometer resolution data from the SPOT-4 satellite. Dates for the data range from 1 November 1999 to 31 December 2000. The 23 land cover classifications used by the GLC2000 are shown in appendix table B.1, along with this report's 7-class aggregation of these classifications.

Table B.1   GLC2000 Land Cover Categories

Code	Type of land cover	Aggregated land cover class
1	Tree cover, broadleaved, evergreen	Forest
2	Tree cover, broadleaved, deciduous, closed	Forest
3	Tree cover, broadleaved, deciduous, open	Forest
4	Tree cover, needle-leaved, evergreen	Forest
5	Tree cover, needle-leaved, deciduous	Forest
6	Tree cover, mixed leaf type	Forest
7	Tree cover, regularly flooded, fresh water	Forest
8	Tree cover, regularly flooded, saline water	Forest
9	Mosaic of tree cover and other natural vegetation	Forest
10	Tree cover, burnt	Forest
11	Shrub cover, closed-open, evergreen	Bush
12	Shrub cover, closed-open, deciduous	Bush
13	Herbaceous cover, closed-open	Bush
14	Sparse herbaceous or sparse shrub cover	Bush
15	Regularly flooded shrub and/or herbaceous cover	Bush
16	Cultivated and managed areas	Agriculture
17	Mosaic of cropland, tree cover, and other natural vegetation	Mosaic
18	Mosaic of cropland, shrub, and/or grass cover	Mosaic
19	Bare areas	Bare
20	Water bodies	Water/missing
21	Snow and ice	Water/missing
22	Artificial surfaces and associated areas	Artificial
23	No data	Water/missing

Source: ECJRC 2003; authors' aggregations.

Forest Situation Typology

The report defines human-affected rural gridcells as being in "agriculture" or "mosaic" classes (using the 7-class aggregation). It then measures the distance from these collections of cells to areas that are forest or bush in the aggregated classification. The nearest 6 kilometers are called *forest edge* or *savanna edge* depending on biome. Forest or bush cells more than 6 kilometers from the nearest human-affected cells are designated as *forest core* or *savanna core*.

But a special rule is applied to small patches of forest and bush cells—those less than 8 square kilometers—that are completely surrounded by agriculture and mosaic cells. These are designated *embedded forests*. *Mosaic forests* consist of embedded forests and mosaic cells. *Mosaiclands* consist of mosaic forests and agricultural cells.

Rural Population Density

The report uses population density figures calculated from the GRUMP (alpha version) population count grid (CIESIN and others 2004b) and the GRUMP area grid (CIESIN and others 2004a). These figures are based on census data reported at a local administrative level—usually the equivalent of a county or *municipio,* or smaller.

Within the administrative unit, GRUMP identifies the population living in cities, towns, and villages of about 2,500 people or more (CIESIN and others 2004c). The rural remainder is assumed to be evenly distributed across the rest of the administrative unit. The assumption of even distribution likely overstates the population density of forested and remote areas of the unit and understates the density of agricultural and mosaic areas. So the forest population densities reported here should be taken with caution—as with all global, spatially explicit population datasets.

Forest Cover Change

The report team is grateful to the Food and Agriculture Organization (FAO) for sharing data from the Forest Resources Assessment Remote Sensing Survey (FRA-RSS) (FAO 2001a; b). The remote sensing survey examined a stratified random sample of 10 percent of the world's tropical forest, using Landsat scenes as a sampling frame. High-resolution (30-meter) images were used to identify nine types of land cover, sampled at 2-kilometer intervals. Change was detected by direct comparison of earlier and later scenes.

In the most forested class we grouped closed canopy, open canopy, and long fallow, followed by a second class consisting of fragmented forest and a third class of agriculture, short fallow, and shrubs (see table 2-4 in FAO 2001a or table 46-1 in FAO 2001b). We defined as degradation any shift from a more to a less densely forested cover. Degradation rates were computed by dividing the number of cells where degradation was observed from one time period to the next by the number of cells that were degradable—that is, neither in the third class nor covered by water or clouds in the earlier period. The changes reported are based on comparison of remote sensing images from around 1990 and 2000. Because of cloud cover, the actual image dates may vary. We did not adjust for the variation in observation period.

In calculating degradation rates, we used a weighting scheme based on the sampling scheme provided by the FAO to accompany the FRA-RSS. The weights used were calculated by dividing the land area computed from all Landsat scenes in the subregion and forest cover stratum by the land area of the sampled Landsat scenes from the respective subregions and strata.

Biomes

WWF (2001) distinguishes 13 biomes. This report's "forests" comprise three WWF tropical and subtropical biomes: moist broadleaf forest, dry broadleaf forest, and coniferous forest. This report's "savannas" correspond to WWF tropical and subtropical grasslands, savannas, and shrublands.

Agricultural Suitability

This measure corresponds to plate 46, "Suitability for rain-fed crops-maximizing technology mix," from the Global Agro-Ecological Zones dataset (FAO and IIASA 2000). This is a gridded dataset with 5 arc-minute resolution. It takes into consideration slope, soil fertility, soil depth, drainage, soil chemical, soil texture, and climate constraints.

Threatened Amphibians

These data are from the Global Amphibian Assessment, which describes the "extent of occurrence" and threat status of almost all known amphibian species (IUCN, Conservation International, and NatureServe 2005). The extent of occurrence is a rough depiction of the known geographic range of the species, based on recorded observations, and may include areas of habitat unsuitable for the species. Figure 1.4 shows the proportion of all gridcells, for each distance category, containing the extent of occurrence of at least one endangered or critically endangered amphibian species, using the classification of the World Conservation Union (IUCN) Redlist (http://www.redlist.org/info/categories_criteria2001.html).

Imminent Extinctions

Data on imminent extinctions are updated from Ricketts and others (2005) using data from the Alliance for Zero Extinction (www.zeroextinction.org, dataset v2.1). Locations of the imminent extinction sites were mapped into the pantropical forest (nonsavanna) gridcells. Figure 1.5 shows, for each distance category, the proportion of gridcells containing an imminent extinction site (multiplied by 100,000).

National Poverty, Forest, and Deforestation Data (Chapter 3 and Figure 2.1)

Brazil

The farmgate price imputation is from an unpublished analysis by IMAZON (Instituto do Homem e Meio Ambiente da Amazônia). Rainfall (annual mean) is 1-kilometer resolution data from Hijmans and others (2004).

Deforestation data are from 1:250,000 scale digital maps of incremental clearing based on remote sensing, and cover primary forests (excluding savannas) covering the officially-defined Amazônian region of Brazil (INPE 2004).

Literacy and population data at the census tract level are from the Brazilian Demographic Census 2000 (IBGE 2003). Municipal income and education data are from UNDP (2004) and derived from the 2000 census.

India

Data on the proportion of forest cover are from India's *State of Forest Report 2003* (Forest Survey of India 2005). Literacy data are from India's 2001 population census (Government of India 2001). Units of observation are at the district level.

Indonesia

Data on forest cover in 2000 are from the Forest Watch Indonesia land cover map, derived from the Ministry of Forests forest cover data for 2003. Forest cover for 1990 was generated from the 1:250,000 land cover map of the National Forest Inventory 1993.

Poverty map data for 2000 were constructed by the Central Bureau of Statistics (BPS 2005) using the method of Elbers, Lanjouw, and Lanjouw (2003), which imputes consumption to census households based on regressions estimated using a separate household survey. There is a tradeoff between spatial precision and precision of the imputed mean consumption level. The *kecamatan*-level estimates shown here have relatively high standard errors and thus are useful for illustrating, for example, relationships between forest cover and poverty, rather than for providing poverty counts for a particular *kecamatan*.

Madagascar

Forest cover and deforestation data are from satellite images interpreted and analyzed by Conservation International for 1990 and 2000 (Harper n.d.; Steininger and others 2004), and from the World Bank poverty map for Madagascar, based on welfare measures computed from the 1993 census of population and housing (Bureau Central du Recensement), as well as from a household survey (Mistiaen, Razafimanantena, and Razafindravonona 2002) again using the method of Elbers, Lanjouw and Lanjouw (2003). Data points were computed at the *firaisana* level. The size of the bubbles is based on the population of the *firaisana* in 1993.

Nicaragua

Extreme rural poverty rates are from *Gobierno de Nicaragua* (2001) and based on the 1995 census and imputed consumption using a 1998 survey. Imputed access time to Managua was computed using GIS methods from a late 1990s road map and assumptions about mean travel speed on four classes of roads. Rural population density was computed as rural population divided by total municipio area—implicitly assuming that urban areas occupy a negligible portion of municipio land area. Tabulations excluded island *municipios* and a few that "fissioned" between 1995 and 2001.

Chapter 5

Data on Brazilian municipal environmental councils and problem perceptions are from IBGE (2002).

Chapter 6

The dataset for parks is the 2005 national IUCN point dataset from WDPA Consortium (2005). Figures 6.1 and 6.2 were produced using it. The analysis was limited to tropical forest and tropical savanna biomes in developing countries, and further excluded marine parks, those without information on establishment date, and those for which accessibility could not be computed.

References

Achard, Frederic, Hugh D. Eva, Philippe Mayaux, Hans-Jürgen Stibig, and Alan Belward. 2004. "Improved Estimates of Net Carbon Emissions from Land Cover Change in the Tropics for the 1990s." *Global Biogeochemical Cycles* 18.

Achard, F., J. P. Malingreau, T. Phulpin, G. Saint, B. Saugier, B. Seguin, and V. Vidal-Madjar. 1994. "A Mission for Global Monitoring of the Continental Biosphere." VEGETATION International Users Committee Secretariat, Joint Research Centre, Ispra, Italy.

Agrawal, Arun. 2001. "Common Property Institutions and Sustainable Governance of Resources." *World Development* 29 (10): 1649–72.

Agrawal, Arun, and Kent Redford. 2006. "Poverty, Development, and Biodiversity Conservation: Shooting in the Dark?" Working paper 26. Wildlife Conservation Society, New York.

Akella, Anita Sundari, and James B. Cannon. 2004. *Strengthening the Weakest Links: Strategies for Improving the Enforcement of Environmental Laws Globally.* Washington, D.C.: Center for Conservation and Government [Conservation International].

Alix-Garcia, Jennifer, Alain de Janvry, Elisabeth Sadoulet, Juan Manuel Torres, Josefina Braña, and Maria Zorilla Ramos. 2005. "An Assessment of Mexico's Payment for Environmental Services Program." Food and Agriculture Organization, Rome.

Alston, Lee J., Gary D. Lipecab, and Bernardo Mueller. 2000. "Land Reform Policies, the Sources of Violent Conflict, and Implication in Deforestation in Brazilian Amazon." *Journal of Environmental Economics and Management* 39 (2): 162–88.

Andersen, L. E., and E. J. Reis. 1997. "Deforestation, Development and Government Policy in the Brazilian Amazon: An Econometric Analysis." Working paper 513. Instituto de Pesquisa Econômica Aplicada (IPEA), Rio de Janeiro.

Andersson, Krister. 2003. "What Motivates Municipal Governments? Uncovering the Institutional Incentives for Municipal Governance of Forest Resources in Bolivia." *Journal of Environment and Development* 12 (1): 5–27.

Angelsen, Arild. 1995. "Shifting Cultivation and 'Deforestation': A study from Indonesia." *World Development* 23 (10): 1713–29.

———. 2006. "A Stylized Model of Incentives to Convert, Maintain, or Establish Forests." Background paper for this report.

Angelsen, Arild, and David Kaimowitz. 2001. *Agricultural Technologies and Tropical Deforestation.* Wallingford, U.K.: CABI Publishing.

Antinori, Camille, and David Barton Bray. 2005. "Community Forest Enterprises as Entrepreneurial Firms: Economic and Institutional Perspectives from Mexico." *World Development* 33 (9): 1529–43.

Antona, M. E. Motte. 2002. "Property Right Transfer in Madagascar's Biodiversity Policies." Paper presented at the BioEcon meeting, Rome.

Araújo, S. Alves de. 2006. "Sistema de Licenciamento Ambiental em Propriedades Rurais do Estado do Mato Grosso." Presentation at the Brazilian Ministry of the Environment workshop "SLAPR na Amazônia Legal—Estudo de Caso das Experiências de Mato Grosso, Rondônia, et Tocantins," February 8–10, Palmas.

Arima, Eugenio Y., Paulo Barreto, and Marky Brito. 2006. *Cattle Ranching in the Amazon: Trends and Implications for Environmental Conservation.* Belém, Brazil: Imazon.

Arima, Eugenio Y., Robert T. Walker, Stephen G. Perz, and Marcellus Caldas. 2005. "Loggers and Forest Fragmentation: Behavioral Models of Road Building in the Amazon Basin." *Annals of the Association of American Geographers* 95 (3): 525–41.

Arnold, J. E. M. 2001. "Forestry, Poverty and Aid." Occasional paper 33. Center for International Forestry Research, Bogor, Indonesia.

Arnold, J. E. M., Gunnar Köhlin, and Reidar Persson. 2006. "Woodfuels, Livelihoods, and Policy Interventions: Changing Perspectives." *World Development* 34 (3): 596–611.

Asner, Gregory P., David E. Knapp, Eben N. Broadbent, Paulo J. C. Oliveira, Michael Keller, and Jose N. Silva. 2005. "Selective Logging in the Brazilian Amazon." *Science* 310 (5747): 480–82.

Aylward, Bruce. 2002. "Strategic Framework." Report to the World Bank under the Program for Sustainable Management of Rural Areas in the Panama Canal Watershed.

———. 2005. "Land-Use, Hydrological Function and Economic Valuation." In M. Bonell and L. A. Bruijnzeel, eds., *Forest, Water and People in the Humid Tropics.* Cambridge, U.K.: Cambridge University Press.

Baillie, J. E. M., C. Hilton-Taylor, and S. N. Stuart, eds. 2004. *2004 IUCN Red List of Threatened Species: A Global Species Assessment.* Gland, Switzerland and Cambridge, U.K.: World Conservation Union (IUCN).

Baland, Jean-Marie, and Jean-Philippe Platteau. 1996. *Halting Degradation of Natural Resources: Is There a Role for Rural Communities?* Oxford: Clarendon Press.

Balk, Deborah, F. Pozzi, Uwe Deichmann, G. Yetman, and A. Nelson. 2004. "The Distribution of People and the Dimension of Place: Methodologies to Improve Global Estimation of Urban Extents." Columbia University, Center for International Earth Science Information Network, Palisades, New York.

Bandyopadhyay, S., P. Shyamsundar, and A. Baccini. 2006. "Forests, Biomass Use and Poverty in Malawi." Draft background paper for the Malawi Poverty Assessment. World Bank, Environment Department, Policy and Economic Team, Washington, D.C.

Barbier, E. B., and Mark Cox. 2004. "An Economic Analysis of Shrimp Farm Expansion and Mangrove Conversion in Thailand." *Land Economics* 80 (3): 389–407.

Barbosa, G. N. 2006. "A experiência de Mato Grosso: uma visão critica do Ministerio Publico Estadual do Mato Grosso." Presentation at the Brazilian Ministry of the Environment workshop "SLAPR na Amazônia Legal—Estudo de Caso das Experiências de Mato Grosso, Rondônia, et Tocantins," February 8–10, Palmas.

Barnes, Douglas F., Kerry Krutilla, and William F. Hyde. 2005. *The Urban Household Energy Transition.* Washington, D.C.: Resources for the Future.

Bartholomé, E., and A. S. Belward. 2005. "GLC2000: A New Approach to Global Land Cover Mapping from Earth Observation Data." *International Journal of Remote Sensing* 26 (May 9, 10): 1959–77.

Batagoda, B. M. S., Kerry R. Turner, Robert Tinch, and Katrina Brown. 2000. "Towards Policy Relevant Ecosystem Services and Natural Capital Values: Rainforest Non-Timber Products." CSERGE Working Paper GEC 2000-06. University of East Anglia, Norwich, U.K.

Baulch, Bob, Truong Thi Kim Chuyen, Dominique Haughton, and Jonathan Haughton. 2004. "Ethnic Minority Development in Vietnam and the Potential for Targeting." In Paul Glewwe, Nisha Agrawal, and David Dollar, eds., *Economic Growth, Poverty, and Household Welfare in Vietnam.* Washington, D.C.: World Bank.

Bennett, Michael T. 2005. "China's Sloping Land Conversion Program: Institutional Innovation or Business as Usual?" Revised version of a paper presented at the ZEF-CIFOR workshop on "Payments for Environmental Services: Methods and Design in Developing and Developed Countries," Titisee, Germany, June 15–18, 2005.

Binswanger, Hans P., Shahidur R. Khandker, and Mark R. Rosenzweig. 1993. "How Infrastructure and Financial Institutions Affect Agricultural Output and Investment in India." *Journal of Development Economics* 41 (2): 337–66.

Boccucci, M., K. D. Muliastra, and G. Dore. 2005. "Poverty Analysis of Indonesia's Forest Land." Draft report. World Bank, Jakarta, Indonesia.

Boltz, Frederick, Douglas R. Carter, Thomas P. Holmes, and Rodrigo Jr. Pereiara. 2001. "Financial Returns under Uncertainty for Conventional and Reduced Impact Logging in Permanent Production Forests of the Brazilian Amazon." *Ecological Economics* (39): 387–98.

Bonell, M., and L. A. Bruijnzeel, eds. 2005. *Forests, Water and People in the Humid Tropics.* Cambridge, U.K.: Cambridge University Press.

Boscolo, Marco, and Jeffrey R. Vincent. 2000. "Promoting Better Logging Practices in Tropical Forests: A Simulation Analysis of Alternative Regulations." *Land Economics* 76 (1): 1–14.

BPS (Biro Pusat Statistik). 2005. *Peta Penduduk Miskin Indonesia*, 2000.

Brandon, Katrina, Larry J. Gorenflo, Ana S. L. Rodrigues, and Robert W. Waller. 2005. "Reconciling Biodiversity Conservation, People, Protected Areas, and Agricultural Suitability in Mexico." *World Development* 33 (9): 1403–18.

Bray, David Barton, Leticia Merino-Perez, Patricia Negreros-Castillo, Gerardo Segura-Warnholtz, Juan Manuel Torres-Rojo, and Henricus F. M. Vester. 2003. "Mexico's Community-Managed Forests as a Global Model for Sustainable Landscapes." *Conservation Biology* 17 (3): 672–77.

Brito, Brenda, Paulo Barreto, and John Rothman. 2005. "Brazil's New Environmental Crimes Law: An Analysis of Its Effectiveness in Protecting the Amazonian Forests." Belém, Imazon.

Brooks, Thomas M., Stuart L. Pimm, and Joseph O. Oyugi. 1999. "Time Lag between Deforestation and Bird Extinction in Tropical Forest Fragments." *Conservation Biology* 13 (5): 1140–50.

Brown, David. 2004. "Review of Independent Forest Monitoring." ODI, London.

Bruijnzeel, L. A. 2004. "Hydrological Functions of Tropical Forests: Not Seeing the Soil for the Trees?" *Agriculture, Ecosystems & Environment* 104: 185–228.

Bruijnzeel, L. A., M. Bonell, D. A. Gilmour, and D. Lamb. 2005. "Forest, Water and People in the Humid Tropics: An Emerging View." In M. Bonell and L. A. Bruijnzeel, eds., *Forest, Water and People in the Humid Tropics*. Cambridge, U.K.: Cambridge University Press.

Bruinsma, J. 2003. *World Agriculture: Towards 2015/2030—An FAO Perspective*. London: Earthscan.

Bruner, Aaron G., Raymond E. Gullison, Richard E. Rice, and Gustavo A. B. Da Fonseca. 2001. "Effectiveness of Parks in Protecting Tropical Biodiversity." *Science* 291: 125–28.

Bureau Central Du Recensement. 1993. *Recensement général de la population et de l'habitat*. Antananarivo, Madagascar: Direction De La Démographie Et Des Statistiques Socials.

Burgess, Neil D., Jennifer D'Amico Hales, Taylor H. Ricketts, and Eric Dinerstein. 2006. "Factoring Species, Non-Species Values and Threats Into Biodiversity Prioritisation across the Ecoregions of Africa and Its Islands." *Biological Conservation* 127 (4): 383–401.

Buys, P., U. Deichmann, and D. Wheeler. 2006. "Road Network Upgrading and Overland Trade Expansion in Sub-Saharan Africa." World Bank, Washington, D.C.

Calder, Ian R. 2005. *The Blue Revolution: Land Use and Integrated Water Resources Management*. London: Earthscan.

Cassman, Kenneth G., and Stanley Wood. 2005. "Cultivated Systems." In Rashid Hassan, Robert Scholes, and Neville Ash, eds., *Ecosystems and Human Well-Being: Current State and Trends*. Washington, D.C.: Island Press.

Castro, Newton de. 2002. "Custos de transporte e produção agrígola no Brasil, 1970–1996." *Agricultura em São Paulo* 49 (2): 87–109.

Ceballos, Gerardo, Paul R. Ehrlich, Jorge Soberón, Irma Salazar, and John P. Fay. 2005. "Global Mammal Conservation: What Must We Manage?" *Science* 309: 603–07.

Cernea, Michael M., and Kai Schmidt-Soltau. 2003. "The End of Forcible Displacement? Conservation Must Not Impoverish People." *Policy Matters* 12: 42–51.

Chazdon, Robin L. 2003. "Tropical Forest Recovery: Legacies of Human Impact and Natural Disturbances." *Perspectives in Plant Ecology, Evolution and Systematics* 6 (1.2): 51–71.

Chomitz, Kenneth M. 2002. "Baseline, Leakage, and Measurement Issues: How Do Forestry and Energy Projects Compare?" *Climate Policy* 2 (1): 35–49.

———. 2004. "Nicaragua Economic Geography: A Snapshot." In *Nicaragua: Drivers of Sustainable Rural Growth and Poverty Reduction in Central America, Vol. II.* Washington, D.C.: World Bank.

Chomitz, K. M. and D. Gray. 1996. "Roads, Land Use, and Deforestation: A Spatial Model Applied to Belize." *The World Bank Economic Review* 10: 487–512.

Chomitz, K. M., and K. Kumari. 1998. "The Domestic Benefits of Tropical Forest Preservation: A Critical Review Emphasizing Hydrological Functions." *The World Bank Research Observer* 13 (1): 13–35.

Chomitz, Kenneth M., and Timothy S. Thomas. 2003. "Determinants of Land Use in Amazônia: A Fine-Scale Spatial Analysis." *American Journal of Agricultural Economics* 85: 1016–28.

Chomitz, Kenneth M., and Sheila Wertz-Kanounnikoff. 2005. "Measuring the Initial Impacts on Deforestation of Mato Grosso's Program for Environmental Control." Policy Research Working Paper 3762. World Bank, Washington, D.C.

Chomitz, K. M, E. Brenes, and L. Constantino. 1999. "Financing Environmental Services: The Costa Rican Experience and Its Implications." *Science of the Total Environment* 240: 157–69.

Chomitz, K. M., Timothy S. Thomas, and Antônio Salazar P. Brandao. 2005. "The Economic and Environmental Impact of Trade in Forest Reserve Obligations: A Simulation Analysis of Options for Dealing with Habitat Heterogeneity." *Revista Economia e Sociologia Rural* 43 (4): 657–82.

Chomitz, K. M, Daniel da Mata, Alexandre Ywata de Carvalho, and João Carlos Magalhaes. 2005a. "Spatial Dynamics of Brazilian Labor Markets." Policy Research Working Paper 3752. World Bank, Washington, D.C.

Chomitz, K. M., K. Alger, T. S. Thomas, H. Orlando, and P. Vila Nova. 2005b. "Opportunity Costs of Conservation in a Biodiversity Hotspot: The Case of Southern Bahia." *Environment and Development Economics* 10 (3): 293–312.

Chomitz, Kenneth M., Gunawan Setiadi, Azrul Azwar, Nusye Ismail, and Widiyarti. 1998. "What Do Doctors Want? Two Empirical Analyses of Indonesian Physicians' Preferences Regarding Service in Rural and Remote Areas." Policy Working Paper Series 1888. World Bank, Washington, D.C.

Chomitz, Kenneth M., G. A. B. Fonseca, D. M. Stoms, M. Honzák, E. C. Landau, T. S. Thomas, D. Thomas, and A. Davis. 2006. "Viable Reserve Networks Arise from Individual Landholder Responses to Conservation Incentives." Unpublished paper.

CIESIN (Center For International Earth Science Information Network), IFPRI (International Food Policy Research Institute), World Bank, and CIAT (Centro Internacional De Agricultura Tropical). 2004a. "Global Rural-Urban Mapping Project (GRUMP), Alpha Version: Land Area Grids." Columbia University, Socioeconomic Data and Applications Center (SEDAC), Palisades, N.Y. [http://sedac.ciesin.columbia.edu/gpw]. Accessed December 22, 2005.

———. 2004b. "Global Rural-Urban Mapping Project (GRUMP), Alpha Version: Population Grids." Columbia University, Socioeconomic Data and Applications Center (SEDAC), Palisades, N.Y. [http://sedac.ciesin.columbia.edu/gpw]. Accessed February 7, 2006.

———. 2004c. "Global Rural-Urban Mapping Project (GRUMP), Alpha Version: Urban Extents." Columbia University, Socioeconomic Data and Applications Center (SEDAC), Palisades, N.Y. [http://sedac.ciesin.columbia.edu/gpw]. Accessed December 22, 2005.

CIFOR (Center for International Forestry Research) and FAO (Food and Agriculture Organization). 2005. "Forests and Floods: Drowning in Fiction or Thriving on Facts?" RAP publication 2005/03. CIFOR and FAO Regional Office for Asia and the Pacific, Bogor, Indonesia.

Cochrane, Mark A., Ane Alencar, Mark D. Schulze, Carlos M. Souza Jr., Daniel C. Nepstad, Paul Lefebvre, and Eric A. Davidson. 1999. "Positive Feedbacks in the Fire Dynamic Of Closed Canopy Tropical Forests." *Science* 284: 1832–35.

Colchester, Marcus. 2006. "Justice in the Forest: Rural Livelihoods and Forest Law Enforcement." Center for International Forestry Research, Bogor, Indonesia.

Colfer, Carol J. Pierce, and Ana Doris Capistrano. 2005. *The Politics of Decentralization: Forest, Power and People.* London: Earthscan.

Contreras-Hermosilla, Arnoldo, and Elisa Peter. 2006. "Best Practices for Improving Law Compliance in the Forestry Sector." FAO and ITTO, Rome.

Contreras-Hermosilla, Arnoldo, and Chip Fay. 2005. "Strengthening Forest Management in Indonesia through Land Tenure Reform: Issues and Framework for Action." Forest Trends, Washington, D.C.

Costa, Marcos Heil, Aurelie Botta, and Jeffrey A. Cardille. 2003. "Effects Of Large-Scale Changes in Land Cover on the Discharge of the Tocantins River, Southeastern Amazonia." *Journal of Hydrology* 283 (1–4): 206–17.

Cowles, Paul D., Soava Rakotoarisoa, Haingolalao Rasolonirinamanana, and Vololona Rasoaromanana. 2001. "Facilitation, Participation, and Learning in an Ecoregion-Based Planning Process: The Case of AGERAS in Toliara, Madagascar." In Louise E. Buck, Charles G. Geisler, John Schelhas, and Eva Wollenberg, eds., *Biological Diversity: Balancing Interests through Adaptive Collaborative Management*. Boca Raton, Fla.: CRS Press.

Cowling, R. M., R. L. Pressey, M. Rouget, and A. T. Lombard. 2003. "A Conservation Plan for a Global Biodiversity Hotspot—The Cape Floristic Region, South Africa." *Biological Conservation* 112 (1–2): 191–216.

Coxhead, Ian, and Bayou Demeke. 2004. "Panel Data Evidence on Upland Agricultural Land Use in the Philippines: Can Economic Policy Reforms Reduce Environmental Damages?" *American Journal of Agricultural Economics* 86 (5): 1354–60.

Cropper, Maureen, Charles Griffiths, and Muthukumara Mani. 1999. "Roads, Population Pressures, and Deforestation in Thailand, 1976–1989." *Land Economics* 75 (1): 58–73.

Cropper, Maureen, Jyotsna Puri, and Charles Griffiths. 2001. "Predicting the Location of Deforestation: The Role of Roads and Protected Areas in North Thailand." *Land Economics* 77 (2): 172–86.

Cruz, Rex Victor O., and Maricel A. Tapia. 2006. "A Review of the Multi-Sectoral Forest Protection Committees in the Philippines." Overseas Development Institute, London.

Curran, L. M., S. N. Trigg, A. K. McDonald, D. Astiani, Y. M. Hardiono, P. Siregar, I. Caniago, and E. Kasischke. 2004. "Lowland Forest Loss in Protected Areas of Indonesian Borneo." *Science* 303 (5660): 1000–03.

Davies, P., and P. Abelson. 1996. "Value Soils in the Tropical Lowlands of Eastern Bolivia." In P. Abelson, ed., *Project Appraisal and Valuation of the Environment, General Principles and Six Case Studies in Developing Countries*. London: Macmillan.

Davis, M. 2005. "Forests and Conflict in Cambodia." *International Forestry Review* 7 (2): 161–64.

Defries, Ruth S., Richard A. Houghton, Matthew C. Hansen, Christopher B. Field, David Skole, and John Townshend. 2002. "Carbon Emissions from Tropical Deforestation and Regrowth Based on Satellite Observations for the 1980s and 1990s." *Proceedings of the National Academy of Sciences* 99 (22): 14256–61.

Deininger, Klaus. 2003. *Land Policies for Growth and Poverty Reduction*. A Policy Research Report. New York: Oxford University Press for the World Bank.

Deininger, Klaus, and Bart Minten. 1999. "Poverty, Politics, and Deforestation: The Case of Mexico." *Economic Development and Cultural Change* 47 (2): 313–44.

———. 2002. "Determinants of Deforestation and the Economics of Protection: An Application to Mexico." *American Journal of Agricultural Economics* 84 (4): 943–60.

De Merode, Emmanuel, Katherine Homewood, and Guy Cowlishaw. 2004. "The Value of Bushmeat and Other Wild Foods to Rural Households Living in Extreme Poverty in Democratic Republic of Congo." *Biological Conservation* 118 (5): 573–81.

Dennis, Rona A., Judith Mayer, Grahame Applegate, Unna Chokkalingam, Carol J. Pierce Colfer, Iwan Kurniawan, Henry Lachowski, Paul Maus, Rizki Pandu Permana, Yayat Ruchiat, Fred Stolle, Suyanto, and Thomas P. Tomich. 2005. "Fire, People and Pixels: Linking Social Science and Remote Sensing to Underlying Causes and Impacts of Fires in Indonesia." *Human Ecology* 33 (4): 465–504.

Deschamps, Vince, and Paul Hartman. 2005. "Trends in Forest Ownership, Forest Resources Tenure and Institutional Arrangements: Are They Contributing to Better Forest Management and Poverty Reduction? Case Studies from Indonesia." Paper prepared for a Food and Agriculture Organization regional workshop, October 17–21, Bangkok, Thailand.

De Vreyer, Philippe, Javier Herrera, and Sandrine Mesple-Somps. 2002. "Consumption Growth and Spatial Poverty Traps: An Analysis of the Effects of Social Services and Community Infrastructures on Living Standards in Rural Peru." Document de travail 2002/17. DIAL, Paris.

Dewi, Sonya, Brian Belcher, and Atie Puntodewo. 2005. "Village Economic Opportunity, Forest Dependence, and Rural Livelihoods in East Kalimantan, Indonesia." *World Development* 33 (9): 1419–34.

Dilley, Maxx, Robert S. Chen, Arthur L. Lerner-Lam, Margaret Arnold, Jonathan Agwe, Piet Buys, Oddvar Kjekstad, Bradfield Lyon, and Gregory Yetman. 2005. "Natural Disaster Hotspots: A Global Risk Analysis." World Bank, Washington, D.C.

Dorosh, Paul, and Bart Minten. 2005. "Rice Price Stabilization in Madagascar: Price and Welfare Implications of Variable Tariffs." Working paper. U.S. Agency for International Development, SAGA, Washington, D.C.

Douglas, Ellen, Stanley Wood, Kate Sebastian, Charles J. Vorosmarty, Kenneth M. Chomitz, and Thomas P. Tomich. Forthcoming. "Policy Implications of a Pan-Tropic Assessment of the Simultaneous Hydrological and Biodiversity Impacts of Deforestation." *Water Resources Management*.

Douglas, Ellen M., Kate Sebastian, K. M Chomitz, Charles J. Vorosmarty, and Stanley Wood. 2005. "The Role of Tropical Forests in Supporting

Biodiversity and Hydrological Integrity." Policy Research Working Paper 3635. World Bank, Washington, D.C.

Dudley, Nigel, and Sue Stolton. 2003. *Running Pure*. Washington, D.C.: World Bank and World Wildlife Fund.

Dudley, Nigel, Kalemani Jo Mulongoy, Sheldon Cohen, Sue Stolton, Victor Charles Barber, and Sarat Babu Gidda. 2005. "Towards Effective Protected Area Systems. An Action Guide to Implement the Convention on Biological Diversity Programme of Work on Protected Areas." Technical Series 18. Secretariat of the Convention on Biological Diversity, Montreal, Canada.

ECJRC (European Commission Joint Research Centre). 2003. "Global Land Cover 2000 Database." [http://www.gvm.jrc.it/glc2000].

Economist Intelligence Unit. 2005. "Country Profile 2005: Brazil." London.

Environmental Law Institute. 2003. "Legal Tools and Incentives for Private Lands Conservation in Latin America: Building Models for Success." Washington, D.C.

Escobal, Javier, and Carmen Ponce. 2002. "The Benefit of Rural Roads: Enhancing Income Opportunities for the Rural Poor." GRADE, Lima, Peru.

ESRI (Environmental Systems Research Institute). 1993. "Digital Chart of the World: Digitized Data, Based On Defense Mapping Agency Maps at 1:1,000,000." [http://www.maproom.psu.edu/dcw].

Etter, Andres, Clive Mcalpine, Kerrie Wilson, Stuart Phinn, and Hugh Possingham. 2006. "Regional Patterns of Agricultural Land Use and Deforestation in Colombia." *Agriculture, Ecosystems & Environment* 114 (2–4): 369–86.

Fa, John E., Dominic Currie, and Jessica Meeuwig. 2003. "Bushmeat and Food Security in the Congo Basin: Linkages between Wildlife and People's Future." *Environmental Conservation* 30 (1): 71–78.

Faith, D. P., P. A. Walker, and C. R Margules. 2001. "Some Future Prospects for Systematic Biodiversity Planning in Papua New Guinea—and for Biodiversity Planning in General." *Pacific Conservation Biology* 6: 325–43.

Faith, D. P., G. Carter, G. Cassis, S. Ferrier, and L. Wilkie. 2003. "Complementarity, Biodiversity Viability Analysis, and Policy-Based Algorithms for Conservation." *Environmental Science and Policy* 6: 311–28.

Fan, Shenngen, and Connie Chan-Kang. 2004. "Returns to Investment in Less-Favored Areas in Developing Countries: A Synthesis of Evidence and Implications for Africa." *Food Policy* 29 (4): 431–44.

Fan, Shenggen, and Xiaobo Zhang. 2004. "Infrastructure and Regional Economic Development in Rural China." *China Economic Review* 15 (2): 203–14.

Fan, Shenngen, Peter Hazell, and T. Haque. 2000. "Targeting Public Investments by Agro-Ecological Zone to Achieve Growth and Poverty Alleviation Goals in Rural India." *Food Policy* 25 (4): 411–28.

255

Fan, Shenggen, David Nyange, and Neetha Rao. 2005. "Public Investment and Poverty Reduction in Tanzania: Evidence from Household Survey Data." Discussion Paper 18. International Food Policy Research Institute, Development Strategy and Government Division, Washington, D.C.

Fan, Shenggen, Xiaobo Zhang, and Linxiu Zhang. 2004. "Reform, Investment, and Poverty in Rural China." *Economic Development and Cultural Change* 52 (2): 395–421.

FAO (Food and Agriculture Organization). 2001a "FRA 2000: Pan-Tropical Survey of Forest Cover Changes 1980–2000." FRA Working Paper 49. Rome.

———. 2001b. "Global Forest Resources Assessment 2000: Main Report." Forestry Paper 140. Rome.

———. 2005. "Global Forest Resources Assessment 2005: Progress towards Sustainable Forest Management." Forestry Paper 147. Rome.

FAO (Food and Agriculture Organization) and IIASA (International Institute For Applied Systems Analysis). 2000. "The Global AEZ CD-ROM." [http://www.iiasa.ac.at/research/luc/gaez/index.htm]. Accessed October 13, 2005.

Fay, Chip, and G. Michon. 2005. "Redressing Forestry Hegemony: When a Forestry Regulatory Framework Is Best Replaced by an Agrarian One." *Agroforestry Systems* 15: 193–209.

Fearnside, Philip M. 1995. "Global Warming Response Options in Brazil's Forest Sector: Comparison of Project-level Costs and Benefits." *Biomass and Bioenergy* 8 (5): 309–22.

———. 2003. "Deforestation Control in Mato Grosso: A New Model for Slowing the Loss of Brazil's Amazon Forest." *Ambio* 35 (5): 343–45.

Feddema, Johannes J., Keith W. Oleson, Gordon B. Bonan, Linda O. Mearns, Lawrence E. Buja, Gerald A. Meehl, and Warren M. Washington. 2005. "The Importance of Land-Cover Change in Simulating Future Climates." *Science* 310 (5754): 1674–78.

Fernandez, Tania, and Carlos Munoz. 2006. "Correlations between Poverty and Deforestation in Mexico." INE-DGIPEA draft report EA-0602. Mexico, D. F.

Ferraro, P. J. 2002. "The Local Costs of Establishing Protected Areas in Low-income Nations: Ranomafana National Park, Madagascar." *Ecological Economics* 43: 261–75.

Ferraro, Paul J., and Agnes Kiss. 2002. "Direct Payments to Conserve Biodiversity." *Science* 298: 1718–19.

Finan, Frederico, Elisabeth Sadoulet, and Alain de Janvry. 2005. "Measuring the Poverty Reduction Potential of Land in Rural Mexico." *Journal of Development Economics* 77: 27–51.

Fisher, R. J., Stewart Maginnis, W. J. Jackson, Edmund Barrow, and Sally Jeanrenaud. 2005. "Poverty and Conservation: Landscape, People and Power." Landscapes and Livelihoods Series 2. World Conservation Union (IUCN), Gland, Switzerland.

FNP Consultoría & Agroinformativos. n.d. "Valor da Terra."

Foley, Jonathan A., Michael T. Coe, Marten Scheffer, and Guiling Wang. 2003. "Regime Shifts in the Sahara and Sahel: Interactions between Ecological and Climatic Systems in Northern Africa." *Ecosystems* 6 (6): 524–32.

Forest Survey of India. 2005. *State of Forest Report 2003*. Dehradun, India: Ministry of Environment and Forests.

Forest Trends. 2006. "Logging, Legality and Livelihoods in PNG: Synthesis of Official Assessments of the Large-Scale Logging Industry Forest Trends." Washington, D.C.

Forman, Richard T. T. 1995. *Land Mosaics: The Ecology of Landscapes and Regions.* Cambridge, U.K.: Cambridge University Press.

Foster, Andrew D., and Mark R. Rosenzweig. 2003. "Economic Growth and the Rise of Forests." *Quarterly Journal of Economics* 118 (2): 601–37.

Fundação Estadual do Meio Ambiente. 2001. "Environmental Control System on Rural Properties." Governo do Estado de Mato Grosso, Cuiabá.

———. 2002. "Relatório dos resultados alcançados na implementação do sistema de controle ambiental de propriedades rurais no estado de Mato Grosso." Governo do Estado de Mato Grosso, Cuiabá.

Fundacão Getulio Vargas. Data series 22716 and 22759. [http://fgvdados .fgv.br]. Accessed June 12, 2005.

FWI (Forest Watch Indonesia) and GFW (Global Forest Watch). 2002. "The State of the Forest: Indonesia." Bogor, Indonesia.

Garrity, D. P., M. Soekardi, M. Noordwijk, R. Cruz, P. S. Pathak, H. P. M. Gunasena, N. So, G. Huijun, and N. M. Majid. 1996. "The *Imperata* Grasslands of Tropical Asia: Area, Distribution, and Typology." *Agroforestry Systems* 36 (1–3): 3–29.

Gautam, A. P., G. P. Shivakoti, and E. L. Webb. 2004. "Forest Cover Change, Physiography, Local Economy, and Institutions in a Mountain Watershed in Nepal." *Environmental Management* 33 (1): 48–61.

Gbetnkom, Daniel. 2005. "Deforestation in Cameroon: Immediate Causes and Consequences." *Environment and Development Economics* 10: 557–72.

GEF (Global Environment Facility). 2006. "The Role of Local Benefits in Global Environmental Programs." Evaluation Report 30. GEF Evaluation Office, Washington, D.C.

Geisler, Charles, and Ragendra de Sousa. 2001. "From Refuge to Refugee: The African Case." *Public Administration and Development* 21: 159–70.

Geist, Helmut J., and Eric F. Lambin. 2001. "What Drives Tropical Deforestation? A Meta-analysis of Proximate and Underlying Causes of Deforestation Based on Subnational Case Study Evidence." LUCC Report Series 4. IHDP and IGBP, Louvain-la-Neuve, Belgium.

Geoghegan, Jacqueline, Sergio Cortina Villar, Peter Klepeis, Pedro Macario Mendoza, Yelena Ogneva-Himmelberger, Rinku Roy Chowdhury, I. I.

Turner, and Colin Vance. 2001. "Modeling Tropical Deforestation in the Southern Yucatan Peninsular Region: Comparing Survey and Satellite Data." *Agriculture, Ecosystems & Environment* 85 (1–3): 25–46.

Ghimire, Krishna B., and Michel P. Pimbert. 1997. *Social Change & Conservation.* London: Earthscan.

Gibson, Clark C., John T. Williams, and Elinor Ostrom. 2005. "Local Enforcement and Better Forests." *World Development* 33 (2): 273–84.

Gibson, John, and Scott Rozelle. 2003. "Poverty and Access to Roads in Papua New Guinea." *Economic Development and Cultural Change* 52 (1): 159–85.

Gilmour, Don, Y. B. Malla, and Mike Nurse. 2004. "Linkages between Community Forestry and Poverty." RECOFTC, Bangkok, Thailand.

Gitz, Vincent, Jean-Charles Hourcade, and Philippe Ciais. 2006. "The Timing of the Biological Carbon Sequestration and Carbon Abatement in the Energy Sector under Optimal Strategies against Climate Risks." *The Energy Journal* 27.

Global Forest Watch. 2005. "Interactive Forestry Atlas of Cameroon (Version 1.0): An Overview." WRI–MINEF, Washington, D.C.

Glomsrod, Solveig, Maria Dolores Monge, and Haakon Vennemo. 1998. "Structural Adjustment and Deforestation in Nicaragua." *Environment and Development Economics* 4: 19–43.

Gobierno de Nicaragua. 2001. Mapa de Pobreza Extrema de Nicaragua, Censo 1995–EMNV 1998.

Gockowski, James, Mathurin Tchatat, Jean-Paul Dondjang, Gisele Hietet, and Terese Fouda. 2006. "The Value of Biodiversity in the Beti Cocoa Agroforests of Southern Cameroon." *Journal of Sustainable Forestry*.

Gorenflo, L., C. Corson, K. M Chomitz, G. Harper, M. Honzák, and B. Ozler. 2006. "Poverty, Population, and Deforestation in Madagascar." Conservation International, Washington, D.C.

Government of India. 2001. *Census of India 2001.* Literacy rates by district available at http://educationforallinindia.com/page157.html.

Grimes, Alicia, Sally Loomis, Paul Jahnige, Margo Burnham, Karen Onthank, Rocio Alercón, Walter Palacios Cuenca, Carlos Cerón Martinez, David Neill, Michael Balick, Brad Bennet, and Robert Mendelsohn. 1994. "Valuing the Rain Forest: The Economic Value of Nontimber Forest Products in Ecuador." *Ambio* 23 (7): 405–10.

Guimaraes, Andrè Loubet, and Christopher Uhl. 1997. "Rural Transport in Eastern Amazonia: Limitations, Options, and Opportunities." *Journal of Rural Studies* 13 (4): 429–40.

Hall, Gillette, and H. A. Patrinos. 2005. *Indigenous People, Poverty and Human Development in Latin America.* United Kingdom: Palgrave Macmillan.

Hamilton, L. S., and P. N. King. 1983. "Tropical Forested Watersheds: Hydrologic and Soils Response to Major Uses and Conversions." Westview Press, Boulder, Colorado.

Hansen, M., and R. DeFries. 2004. "Detecting Long Term Forest Change Using Continuous Fields of Tree Cover Maps from 8km AVHRR Data for the Years 1982–1999." *Ecosystems* 7: 695–716.

Harper, G. n.d. "Madagascar: Forest Cover and Deforestation, 1990–2000." Conservation International, Center for Applied Biodiversity Science, Washington, D.C.

Harvey, C. A., C. Villanueva, J. Villacís, M. Chacón, D. Muñoz, M. López, M. Ibrahim, R. Gómez, R. Taylor, J. Martinez, A. Navas, J. Saenz, D. Sánchez, A. Medina, S. Vilchez, B. Hernández, A. Perez, F. Ruiz, F. López, I. Lang, and F. L. Sinclair. 2005. "Contribution of Live Fences to the Ecological Integrity of Agricultural Landscapes." *Agriculture, Ecosystems & Environment* 111: 200–30.

Hettige, Hemamala. 2006. "When Do Rural Roads Benefit the Poor and How?" Asian Development Bank, Manila, Philippines.

Hijmans, R. J., S. E. Cameron, J. L. Parra, P. G. Jones, and A. Jarvis. 2004. "The WorldClim Interpolated Global Terrestrial Climate Surfaces, Version 1.3." [http://biogeo.berkeley.edu/].

Hoare, Alison E. 2006. "Divided Forests: Towards Fairer Zoning of Forest Lands." Rainforest Foundation, London, U.K.

Holden, Stein. 2001. "A Century of Technological Change and Deforestation in the *Miombo* Woodlands of Northern Zambia." In Arild Angelsen and David Kaimowitz, eds., *Agricultural Technologies and Tropical Deforestation*. Wallingford, U.K.: CABI Publishing.

House, J., V. Brovkin, R. Betts, R. Costanza, M. Assunçao Silva Dias, E. Holland, C. Le Quéré, N. Kim Phat, U. Riebesell, M. Scholes, A. Arneth, D. Barratt, K. Cassman, T. Christensen, S. Cornell, J. Foley, L. Ganzeveld, T. Hickler, S. Houweling, M. Scholze, F. Joos, K. Kohfeld, M. Manizza, D. Ojima, I. C. Prentice, C. Schaaf, B. Smith, I. Tegen, K. Thonicke, and N. Warwick. 2006. "Climate and Air Quality." In *Millennium Ecosystem Assessment 2005—Current State and Trends: Findings of the Condition and Trends Working Group. Ecosystems and Human Well-being*. Washington, D.C.: Island Press.

Howard, Andrew F., and Juvenal Valerio. 1996. "Financial Returns from Sustainable Forest Management and Selected Agricultural Land-use Options in Costa Rica." *Forest Ecology and Management* 81: 35–49.

Hyde, William F. Forthcoming. *The Global Economics of Forestry.*

———. 2005. "Institutions, Sustainability, and Natural Resources: Institutions for Sustainable Forest Management." In S. Kant and R. Berry, eds., *The Limitations to SFM: An Economic Perspective*. Dordrecht, Netherlands: Springer.

Hyde, William F., M. Dalmacio, E. Guiang, and B. Harker. 1997. "Forest Charges and Trusts: Shared Benefits with a Clear Definition of Responsibilities." *Journal of Philippine Development* XXIV (2): 56–223.

IBGE (Instituto Brasileiro de Geografia e Estadística). 1998. "Censo Agropecuário 1995–1996—No. 24 Mato Grosso." Rio de Janeiro.

———. 2003. "Censo demográfico 2000—agregado por setores censitários dos resultados do universo, 2nd edition." Rio de Janeiro.

———. 2006. "Produção agrícola municipal." [http://www.sidra.ibge.gov.br].

IBGE (Instituto Brasileiro de Geografia e Estatistica) 2005 "Perfil dos municipios Brasileiros—meio ambiente." Rio de Janeiro.

INPE 2004. "Projeto prodes." [http://www.obt.inpe.br/prodes/]. Accessed January 2005.

———. 2006. "Mean Rate Gross Deforestation (km^2/year) from 1978 to 2000, Projeto Prodes." [http://www.obt.inpe.br/prodes/prodes_1988_2003.htm].

Insan Hitawasana Sejahtera. 2003. "Indonesia Forest and Media (INFORM) Campaign Monitoring and Evaluation: Results of the Baseline Survey" Jakarta.

Instituto Cuanto. 2005. "Evaluacion economica, social, ambiental e institucional del provias rural fase I." Lima, Peru.

Instituto Socioambiental. 2005. "Mato Grosso, Amazônia (i) legal—desmatamentos de florestas em propriedades rurais integradas ao Sistema de Licenciamento Ambiental Rural entre 2001 e 2004." Brasilia.

ITTC (International Tropical Timber Council). 2005. "Achieving the ITTO Objective 2000 and Sustainable Forest Management in Mexico." Yokohama, Japan.

ITTO (International Tropical Timber Organization). 2006. "Status of Tropical Forest Management 2005." Technical Series 24. Yokohama, Japan.

IUCN (World Conservation Union). 1994. "Guidelines for Protected Area Management Categories." Gland, Switzerland. [http://www.iucn.org/themes/wcpa/pubs/pdfs/iucncategories.pdf].

IUCN (World Conservation Union), Conservation International, and NatureServe. 2005. "Global Amphibian Assessment." [http://www.globalamphibians.org].

Jacoby, H. G. 2000. "Access to Markets and the Benefits of Rural Roads." *The Economic Journal* 110: 713–37.

Jalan, Jyotsna, and Martin Ravallion. 2002. "Geographic Poverty Traps? A Micro Model of Consumption Growth in Rural China." *Journal of Applied Econometrics* 17 (4): 329–46.

Jensen, Henning Tarp, Sherman Robinson, and Finn Tarp. 2004. "General Equilibrium Measures of Agricultural Policy Bias in Fifteen Developing Countries." Discussion Paper 04-25. University of Copenhagen, Institute of Economics, Denmark.

Joshi, L., G. Wibawa, G. Vincent, D. Boutin, R. Akiefnawati, G. Manurung, M. Van Noordwijk, and S. Williams. 2002. "Jungle Rubber: A Traditional Agroforestry System Under Pressure." World Agroforestry Centre (ICRAF), Bogor, Indonesia.

Kaimowitz, David, and Arild Angelsen. 1998. "Economic Models of Tropical Deforestation: A Review." Center for International Forestry Research, Bogor, Indonesia.

Kaimowitz, David, and Joyotee Smith. 2001. "Soybean Technology and the Loss of Natural Vegetation in Brazil and Bolivia." In Arild Angelsen and David Kaimowitz, eds., *Agricultural Technologies and Tropical Deforestation*. Wallingford, U.K.: CABI Publishing.

Kaimowitz, David, Benoit Mertens, Sven Wunder, and Pablo Pacheco. 2004. "Hamburger Connection Fuels Amazon Destruction." Center for International Forestry Research, Bogor, Indonesia.

Kazianga, Harounan, and William A. Masters. 2005. "Property Rights, Production Technology and Deforestation: Cocoa in Cameroon." [http://www.columbia.edu/~hk2252/KaziangaMasters.pdf].

Khan, Asmeen, Paul Jepson, Michael Wells, Scott Guggenheim, and Wahjudi Wardojo. 1999. "Investing in Biodiversity: A Review of Indonesia's Integrated Conservation Development Projects." World Bank, Washington, D.C.

Khanna, Madhu, Wanhong Yang, Richard Farnsworth, and Hayri Onal. 2003. "Cost-Effective Targeting of Land Retirement to Improve Water Quality with Endogenous Sediment Deposition Coefficients." *American Journal of Agricultural Economics* 85 (3): 538–53.

Kiersch, B., and S. Tognetti. 2002. "Land-water Linkages in Rural Watersheds." *Land Use and Water Resources Research* 2.

Kihiyo, Vincent B. M. S. 1996. "Economic Evaluation of Rural Woodlots in a Developing Country: Tanzania." *Journal of Environmental Management* 46 (3): 271–79.

Kirby, Kathryn R., William F. Laurance, Ana K. Albernaz, Gotz Schroth, Philip M. Fearnside, Scott Bergen, Eduardo M. Venticinque, and Carlos da Costa. 2006. "The Future of Deforestation in the Brazilian Amazon." *Futures* 38 (4): 432–53.

Kishor, M. Nalin, and Luis F. Constantino. 1993. "Forest Management and Competing Land Uses: An Economic Analysis for Costa Rica." Dissemination Note 7. World Bank, LATEN, Washington, D.C.

Kloss, Dirk. 2006. "Forest Conservation through Protected Area Establishment and Maintenance." Background paper.

Köhlin, Gunnar, and Gregory S. Amacher. 2005. "Welfare Implications of Community Forest Plantations in Developing Countries: The Orissa Social Project." *American Journal of Agricultural Economics* 87 (4): 855–69.

Lamb, David, Peter D. Erskine, and John A. Parrotta. 2005a. "Restoration of Degraded Tropical Forest Landscapes." *Science* 310: 1628–32.

———. 2005b. "Restoration of Degraded Tropical Forest Landscapes—Supporting Material." [http://www.sciencemag.org/cgi/content/full/310/5754/1628/DC1].

Larson, Anne M. 2004. "Democratic Decentralisation in the Forestry Sector: Lessons Learned from Africa, Asia and Latin America." Center for International Forestry Research, Bogor, Indonesia.

Laurance, William F., Barbara M. Croes, Landry Tchignoumba, Sally A. Lahm, Alfonso Alonso, Michelle E. Lee, Patrick Campbell, and Claude Ondzeano. 2006. "Impact of Roads and Hunting on Central African Rainforest Mammals." *Conservation Biology* 20 (4): 1251–61.

Laurance, W. F., T. E. Lovejoy, H. L. Vasconcelos, E. M. Bruna, R. K. Didham, P. C. Stouffer, C. Gascon, R. O. Bierregaard, S. G. Laurance, and E. Sampaio. 2002. "Ecosystem Decay of Amazonian Forest Fragments: A 22-year Investigation." *Conservation Biology* 16: 605–18.

Lawton, R. O., U. S. Nair, R. A. Pielke Sr., and R. M. Welch. 2001. "Climatic Impact of Tropical Lowland Deforestation on Nearby Montane Cloud Forests." *Science* 294 (5542): 584–87.

Ledec, George, and Paula J. Posas. 2006. "Biodiversity Conservation in Road Projects: Lessons from World Bank Experience in Latin America." *Transportation Research Record* 1 (1819): 198–202.

Lescuyer, Guillaume, Alexandre Emerit, Edouard Essiane Mendoula, and Joseph Junior Seh. 2001. "Community Involvement in Forest Management: A Full-scale Experiment in the South Cameroon Forest." RDFN Paper 25c. ODI, London.

Lima, A., C. T. Irigaray, J. C. Figueira, S. Guimarães, R. T. de Silva, and S. Araújo. 2005. "Sistema de Licenciamento Ambienal em propriedades rurais do estado do Mato Grosso: Análise de lições na sua implementação." Final report to the Brazilian Ministry of the Environment, Brasilia.

Lofgren, Hans, James Thurlow, and Sherman Robinson. 2004. "Prospects for Growth and Poverty Reduction in Zambia, 2001–2015." Discussion paper 11. International Food Policy Research Institute, Washington, D.C.

Lombardini, C. 1994. "Deforestation in Thailand." In K. Brown and D. Pearce, eds., *The Causes of Tropical Deforestation*. London: UCL Press.

Mace, Georgina, Hillary Masundire, and Jonathan Baillie. 2005. "Biodiversity." In Rashid Hassan, Robert Scholes, and Neville Ash, eds., *Ecosystems and Human Well-being: Current State and Trends*. Washington, D.C.: Island Press.

MacKinnon, Kathi. 2005. "Parks, People and Policies: Conflicting Agendas for Forests in Southeast Asia." In E. Bermingham, C. W. Dick, and C. Moritz, eds., *Tropical Rainforests. Past, Present and Future*. Chicago: University of Chicago Press.

Mahapatra, Krushna, and Shashi Kant. 2005. "Tropical Deforestation: A Multinomial Logistic Model and Some Country-specific Policy Prescriptions." *Forest Policy and Economics* 7 (1): 1–24.

Mahar, D. J. 2000. "Agro-ecological Zoning in Rondônia, Brazil: What Are the Lessons?" In Anthony Hall, ed., *Amazonia at the Crossroads: The*

Challenge of Sustainable Development. University of London, Institute of Latin American Studies.

Malla, Y. B. 2000. "Impact of Community Forestry Policy on Rural Livelihoods and Food Security in Nepal." *Unasylva* 51 (202): 37–45.

Margules, C. R., and R. L. Pressey. 2000. "Systematic Conservation Planning." Tropical Forest Research Centre and Rainforest Cooperative Research Centre, Atherton, Australia.

Margulis, Sergio. 2004. "Causes of Deforestation of the Brazilian Amazon." Working paper 22. World Bank, Washington, D.C.

Mather, A. S. 1992. "The Forest Transition." *AREA—Institute of British Geographers* 24 (4): 367–79.

Mayers, James, and Stephen Bass. 1999. *Policy That Works for Forests and People.* London: IIED.

McAndrew, John P., Mam Sambath, Hong Kimly, and Ky Bunthai. 2004. "Phnong Villagers Adapt to Decline in Natural Resources." *Cambodia Development Review* 8 (1): 9–12.

McConnell, William J., Sean P. Sweeney, and Bradley Mulley. 2004. "Physical and Social Access to Land: Spatio-temporal Patterns of Agricultural Expansion in Madagascar." *Agriculture, Ecosystems & Environment* 101 (2–3): 171–84.

McKenney, Bruce, Yim Chea, Prom Tola, and Tom Evans. 2004. "Focusing on Cambodia's High Value Forests: Livelihoods and Management." Cambodian Development Resource Institute and Wildlife Conservation Society, Phnom Penh.

McNeely, Jeffrey A., and Sara J. Scherr. 2003. *Ecoagriculture: Strategies to Feed the World and Save Wild Biodiversity.* Washington, D.C.: Island Press.

Meinzen-Dick, Ruth S., and Monica Di Gregorio. 2004. "Collective Action and Property Rights for Sustainable Development 2020." Focus 11. CAPRI, Washington, D.C.

Mendelsohn, Robert, Ariel Dinar, and Apurva Sanghi. 2001. "The Effect of Development on the Climate Sensitivity of Agriculture." *Environment and Development Economics* 6: 85–101.

Merry, F. D., P. E. Hildebrand, P. Pattie, and D. R. Carter. 2002. "An Analysis of Land Conversion from Sustainable Forestry to Pasture: A Case Study in the Bolivian Lowlands." *Land Use Policy* 19 (3): 207–15.

Mertens, B., R. Poccard-Chapuis, M.-G. Piketty, A.-E. Lacques, and A. Venturieri. 2002. "Crossing Spatial Analyses and Livestock Economics to Understand Deforestation Processes in the Brazilian Amazon: The Case of Sao Felix do Xingu in South Pará." *Agricultural Economics* 27 (3): 269–94.

Mertens, Benoit, David Kaimowitz, Atie Puntodewo, Jerry Vanclay, and Patricia Mendez. 2004. "Modeling Deforestation at Distinct Geographic

Scales and Time Periods in Santa Cruz, Bolivia." *International Regional Science Review* 27 (3): 271–96.

Millennium Ecosystem Asssessment. 2005. *Ecosystems and Human Well-being: Synthesis.* Washington, D.C.: Island Press.

Ministry of Environment and Forests. 2005. *State of Forest Report 2003.* Dehradun, India.

Minten, Bart. 1999. "Infrastructure, Market Access, and Agricultural Prices: Evidence from Madagascar." MSSD Discussion Paper 26. International Food Policy Research Institute, Washington, D.C.

Minten, Bart, and Philippe Méral. 2005. "International Trade and Environmental Degradation: A Case Study on the Loss of Spiny Forest Cover in Madagascar." In Bart Minten, ed., *Trade, Liberalization, Rural Poverty, and the Environment: The Case of Madagascar.* Washington, D.C.: World Wildlife Fund.

Mistiaen, J., B. Soler, T. Razafimanantena, and J. Razafindravonona. 2002. "Putting Welfare on the Map in Madagascar." Working Paper 34. World Bank, Africa Region, Washington, D.C.

Molnar, Augusta, Sara J. Scherr, and Arvind Khare. 2004. "Who Conserves the World's Forests? A New Assessment of Conservation and Investment Trends." Forest Trends, Washington, D.C.

Monela, G. C., S. A. O. Chamshama, R. Mwaipopo, and D. M. Gamassa. 2004. "A Study on the Social, Economic and Environmental Impacts of Forest Landscape Restoration in Shinyanga Region, Tanzania." Ministry of Natural Resources and Tourism (Forestry and Beekeeping Division) and World Conservation Union (Eastern Africa Regional Office), Dar es Salaam, Tanzania.

Moser, Christine, Christopher B. Barrett, and Bart Minten. 2005. "Missed Opportunities and Missing Markets: Spatio-temporal Arbitrage of Rice in Madagascar." Working paper 180. SAGA. Working paper. 180, U.S. Agency for International Development, SAGA, Washington, D.C.

Müller, Daniel, and Darla K. Munroe. 2005. "Tradeoffs between Rural Development Policies and Forest Protection: Spatially Explicit Modeling in the Central Highlands of Vietnam." *Land Economics* 81 (3): 412–25.

Müller, Daniel, and Manfred Zeller. 2002. "Land Use Dynamics in the Central Highlands of Vietnam: A Spatial Model Combining Village Survey Data with Satellite Imagery Interpretation." *Agricultural Economics* 27 (3): 333–54.

Muñoz-Piña, Carlos, Alejandro Guevara, Juan Manuel Torres, and Josefina Braña. 2005. "Paying for the Hydrological Services of Mexico's Forests: Analysis, Negotiations and Results." Revised version of a paper presented at the ZEF-CIFOR workshop on "Payments for Environmental Services: Methods and Design in Developing and Developed Countries," Titisee, Germany, June 15–18, 2005.

Munroe, Darla K., Jane Southworth, and Catherine M. Tucker. 2002. "The Dynamics of Land-cover Change in Western Honduras: Exploring Spatial and Temporal Complexity." *Agricultural Economics* 27: 355–69.

——. 2004. "Modeling Spatially and Temporally Complex Land-Cover Change: The Case of Western Honduras." *The Professional Geographer* 56 (4): 544–59.

Murali, K. S., Indu K. Murthy, and N. H. Ravindranath. 2002. "Joint Forest Management in India and Its Ecological Impacts." *Environmental Management and Health* 13 (5): 512–28.

Murray, Brian C., Bruce A. McCarl, and Hemg-Chi Lee. 2004. "Estimating Leakage from Forest Carbon Sequestration Programs." *Land Economics* 80 (1): 109–24.

Myers, Norman, Russell A. Mittermeier, Cristina G. Mittermeier, Gustavo A. B. da Fonseca, and Jennifer Kent. 2000. "Biodiversity Hotspots for Conservation Priorities." *Nature* 403: 853–58.

Naidoo, Robin, and Wiktor L. Adamowicz. 2005. "Economic Benefits of Biodiversity Exceed Costs of Conservation at an African Rainforest Reserve." *Proceedings of the National Academy of Sciences* 102 (46): 16712–16.

——. 2006. "Modeling Opportunity Costs of Conservation in Transitional Landscapes." *Conservation Biology* 20 (2): 490–500.

National Research Council, Water Science and Technology Board. 2004. *Valuing Ecosystem Services: Towards Better Environmental Decision-Making*. National Academies Press, Washington, D.C.

Ndjanyou, L., and C. H. Majerowitz. 2004. "Actualisation de l'audit de la fiscalité décentralisée du secteur forestier camerounais." Institutions et Developpement, Boulogne, France.

Nelson, Andrew, and Kenneth M. Chomitz. 2006. "The Forest-Hydrology-Watershed Nexus in Central America: An Heuristic Analysis." *Environment, Development and Sustainability.*

Nelson, G. C., and D. Hellerstein. 1997. "Do Roads Cause Deforestation? Using Satellite Images in Econometric Analysis of Land Use." *American Journal of Agricultural Economics* 79: 80–88.

Nelson, Gerald, Alessandro de Pinto, Virginia Harris, and Steven W. Stone. 2004. "Land Use and Road Improvements: A Spatial Perspective." *International Regional Science Review* 27 (3): 297–325.

Nelson, Gerald C., Virginia Harris, and Steven W. Stone. 2001. "Deforestation, Land Use, and Property Rights: Empirical Evidence from Darien, Panama." *Land Economics* 77 (2): 187–205.

Nepstad, D. C., G. Carvalho, A. C. Barros, A. Alencar, J. P. Capobianco, J. Bishop, Moutinho, P. Lefebvre, U. Lopes Silva Jr., and E. Prins. 2001. "Road Paving, Fire Regime Feedbacks, and the Future of Amazon Forests." *Forest Ecology and Management* 154: 395–407.

Nepstad, D. C., S. Schwartzmann, B. Bamberger, M. Santilli, D. Ray, P. Schlesinger, P. Lefebvre, A. Alencar, E. Prinz, G. Fiske, and A. Rolla. 2006. "Inhibition of Amazon Deforestation and Fire by Parks and Indigenous Lands." *Conservation Biology* 20 (1): 65–73.

Nguyen, Quang Tan. 2006. "Trends in Forest Ownership, Forest Resources Tenure and Institutional Arrangements: Are They Contributing to Better Forest Management and Poverty Reduction? The Case of Viet Nam." Food and Agriculture Organization, Rome.

Ninan, K. N., and Jyothis Sathyapalan. 2005. "The Economics of Biodiversity Conservation: A Study of a Coffee Growing Region in the Western Ghats of India." *Ecological Economics* 55 (1): 61–72.

Nittler, John, and Henry Tschinkel. 2005. "Community Forest Management in Maya Biosphere Reserve of Guatemala." Submitted to USAID; Steering Committee on Nature, Wealth and Power (NWP); Sustainable Agriculture and Natural Resource Management (SANREM); and Collaborative Research Support Program (CRSP), University of Georgia.

Norton-Griffiths, Michael, and Clive Southey. 1995. "The Opportunity Costs of Biodiversity Conservation in Kenya." *Ecological Economics* 12 (2): 125–39.

Olschewski, Roland, and Pablo C. Benitez. 2005. "Secondary Forests as Temporary Carbon Sinks? The Economic Impact of Accounting Methods on Reforestation Projects in the Tropics." *Ecological Economics* 55 (3): 380–94.

Olson, D. M., and E. Dinerstein. 1998. "The Global 200: Priority Ecoregions for Global Conservation." *Annals of the Missouri Botanical Garden* 89: 125–26.

Olson, David M., Eric Dinerstein, Eric D. Wikramanayake, Neil D. Burgess, George V. N. Powell, Emma C. Underwood, Jennifer A. D'Amico, Illanga Itoua, Holly E. Strand, John C. Morrison, Colby J. Loucks, Thomas F. Allnutt, Taylor H. Ricketts, Yumiko Kura, John F. Lamoreux, Wesley W. Wettengel, Prashant Hedao, and Kenneth R. Kassem. 2001. "Terrestrial Ecoregions of the World: A New Map of Life on Earth." *BioScience* 51 (11): 933–38.

Osgood, D. 1994. "Government Failure and Deforestation in Indonesia." In K. Brown and D. Pearce, eds., *The Causes of Tropical Deforestation*. London: UCL Press.

Ostrom, Elinor. 1990. *Governing the Commons: The Evolution of Institutions for Collective Action.* Cambridge, U.K.: Cambridge University Press.

———. 1999. "Self-Governance and Forest Resources." Occasional paper 20. Center for International Forestry Research, Bagor, Indonesia.

Oyono, P. Rene. 2005. "Profiling Local-level Outcomes of Environmental Decentralizations: The Case of Cameroon's Forests in the Congo Basin." *Journal of Environment and Development* 14 (3): 317–37.

Pacala, S., and R. Socolow. 2004. "Stabilization Wedges: Solving the Climate Problem for the Next 50 Years with Current Technologies." *Science* 305.

Pacheco, Pablo. 2002. "Deforestation and Degradation in Lowland Bolivia." In Charles H. Wood and Roberto Porro, eds., *Deforestation and Land Use in the Amazon*. Gainesville: University of Florida Press.

Pagiola, Stefano. 2005. "Payments for Environmental Services in Costa Rica." Revised version of a paper presented at the ZEF-CIFOR workshop on Payments for environmental services: Methods and design in developing and developed countries, Titisee, Germany, June 15–18, 2005.

Pagiola, Stefano, Agustin Arcenas, and Gunars Platais. 2005. "Can Payments for Environmental Services Help Reduce Poverty? An Exploration of the Issues and the Evidence to Date from Latin America." *World Development* 33 (2): 237–53.

Pagiola, Stefano, Elías Ramírez, José Gobbi, Cees de Haan, Muhammad Ibrahim, Enrique Murgueitio, and Juan Pablo Ruíz. 2006. "Paying for the Environmental Services of Silvopastoral Practices in Nicaragua." Prepared for submission to Special Issue of *Ecological Economics* on "Ecosystem Services and Agriculture," edited by S. M. Swinton, F. Lupi, S. H. Hamilton, and G. P. Robertson.

Pagiola, Stefano, Paola Agostini, Gobbi José, Cees de Haan, Muhammad Ibrahim, Enrique Murgueitio, Elías Ramírez, Mauricio Rosales, and Juan Pablo Ruíz. 2004. "Paying for Biodiversity Conservation Services in Agricultural Landscapes." Environmental Economics Series 96. World Bank, Washington, D.C.

Palm, Cheryl, Stephen A. Vosti, Pedro Sanchez, and Polly J. Ericksen. 2005. *Slash-and-Burn Agriculture: The Search for Alternatives.* New York: Columbia University Press.

Palmer, Charles, and Stefanie Engel. 2006. "For Better or for Worse? Local Impacts of the Decentralization of Indonesia's Forest." ETH, Zürich.

Pan, William K. Y., Stephen J. Walsh, Richard E. Bilsborrow, Brian G. Frizzelle, Christine M. Erlien, and Francis Baquero. 2004. "Farm-level Models of Spatial Patterns of Land Use and Land Cover Dynamics in the Ecuadorian Amazon." *Agriculture Ecosystems and Environment* 101: 117–34.

Panayotou, T., and S. Sungsuwan. 1994. "An Econometric Analysis of the Causes of Tropical Deforestation: The Case of Northeast Thailand." In K. Brown and D. Pearce, eds., *The Causes of Tropical Deforestation*. London: UCL Press.

Pearce, David, Francis E. Putz, and Jerome K. Vanclay. 2003. "Sustainable Forestry in the Tropics: Panacea or Folly?" *Forest Ecology and Management* 172 (2–3): 229–47.

Pender, John, Pamela Jagger, Ephraim Nkonya, and Dick Sserunkuuma. 2004. "Development Pathways and Land Management in Uganda." *World Development* 32 (5): 767–92.

Pendleton, Linwood H., and E. Lance Howe. 2002. "Market Integration, Development, and Smallholder Forest Clearance." *Land Economics* 78 (1): 1–19.

Perotto-Baldiviezo, H. L., T. L. Thurow, C. T. Smith, R. F. Fisher, and X. B. Wu. 2004. "GIS-based Spatial Analysis and Modeling for Landslide Hazard Assessment in Steeplands, Southern Honduras." *Agriculture, Ecosystems & Environment* 103 (1): 165–76.

Pfaff, A. S. P. 1999. "What Drives Deforestation in the Brazilian Amazon? Evidence from Satellite and Socioeconomic Data." *Journal of Environmental Economics and Management* 37: 26–43.

Pichón, Francisco J. 1997. "Colonist Land-Allocation Decision, Land Use, and Deforestation in the Ecuadorian Amazon Frontier." *Economic Development and Cultural Change* 45 (4): 707–44.

Pinedo-Vasquez, Miguel, Daniel Zarin, and Peter Jipp. 1992. "Economic Returns from Forest Conversion in the Peruvian Amazon." *Ecological Economics* 6 (2): 163–73.

Putz, Francis E., Geoffrey M. Blate, Kent H. Redford, Robert Fimbel, and John Robinson. 2001. "Tropical Forest Management and Conservation of Biodiversity: An Overview." *Conservation Biology* 15 (1): 7–20.

Randrianarisoa, J. C. 2003. "Analyse spatial de la production rizicole malgache." Presented at Cornell University and International Labour Organization conference on developpement économique, services sociaux et pauvreté à Madagascar.

Ravindranath, N. H., and B. S. Somashekhar. 1995. "Potentials and Economics of Forestry Options for Carbon Sequestration in India." *Biomass and Bioenergy* 8 (5): 323–36.

Reardon, Thomas, Julio Berdegue, and German Escobar. 2001. "Rural Nonfarm Employment and Incomes in Latin America: Overview and Policy Implications." *World Development* 29 (3): 395–409.

Redford, Kent, and Michael Painter. 2006. "Natural Alliances between Conservationists and Indigenous Peoples." Working paper 25. Wildlife Conservation Society, New York.

Reis, E. J., and R. Guzmán. 1994. "An Econometric Model of Amazon Deforestation." In K. Brown and D. Pearce, eds., *The Causes of Tropical Deforestation*. London: UCL Press.

Renkow, Mitch, Daniel G. Hallstrom, and Daniel D. Karanja. 2004. "Rural Infrastructure, Transactions Costs and Market Participation in Kenya." *Journal of Development Economics* 73 (1): 349–67.

Ribot, Jesse. 2002. "Democratic Decentralization of Natural Resources: Institutionalizing Popular Participation." World Resources Institute, Washington, D.C.

———. 2003. "Democratic Decentralization of Natural Resources: Institutional Choice and Discretionary Power Transfer in Sub-Saharan Africa." *Public Administration and Development* 23: 53–65.

Ribot, Jesse, and Anne M. Larson. 2005. *Democratic Decentralisation through a Natural Resource Lens.* London: Routledge.

Ricker, Martin, Robert O. Mendelsohn, Douglas C. Daly, and Guillermo Angeles. 1999. "Enriching the Rainforest with Native Fruit Trees: An Ecological and Economic Analysis in Los Tuxtlas (Veracruz, Mexico)." *Ecological Economics* 31 (3): 439–48.

Ricketts, Taylor H., Gretchen C. Daily, Paul R. Ehrlich, and Charles D. Michener. 2004. "Economic Value of Tropical Forest to Coffee Production." *Proceedings of the National Academy of Sciences* 101 (34): 12579–82.

Ricketts, T. H., E. Dinerstein, Tim Boucher, Thomas Brooks, S. H. M. Butchart, Michael Hoffmann, J. F. Lamoreux, J. Morrison, M. Parr, J. D. Pilgrim, A. S. L. Rodrigues, W. Sechrest, G. Wallace, K. Berlin, J. Bielby, N. D. Burgess, D. R. Church, N. Cox, D. Knox, C. Loucks, G. W. Luck, L. L. Masterl, R. Moore, Robin Naidoo, R. Ridgely, G. E. Schatz, G. Shire, H. Strand, W. Wettengel, and E. Wikramanayake. 2005. "Pinpointing and Preventing Imminent Extinctions." *PNAS* 102 (51): 18497–501.

Ridder, Ralph. 2006. Presentation at University of Montana workshop on Long-term Monitoring of Vegetation Variables Using Moderate Resolution Satellites, August 9, Missoula, Mont.

Rodrigues, A. S. L., S. J. Andelman, M. I. Bakarr, L. Boitani, T. M. Brooks, L. D. C. Fishpool, G. A. B. da Fonseca, K. J. Gaston, M. Hoffmann, J. S. Long, P. A. Marquet, J. D. Pilgrim, R. L. Pressey, J. Schipper, W. Sechrest, S. N. Stuart, L. G. Underhill, R. W. Waller, M. E. J. Watts, and X. Yan. 2004. "Effectiveness of the Global Protected Areas Network in Representing Species Diversity." *Nature* 428: 640–43.

Rojas, Manrique, and Bruce Aylward. 2002. "Cooperation between a Small Private Hydropower Producer and a Conservation NGO for Forest Protection: The Case of La Esperanza, Costa Rica." Land-Water Linkages in Rural Watersheds Case Study Series. Food and Agriculture Organization, Rome.

Roldan Ortega, Roque. 2004. "Models for Recognizing Indigenous Land Rights in Latin America." Environment Department Paper 99. World Bank, Washington, D.C.

Romano, Francesca, and Dominique Reeb. 2006. "Understanding Forest Tenure: What Rights and for Whom? Secure Forest Tenure for Sustainable Forest Management and Poverty Alleviation: The Case of Southeast Asia." Food and Agriculture Organization, Forestry Department, Forest Policy and Information Division, Rome.

Roper, J. Montgomery. 2003. "An Assessment of Indigenous Participation in Commercial Forestry Markets: The Case of Nicaragua's Northern Atlantic Autonomous Region." Forest Trends, Washington, D.C.

Rosenzweig, M. L. 2001. "Loss of Speciation Rate Will Impoverish Future Diversity." *PNAS* 98 (10): 5404–10.

———. 2003. *Win-Win Ecology: How the Earth's Species Can Survive in the Midst of Human Enterprise.* New York: Oxford University Press.

Ross, Michael L. 2001. *Timber Booms and Institutional Breakdown in Southeast Asia.* Cambridge, U.K.: Cambridge University Press.

Rudel, Thomas K. 2005. *Tropical Forests.* New York: Columbia University Press.

Rudel, Thomas K., Marla Perez-Lugo, and Heather Zichal. 2000. "When Fields Revert to Forest: Development and Spontaneous Reforestation in Post-War Puerto Rico." *Professional Geographer* 52 (3): 386–97.

Rudel, Thomas K., Oliver T. Coomes, Emilio Moran, Frederic Achard, Arild Angelsen, Jianchu Xu, and Eric Lambin. 2005. "Forest Transitions: Towards a Global Understanding of Land Use Change." *Global Environmental Change Part A* 15 (1): 23–31.

Ruf, François. 2001. "Tree Crops as Deforestation and Reforestation Agents: The Case of Cocoa in Côte d'Ivoire and Sulawesi." In Arild Angelsen and David Kaimowitz, eds., *Agricultural Technologies and Tropical Deforestation*. Wallingford, U.K.: CABI Publishing.

Sanchez-Azofeifa, G. Arturo, G. C. Daily, A. S. P. Pfaff, and Christopher Busch. 2003. "Integrity and Isolation of Costa Rica's National Parks and Biological Reserves: Examining the Dynamics of Land-cover Change." *Biological Conservation* 109: 123–35.

Sarin, Madhu, Lipika Ray, Manju S. Raju, Mitali Chattarjee, Narayan Banerjee, and Shyamala Hiremath. 1998. "Who is Gaining? Who is Losing? Gender and Equity Concerns in Joint Forest Management." Society for Promotion of Wasteland Development, New Delhi.

Sathaye, J., W. Makundi, L. Dale, P. Chan, and K. Andrasko. Forthcoming. "GHG Mitigation Potential, Costs and Benefits in Global Forests: A Dynamic Partial Equilibrium Approach." *Energy Journal.*

Scherr, Sara J., Andy White, and David Kaimowitz. 2003. "A New Agenda for Forest Conservation and Poverty Reduction: Making Forest Markets Work for Low-income Producers." Forest Trends, Washington, D.C.

Schmidt-Soltau, Kai. 2003. "Conservation-related Resettlement in Central Africa: Environmental and Social Risks." *Development and Change* 34 (3): 525–51.

Schneider, R. R. 1995. "Government and Economy on the Amazon Frontier." Environment Paper 11. World Bank, Washington, D.C.

Schneider, S. H. 2004. "Abrupt Non-linear Climate Change, Irreversibility and Surprise." *Global Environmental Change* 14: 245–58.

Schweik, Charles M., Harini Nagendra, and Deb Ranjan Sinha. 2003. "Using Satellite Imagery to Locate Innovative Forest Management Practices in Nepal." *Ambio* 32 (4): 312–19.

Serneels, Suzanne, and Eric F. Lambin. 2001. "Proximate Causes of Land-use Change in Narok District, Kenya: A Spatial Statistical Model." *Agriculture, Ecosystems & Environment* 85 (1–3): 65–81.

Shively, Gerald, and Elmer Martinez. 2001. "Deforestation, Irrigation, Employment and Cautious Optimism in Southern Palawan, the Philippines." In Arild Angelsen and David Kaimowitz, eds., *Agricultural Technologies and Tropical Deforestation*. Wallingford, U.K.: CABI Publishing.

Shively, Gerald, and S. N Pagiola. 2004. "Agricultural Intensification, Local Labor Markets, and Deforestation in the Philippines." *Environment and Development Economics* 9: 241–66.

Shone, Bryan M., and Jill L. Caviglia-Harris. 2005. "Quantifying and Comparing the Value of Non-timber Forest Products in the Amazon." *Ecological Economics* 58 (2): 249–267.

Shyamsundar, Priya, and S. Bandyopadhyay. 2004. "Fuelwood Consumption and Participation in Community Forestry in India." Policy Research Working Paper 3331. World Bank, Washington, D.C.

Shyamsundar, Priya, and Randall A. Kramer. 1996. "Tropical Forest Protection: An Empirical Analysis of the Costs Borne by Local People." *Journal of Environmental Economics and Management* 31: 129–44.

Shyamsundar, Priya, Eduardo Araral, and Suranjan Weeraratne. 2005. "Devolution of Resource Rights, Poverty, and Natural Resource Management: A Review." Environmental Economics Series, Working Paper no. 104, World Bank, Washington, D.C.

Simpson, R. David, Roger A. Sedjo, and John W. Reid. 1996. "Valuing Biodiversity for Its Use in Pharmaceutical Research." *Journal of Political Economy* 104 (1): 163–85.

Somanathan, E., R. Prabhakar, and Bhupendra Singh Metha. 2005. "Does Decentralization Work? Forest Conservation in the Himalayas." Discussion Paper in Economics 05-04. Indian Statistical Institute, Delhi.

Southgate, Douglas, Rodrigo Sierra, and Lawrence Brown. 1991. "The Causes of Tropical Deforestation in Ecuador: A Statistical Analysis." *World Development* 19 (9): 1145–51.

Southworth, Jane, Harini Nagendra, Laura A. Carlson, and Catherine Tucker. 2004. "Assessing the Impact of Celaque National Park on Forest Fragmentation in Western Honduras." *Applied Geography* 24 (4): 303–22.

Steinberg, Paul F. 2001. *Environmental Leadership in Developing Countries: Transnational Relations and Biodiversity Policy in Costa Rica and Bolivia.* Cambridge, Mass.: MIT Press.

———. 2005. "From Public Concern to Policy Effectiveness: Civic Conservation in Developing Countries." *Journal of International Wildlife Law and Policy* 8: 341–65.

Steininger, M. K., G. Harper, C. J. Tucker, D. Juhn, and F. Hawkins. 2004 "Forest Clearance and Fragmentation in Madagascar." unpublished digital map. Washington, Conservation International.

Stockholm Environment Institute. 2002. "Charcoal Potential in Southern Africa—CHAPOSA." Final report. Stockholm.

Stocks, A., B. McMahan, and P. Taber. 2006. "Beyond the Map: Indigenous and Colonist Impacts and Territorial Defense in Nicaragua's Bosawas Reserve." Unpublished.

Stolle, F., K. M. Chomitz, Eric Lambin, and Thomas P. Tomich. 2003. "Spatial Determinants of Vegetation Fires in Jambi Province, Sumatra, Indonesia." *Forest Ecology and Management* 179 (July): 277–92.

Stolton, Sue, Marc Hockings, Nigel Dudley, Kathy MacKinnon, and Tony Whitten. 2003. "Reporting Progress at Protected Area Sites: A Simple

Site-level Tracking Tool Developed for the World Bank and WWF." World Bank, Washington, D.C.

Stoms, David M., Kenneth M. Chomitz, and F. W. Davis. 2004. "TAMARIN: A Landscape Framework for Evaluating Economic Incentives for Rainforest Restoration." *Landscape and Urban Planning* 68 (1 May): 95–108.

Stone, Steven W. 1998. "Using a Geographic Information System for Applied Policy Analysis: The Case of Logging in the Eastern Amazon." *Ecological Economics* 27 (1): 43–61.

Stoneham, Gary, Vivek Chaudhri, Arthur Ha, and Loris Strappazzon. 2003. "Auctions for Conservation Contracts: An Empirical Examination of Victoria's BushTender Trial." *Australian Journal of Agricultural and Resource Economics* 47 (4): 477–500.

Sunderlin, William D., Sonya Dewi, and Atie Puntodewo. 2006. "Forests, Poverty, and Poverty Alleviation Policies." Background paper.

Sunderlin, William D., Arild Angelsen, Brian Belcher, Paul Burgers, Robert Nasi, Levania Santoso, and Sven Wunder. 2005. "Livelihoods, Forests, and Conservation in Developing Countries: An Overview." *World Development* 33 (9): 1383–1402.

Tacconi, Luca. 2003. "Fires in Indonesia: Causes, Costs, and Policy Implications." CIFOR Occasional paper no. 38, Center for International Forestry Research, Bogor.

ten Kate, K., J. Bishop, and R. Bayon. 2004. "Biodiversity Offsets: Views, Experience, and the Business Case." IUCN, Gland, Switzerland and Cambridge, UK and Insight Investment, London, UK.

Thanapakpawin, Porranee, Jeffrey E. Richey, David Thomas, Sarah D. Rodda, Bruce Campbell, and Miles G. Logsdon. 2006. "Effects of Land Use Change on the Hydrologic Regime of the Mae Chaem River Basin, NW Thailand." Submitted for publication. River Systems Research Group, University of Washington, Seattle.

Tiffen, Mary, and Michael Mortimore. 1994. "Environment, Population Growth and Productivity in Kenya: A Case Study of Machakos District." International Institute for Environment and Development, London.

Tomich, Thomas P., Hubert de Foresta, Rona Dennis, Quirine Ketterings, Daniel Murdiyarso, Cheryl Palm, Fred Stolle, Suyanto, and Meine Van Noordwijk. 2002. "Carbon Offsets for Conservation and Development in Indonesia?" *American Journal of Alternative Agriculture* 17 (3): 125–37.

Tomich, Thomas P., Andrea Cattaneo, Simon Chater, Helmut J. Geist, James Gockowski, David Kaimowitz, Eric Lambin, Jessa Lewis, Ousseynou Ndoye, Cheryl Palm, Fred Stolle, William D. Sunderlin, Judson F. Valentim, Meine Van Noordwijk, and Stephen A. Vosti. 2005. "Balancing Agricultural Development and Environmental Objectives: Assessing Tradeoffs in the Humid Tropics." In Cheryl Palm, Stephen A. Vosti, Pedro Sanchez, and Polly J. Ericksen, eds., *Slash-and-Burn Agriculture: The Search for Alternatives.* New York: Columbia University Press.

Tucker, Catherine M., Darla K. Munroe, Harini Nagendra, and Jane South-worth. 2005. "Comparative Spatial Analyses of Forest Conservation and Change in Honduras and Guatemala." *Conservation and Society* 3 (1): 174–200.

UNDP (United Nations Development Programme). *Atlas do Desenvolvimento Humano no Brasil.* [http://www.pnud.org.br/atlas/].

UNEP. 2005. *One Planet Many People: Atlas of Our Changing Environment.* UNEP: Nairobi.

UN Population Division. 2004. "World Population Prospects 2004, Medium Variant." New York.

Uphoff, N. 2003. "Higher Yields with Fewer External Inputs? The System of Rice Intensification and Potential Contributions to Agricultural Sustainability." *International Journal of Agricultural Sustainability* 1 (1): 38–50.

USDA (U.S. Department of Agriculture). 2006. "Oilseeds: World Markets and Trade." Circular Series FOP 3-06. Foreign Agricultural Service, Washington, D.C.

van der Molen, M. K., A. J. Dolman, M. J. Waterloo, and L. A. Bruijnzeel. Forthcoming. "Climate Is Affected More by Maritime Than by Continental Land Use Change: A Multiple Scale Analysis." *Global and Planetary Change.*

Van Noordwijk, Meine, F. Agus, B. Verbist, K. Hairiah, and Thomas P. Tomich. 2006. "Managing Watershed Services in Ecoagriculture Landscapes." In Jeffrey A. McNeely and Sara J. Scherr, eds., *The State-of-the-Art of Ecoagriculture.* Washington, D.C.: Island Press.

van Wilgen, B. W., C. Marais, D. Magadlela, N. Jezile, and D. Stevens. 2002. "Win-Win-Win: South Africa's Working for Water Programme." In S. M. Pierce, R. M. Cowling, T. Sandwith, and K. MacKinnon, eds., *Mainstreaming Biodiversity in Development: Case Studies from South Africa.* Washington, D.C.: World Bank.

Vance, Colin, and Jacqueline Geoghegan. 2002. "Temporal and Spatial Modelling of Tropical Deforestation: A Survival Analysis Linking Satellite and Household Survey Data." *Agricultural Economics* 1683: 1–16.

Vedeld, Paul, Arild Angelsen, Espe Sjaastad, and Gertrude K. Berg. 2004. "Counting on the Environment: Forest Incomes and the Rural Poor." Environmental Economics Series, Working Paper 98. World Bank, Washington, D.C.

Vincent, R. Jeffrey, C. Clark Gibson, and Marco Boscolo. 2003. "The Politics and Economics of Forest Reforms in Cameroon." World Bank, Washington, D.C.

von Amsberg, J. 1998. "Economic Parameters of Deforestation." *The World Bank Economic Review* 12: 133–53.

von Thünen, Johann Heinrich. 1966 *Isolated state* (an English edition of *Der isolierte Staat*). Translated by Carla M. Wartenberg. Edited with an introduction by Peter Hall, Oxford. New York: Pergamon Press.

Vosti, Stephen A., James Gockowski, and Thomas P. Tomich. 2005. "Land Use Systems at the Margins of Tropical Moist Forest: Addressing Smallholder Concerns in Cameroon, Indonesia, and Brazil." In Cheryl Palm, Stephen A. Vosti, Pedro Sanchez, and Polly J. Ericksen, eds., *Slash-and-Burn Agriculture: The Search for Alternatives.* New York: Columbia University Press.

Warnken, Philip F. 1999. *The Development and Growth of Soybean Industry in Brazil.* Ames, Iowa: Iowa State University Press.

Warr, Peter. 2005. Roads and Poverty in Rural Laos. Working paper 4. RSPAS, The Australian National University.

Watson, Robert T. and the Core Writing Team, eds. 2001. *Climate Change 2001: Synthesis Report. A Contribution of Working Groups I, II and III to the Third Assessment Report of the Intergovernmental Panel on Climate Change.* Cambridge, U.K.: Cambridge University Press.

WDPA Consortium. 2005. "World Database on Protected Areas 2005." World Conservation Union (IUCN) and United Nations Environment Programme–World Conservation Monitoring Centre.

Wertz-Kanounnikoff, Sheila. 2005. "Deforestation in Amazônia: An Inquiry into the Effect of Land Tenure and Population from 2000 to 2003." World Bank.

White, Andy, and Alejandra Martin. 2002. "Who Owns the World's Forests?" Forest Trends, Washington, D.C.

Whitten, Tony, Sengli J. Damanik, Jazanul Anwar, and Nazaruddin Hisyam. 2000. *The Ecology of Sumatra.* Singapore: Periplus Edition.

Wigmosta, M. S., L. Vail, and D. P. Wittenmaier. 1994. "A Distributed Hydrology-vegetation Model for Complex Terrain." *Water Resources Research* 30 (6): 1665–79.

Wilson, Kerrie, Adrian Newton, Cristian Echeverria, Chris Weston, and Mark Burgman. 2005. "A Vulnerability Analysis of the Temperate Forests of South Central Chile." *Biological Conservation* 122 (1): 9–21.

World Bank. 2001. "Peru Second Rural Roads Project." Project Appraisal Document 22110. Washington, D.C.

———. 2002. *World Development Report 2003: Sustainable Development in a Dynamic World: Transforming Institutions, Growth, and the Quality of Life.* New York: Oxford University Press.

———. 2003. "Implementation Completion Report (CPL-34440) on a Loan in the Amount of US$167.0 Million to the Federative Republic of Brazil for a Rondônia Natural Resources Management Project." Report 26080. Washington, D.C.

———. 2004. "Sustaining Forests: A Development Strategy." Washington, D.C.

———. 2005. "India. Unlocking Opportunities for Forest-dependent People in India." Report 34481-IN. Washington, D.C.

WRI (World Resources Institute). 2005. *The Wealth of the Poor: Managing Ecosystems to Fight Poverty.* Washington, D.C.

Wu, JunJie. 2000. "Slippage Effects of the Conservation Reserve Program." *American Journal of Agricultural Economics* 82 (4): 979–92.

Wunder, S. 2000. *The Economics of Deforestation.* New York: St. Martin's.

Wunder, Sven, and William D. Sunderlin. 2004. "Oil, Macroeconomics, and Forests: Assessing the Linkages." *The World Bank Research Observer* 19 (2): 231–57.

WWF (World Wildlife Fund). 2001. "Terrestrial Ecoregions GIS Database." [http://www.worldwildlife.org/science/data/terreco.cfm]. Accessed May 25, 2005.

Xu, Zhigang, Michael T. Bennett, Ran Tao, and Jintao Xu. 2004. "China's Sloping Land Conversion Programme Four Years On: Current Situation, Pending Issues." *International Forestry Review* 6 (3–4): 317–26.

Yaron, Gil. 2001. "Forest, Plantation Crops or Small-scale Agriculture? An Economic Analysis of Alternative Land Use Options in the Mount Cameroon Area." *Journal of Environmental Planning and Management* 44 (1): 85–108.

Yin, Hongfu, and Changan Li. 2001. "Human Impact on Floods and Flood Disasters on the Yangtze River." *Geomorphology* 41 (2–3): 105–09.

Yohe, Gary, Natasha Andronova, and Michael Schlesinger. 2004. "CLIMATE: To Hedge or Not Against an Uncertain Climate Future?" *Science* 306 (5695): 416–17.

Zbinden, Simon, and David R. Lee. 2004. "Paying for Environmental Services: An Analysis of Participation in Costa Rica's PSA Program." *World Development* 33 (2): 255–72.

Zelek, C. A., and G. E. Shively. 2003. "Measuring the Opportunity Cost of Carbon Sequestration in Tropical Agriculture." *Land Economics* 79 (3): 342–54.

Zeller, Manfred, Aliou Diagne, and Charles Mataya. 1998. "Market Access by Smallholder Farmers in Malawi: Implications for Technology Adoption, Agricultural Productivity and Crop Income." *Agricultural Economics* 19 (1–2): 219–29.

Zhang, X., and S. Fan. 2001. "How Productive is Infrastructure? New Approach and Evidence from Rural India." Discussion paper 84. International Food Policy Research Institute, Washington, D.C.

Ziegler, Alan D., Thomas W. Giambelluca, Ross A. Sutherland, Mike A. Nullet, Sanay Yarnasarn, Jitti Pinthong, Pornchai Preechapanya, and Sathaporn Jaiaree, 2004. "Toward Understanding the Cumulative Impacts of Roads in Upland Agricultural Watersheds of Northern Thailand." *Agriculture, Ecosystems & Environment* 104 (2004): 145–58.

Index

Note: Page numbers followed by letters b, f, m, n, p, and t refer to entries in boxes, figures, maps, notes, photos, and tables, respectively.